AF644265

Indo-US Relations

Indo-US Relations

Dimensions and Emerging Trends

Edited by
Mohammed Badrul Alam

SHIPRA

All rights reserved. No part of this publication may be reproduced, stored in a retrival system, or transmitted in any form or by any means, electronic, mechanical, photocopying, recording or otherwise, without the prior written permission of the Publisher. The views expressed in this volume are of the individual contributor or author and do not represent the viewpoint of the Editor/Institute.

ISBN: 978-81-7541-671-0

First Published in India in 2013

Indo-US Relations: Dimensions and Emerging Trends

© *Editor*

Published by:
SHIPRA PUBLICATIONS
H.O.: LG 18-19, Pankaj Central Market, Patparganj,
I.P. Ext., Delhi-110092, Tel: 91-11-2223 5152, 2223 6152
Br.Off.: 4617/18, Ansari Road, Darya Ganj,
New Delhi-110002, Tel: 6594 6453, 9810522367
E-mail: info@shiprapublications.com
www.shiprapublications.com

Foreword

Indo-US relations in the 21st century have been marked by strategic partnership rapid growth in economic cooperation; massive educational collaborations and unprecedented social and cultural interactions between the civil society groups.

Former Indian Prime Minister Atal Behari Vajpayee's description of the United States as a "natural ally" of India and President Barak Hussein Obama's portrayal of India as an "indispensable partner" of the United States cannot be dismissed as political rhetoric. Academics of all hues have witnessed over the years a palpable shift in the paradigm that explained the relationship between these two countries during the Cold War years. The scholastic depiction of this relationship is better captured by what Denis Kux interprets as a movement from "estrangement" to "engagement".

The powerful and prosperous democracy—the United States and the dynamic, but developing democracy—India suffered from strategic divergences, incompatible economic policies and inexplicable political complexities during the Cold War years. What resulted from this was mutual misperception and reciprocal apprehensions over each other's critical motivations. Consequently, Washington and New Delhi could manage only a working relationship that was not optimally productive.

The opportunity cost of Cold War-tainted ties between the US and India was quickly understood in both the capitals once the Soviet Union crumbled and the structure of international politics fell apart. Indian and American leaders in the new context of the post-Cold War era made quick and sustainable amendments to their outlook towards each other and used their insights to craft a new structure of bilateral rapport.

However, it was not an unproblematic effort, and the birth pang of the current "indispensable" relationship was discernible during the last decade of the 20th century. The US leadership stopped worrying about India as a strategic collaborator of its erstwhile enemy; hailed the dynamism and resilience in Indian democratic polity; got excited about the prospects of doing business with the rising middle class in India, but stuck to its nonproliferation fundamentalism and pushed hard its policy of exporting "Washington Consensus" based economic ideas.

India appreciated the tougher US stand on Pakistan related to terrorism and WMD proliferation; altered its economic policy by replacing "Licensing Raj" by liberal reforms; toned down its foreign policy rhetoric of non-aligned years; expressed its aspiration to design a new cooperative rapport with the United States; but vehemently opposed Washington's South Asia-specific nonproliferation agenda and eagerly watched the evolution of US ties with China in the emerging world order.

The bumps on the road were more strongly felt when India decided to go nuclear and conducted a series of nuclear test explosions at Pokharan in 1998. The relatively rosy road of Indo-US relations suddenly got enveloped with gloomy clouds that faded away only after President Bill Clinton made a historic and path-breaking visit to India in March 2000. The sanctions-affected ties were not only restored but the two countries also laid the foundation stone of a new strategic partnership that has metamorphosed the edifice of Indo-US relationship.

President Bill Clinton first tolerated and then accommodated the US nonproliferation policy with the new nuclear reality of South Asia. But his successor, President George W. Bush, marched several steps ahead and decided to permanently erase the nuclear tension between the two countries. The outcome was an unprecedented chapter in the global nuclear history in the form of a civilian nuclear cooperation agreement signed by the two countries. President Bush in the process has carved out a place for himself in the present and future textbook on Indo-US relations.

President Bush can also be credited with forging a sophisticated military-to-military cooperation with India. It encompassed fight against low intensity conflict, such as terrorism and wider areas of cooperation in the maritime and space spheres as well. When President Barak Obama created history by being the first African-American to be elected to the White House, many in India doubted whether he would be able to carry forward the fast emerging friendly and cooperative ties of his country with India.

Obviously, he found it difficult to propose any big-ticket item like the 123 agreement his predecessor came up with. But his highly commendable and successful India visit in November 2010 left none in doubt that there would be no going back on the emerging strategic partnership between India and the US. He endorsed Indian membership in UN Security Council and India's entry into a host of international nonproliferation regimes.

However, there is a long way before the promises and plans can be fruitfully put into operation. The strategic partnership is "indispensable" but at the same time it requires sustained attention and endeavour. Social, political and financial and technological hurdles have cropped up now and will do so in the future.

Prof. M.B. Alam has made a commendable attempt in producing an edited volume to debate and discuss these issues and events. Books and articles on Indo-US relations are numerous, but what is novel in Prof. Alam's project is an effort to tap relatively younger minds and make their views on the subject known to the outside world.

Prof. Chintamani Mahapatra
School of International Studies
Jawaharlal Nehru University
New Delhi-110067

Preface

The primary purpose of this book is to analyze, examine, and evaluate bilateral relations between India and the United States in the 21st century. Both India and the United States are stable democracies – one the largest in the world, the other the oldest. From America's standpoint, post-World War II, a new democratic regime in India was counted upon as a strategic ally for containing Soviet influence in Asia. Yet, India refused to be an ally of the US. Strongly allied with Britain through both World Wars, the United States had a policy of ambivalence towards colonial India. F.D.Roosevelt and Truman paid scant attention to the cause of Indian independence and did not press hard either Churchill or Atlee, the British Premiers during World War II to give independence to India. In the wake of World War II, when America emerged as the world's leading economic and military superpower, India, endowed with abundant raw goods, emerged as an attractive potential trade partner for the US. With India emerging fast as a hard power and soft power, defense, economic and political ties between the two countries have grown to a more popular level of mainstream American society. Similarly, the Indian diaspora residing in the US have been extremely proactive and visible in presenting themselves as a model minority due to their high educational profile, economic affluence and political participation. The year 2008 was a significant turning point in the course of Indo-US relations. The controversial civilian nuclear agreement between India and the United States that was signed during Indian Prime Minister Dr. Manmohan Singh's visit to Washington in July 2005, received US Congress' approval to go forward. Intense negotiations by both sides led to the accord, known as the 123 Agreement. Under the landmark treaty, India would subject its civilian nuclear program under IAEA safeguards, support nuclear non-proliferation programs, work to prevent the export of nuclear related materials, and abide by a self-imposed moratorium on nuclear weapons testing. In spite of policy divergences from time to time, India and the United States are committed to the formation of a strong, viable partnership in multiple spheres based on shared common values including respect for individual liberty, justice, rule of law and democracy.

Chapter One deals with Bush administration's orientations toward India during the first decade of 21st century. Mohammed Badrul Alam also analyzes and examines how despite generic problems, both the United States and India have opted in favour of democratic path of free and open dialogue and discourse in bridging the cultural divide and in exploring newer avenues toward a synergized US-India relations well in to the future.

Chapter Two covers the gamut of the strategic partnership between India and the United States during Obama administration towards a meaningful dialogue, cooperation, and engagement. B.V. Muralidhar and M.Vishnu Prakash have delineated the pattern of this relationship from 'estranged democracies' to 'engaged democracies'.

Chapter Three provides the backdrop to the transformational change that can be attributed to the changing balance of power in world politics (particularly in Asia), increased recognition of common interests and shared values, India's economic growth and the increased influence of the Indian American lobby in the US. Uma Purushothaman succinctly explains how Indo-US defence cooperation is in the long-term mutual interest of both countries and must be enhanced in the future.

Chapter Four provides the context under which steps toward Indo-US Civil Nuclear Agreement was initiated. Muzaffar Ahemad Ganaie describes how with this initiative, Bush not only reversed decades old US policy on non-proliferation but also removed the biggest obstacle which for years had clouded the relations between two countries

Chapter Five deals with the changing global environment in the post Cold War wherein have emerged diverse new issues ranging from poverty to refugee crises, information privacy to cyber- terrorism, environmental problems to natural disasters—which require non-military policies and strategies. Narottam Gaan elaborates on environmental security considered as a major component of non-traditional security concept.

Chapter Six provides the contours of strategic cooperation as has been laid by the emergence of India as a nation with converging interests and principles with those of the US. Reyaz Ahmad Ganaie analyses the emergence of India and the US as strategic allies in the 21st century and how it marks a complete shift in their respective foreign policies.

Chapter Seven analyses and examines the case of Asian Indians living in the United States, in the context of 'cultural pluralism' model. Mohammed Badrul Alam also addresses and evaluates the perception of Asian Indians as a 'model minority' and their attitudes toward family, education, religion, political participation, ethnic association, media and communication.

Chapter Eight describes how Indo-US relations has come a long way since the Cold War days when America's obsession with anti-Communism and India's adherence to Non-Alignment created gaps that could not be easily be bridged. Monish Tourangbam explains how the strength of India as an ally lies in the fact that India will never blindly toe the US line, in the fact that an emerging power like India, will never become the kind of ally that Pakistan typifies.

Chapter Nine summarizes how in the fragile environment when US troops are about to leave Afghanistan and the Talibans are a still a force to reckon with, India and the US as the main stakeholders in Afghanistan are trying to play the stability card in this war ravaged country. Akhilesh Kumar Tiwari analyzes the role of India and the United States in reconstructions and development process of Afghanistan and in their efforts to bolster the legitimacy of Hamid Karzai government.

Chapter Ten describes the transformation of the status of terrorism as an outcome of the attacks of 9/11 on the twin-towers of World Trade Center and Pentagon—the chief symbols of American economic and military supremacy. Amulya Kumar Tripathy elaborates how India and the United States have a shared interest in strengthening counter international terrorism and in the process enhancing cooperation between the two countries.

Chapter Eleven provides an overview of how with the changing geopolitical long term interests of the US, on the one hand, and its search for a natural and dependable ally in both countering terror and promoting international peace and security, on the other, appear to have catapulted India to a position where it becomes a coveted partner of the US, not only in the context of South Asia but in global politics as well. Rajendra Kumar Pandey questions whether after decimating al-Qaida and wiping out all probable terrorist threats to its interests and installations, US would continue to be interested in carrying forward the counter-terror cooperation with India by treating it as a valuable partner.

Chapter Twelve describes how South Asia has emerged as one of the core areas for US foreign policy interest. Kaustav Padmapati analyses how being the dominant actor in the region, India was considered as a promising power and 'indispensible partner' of the United States.

Chapter Thirteen explains how the Bush Jr Administration's efforts to broad base its ties with India is a recognition to the fact that New Delhi does and can have a very important role to play in guaranteeing strategic stability in the Indian Ocean Region and in promoting a viable balance of power in Asia. Biswajit Mohapatra elaborates how strategic partnership is intensified while protecting each country's independence and independent way of promoting economic growth for the benefit of the large public.

Chapter Fourteen describes the historiography of Indian Americans and how this ethnic group has shaped and influenced policy making germane to Indo-US relations. Mukesh Bagoria explains how the Indian Diaspora in the United States has played a very important role in bridging the gap and in the restructuring of the bilateral relations.

Chapter Fifteen highlights the complex dynamics of US-Pakistan relations particularly since 9/11 and 26/11. M.J.Vinod evaluates Obama administration's approach towards improved relations between India and Pakistan by the US acting as a facilitator in the peace process.

Acknowledgements

This book has its inspiration from teaching a wide range of students in India, USA and Japan over the past three decades. As for my inculcation to American Studies discourse, it commenced long time ago in early 1980s in Jawaharlal Nehru University, New Delhi where I earned my M.Phil degree in American Studies at the School of International Studies. My professors, Dr. B.K.Shrivastava, Dr. M.S.Venkatramani and Dr. R.P. Kaushik, taught me the various aspects and various of American Studies and its implications. My long stint working at the American Center library in New Delhi opened up my eyes to the scope and breadth of literature on almost all important facets of American Studies.

In the United States, where I attended Cornell University in Ithaca, New York, and earned my M.A and Ph. D degrees in International Studies, many high profile professors such as Prof. Mary Katzenstein, Prof. Milton Esman, Prof. Richard Polenberg, Prof Water LaFeber, instilled in me the various intricacies and complexities of issues related to US-India relations.

In Japan, where I have been teaching at Miyazaki International University in Southern Japan from 1998 to 2005, a number of colleagues such as Dr. Kate Greenfield, Dr. Getachew Felleke, Amanda Bradley, Dr. Jeong Pyong-Hong, Dr. Mika Mervio and Dr.Yasu Izumikawa, helped me in shaping my ideas and in bringing in the right focus on complex dynamics of Indo-US relations.

At Jamia Millia Islamia University, Delhi, where I am presently a Professor of Political Science, all of my colleagues were of assistance in one way or the other. A number of my colleagues in the Department of Political Science including Prof. Rumki Basu, Prof. Nisar Ul Haq, Prof. Furqan Ahmad, and from the Economics department, Prof. Shahid Ashraf, were great source of inspiration and motivation. A number of doctoral research scholars including Reyaz Ahmad Ganie, Muzaffar Ahmad Ganie, Akhilesh Tiwari, Digvijay Singh Sekhawat, Sarish Sebastian, Kuldeep Singh, Amit Gupta were of immense help in collecting the source materials.

A special word of thanks to Shri D. Kumar, Shipra Publications, New Delhi, India, for showing genuine interest in the manuscript and for its subsequent publication.

The greatest gratitude is owed to my mother, Mrs. Hedatun Nisa and brothers: Dr. Mohammed Shamsul Alam and Mohammed Aminul Alam, and sisters: Dr. (Mrs.) Swaleha Khatun, Mrs. Rahima Khatun, Mrs. Sofia Khatun, my wife: Mrs. Gahartaj Rokeya and my children: Saira Alam, Zubair Alam, Sadaf Alam and Munawar Alam. Although quite demanding and at times frustrating, everyone allowed me the time and necessary emotional support I needed to complete my work. Much of my success is due to their love and affection at all times.

Delhi, India **Prof. Mohammed Badrul Alam**

Contents

1

Indo-US Relations during the First Decade of the 21st Century: An Evaluation

Mohammed Badrul Alam

Upon assuming the US Presidency in January 2001, President George Bush, Jr.; had identified India as an important actor in the globe and a pre-eminent power in South Asia. Although the relationship between the United States and India has been on a roller coaster ride for the previous five decades, the changing contours of strategic and economic interests and priorities have brought both the nations closer in the current international and regional environments. This chapter deals with Bush administration's orientations toward India during its first term, 2001-2004.

In the past, during India's pre-independence years prior to 1947, US administration, in particular, President Franklin D. Roosevelt's, showed keen interest in favour of speedy transfer of power to India and had exerted pressure on the British government to do the needful.[1] From 1950s onwards, Indo-US relations were shaped and overshadowed by Cold War politics. Within the bipolar framework, the India-Soviet friendship and the US-Pakistan alliance were the two major developments during this phase. Though economic aid relations prevailed during 1950s and 1960s, New Delhi and Washington saw each other on opposite sides of the fence during this period. However, Presidents Kennedy and Lyndon Johnson were in favour of maintaining warm relations with India. It was possible primarily due to the excellent personal chemistry between the US President Kennedy and later Johnson, with India's Prime Minister, mainly, Jawaharlal Nehru. Recently declassified papers show that Kennedy was more greatly interested in India than Pakistan. The Sino-Indian dispute in 1962 brought about enhanced bilateral cooperation between the two countries the when US supported actively India's territorial integrity against the Chinese intrusion. But the 1965 Indo-Pak War undid everything; Washington lost interest in the region. Though President Carter showed some interest, the Afghan war witnessed US political support tilting again towards Islamabad due to Pakistan's geo-strategic location.

President Reagan literally wrote off India. Later, in the mid-1980s the US strategy was to wean India away from the Soviet Union. Dramatic turn occurred in the 1990s—the Cold War was terminated with the disintegration of the Soviet Union and the US-Pak relations nosedived, because of the latter's clandestine nuclear programme. The 1990s also witnessed the liberalization of India's closed economic sector to US big business houses and multinational companies and a noticeable, upward trend in US-India perception of a new strategic reality in the South Asian region became visible.

Beginning with 2000, a number of high profile reciprocal visits took place in Washington and New Delhi to work towards a policy of adjustment and accommodation in a number of core areas of mutual interests.

These improvements culminated with President Clinton's visit to India in March 2000. His visit assumed significant media interest as it was the first ever visit made by a visiting US President to India since President Jimmy Carter visited India in 1978. The then Indian Prime Minister Vajpayee and then US President Clinton signed the Vision Statement that had outlined the future of Indo-US relations. The highlights of the Vision Statement were:[2]

a. As a part of the vision for future relationship, a regular, wide-ranging dialogue is important for achieving the goal of establishing closer and multi-faceted relations between India and the US and for the two countries to work jointly for the promotion of peace and prosperity in the 21st century.
b. The US president and the Indian prime minister will hold regular bilateral 'summits' in alternating capitals or elsewhere, including on the occasions of multilateral meetings, to review bilateral relations and consult on international developments and issues.
c. The two countries will also hold an annual foreign policy dialogue at the level of secretary of state of the United States and external affairs minister of India.
d. The two countries also consider the ongoing dialogue on security and non-proliferation between the deputy secretary of state of the United States and the external affairs minister of India important for improving mutual understanding on bilateral, regional and international security matters.
e. Foreign Office consultations between the under secretary of state for political affairs of the United States and the Indian foreign secretary will continue.
f. The two leaders consider combatting international terrorism as one of the most important global challenges.

g. The two leaders see an enormous potential for enhancement of economic and business relations between the two countries in the Knowledge Age. They have decided to institutionalise bilateral economic dialogue.
h. The two leaders consider cooperation between the two countries in the energy and environment sectors an important part of their vision for the future. They have agreed to set up a Joint Consultative Group on Clean Energy and Environment.
i. The two leaders believe that the strong scientific resources of the two countries provide excellent opportunities for scientific collaboration between them.

Though all these proposed points laid a strong foundation for enhanced bilateral relations between India and the US, the Clinton Administration appeared unable or unwilling to make the final break with its failed nuclear non-proliferation policy in the region. As long as nuclear non-proliferation remained the benchmark from the US standpoint, there were strict limits beyond which the bilateral relationship could not improve. Nevertheless, the Clinton Administration's policies had provided the framework on which the new, incoming Bush Administration could build further momentum.

India in Bush's Asia Policy

South Asia may not have figured very high during the election campaign, but whatever little Bush had to say on India was quite positive. For instance, during the foreign policy speech made on November 19, 1999, he said as follows:

> "Often overlooked in our strategic calculations is that great land that rests at the south of Eurasia. This coming century will see democratic India's arrival as a force in the world. A vast population, before long the world's most populous nation. A changing economy, in which 3 of its 5 wealthiest citizens are software entrepreneurs. India is now debating its future and strategic path, and the United States must pay it more attention. We should establish more trade and investment with India as it opens to the world. And we should work with the Indian government, ensuring it is a force for stability and security in Asia. This should not undermine our longstanding relationship with Pakistan, which remains crucial to the peace of the region."[3]

Similarly, in the RNC (Republican National Committee) election platform of George Bush, on India, it was stated that "India is emerging as one of the greatest democracies of the twenty-first century. Soon, it will be the world's most populous state. India is now redefining its identity and future strategy. The United States should engage India, respecting its great multicultural achievements and encouraging India's choices for a more open world."[4] India's pre-eminence in South Asia as well as its potential in the global arena as an emerging upper tier country was thus taken in to serious consideration by the Bush administration.

The Heritage Foundation's paper of December 11, 2000, said, "The United States and India must begin to view themselves as friendly countries that have complementary, though not identical goals."[5] What it meant was both the United States and India as vibrant democracies could find multiple avenues in cementing their bilateral ties and taking it further to greater heights for a win-win relationship.

Also, US Secretary of State Colin Powell made some significant remarks on India: "...India has the potential to keep the peace in the vast Indian Ocean area and its periphery. We need to work harder and more consistently to assist India in this endeavour, while not neglecting our friends in Pakistan."[6] Hence, one could say that Bush was likely to pursue a more intense and proactive pattern of cooperation between India and the United States.

Trade Relations

During the Bush administration, trade relations with India increased dramatically comparable tc previous years. As per US trade data released by the US Department of Commerce, worldwide merchandise exports to US grew during calendar year 2002 by +1.98 per cent. Out of the top 25 exporting countries to the US, growth rates for 14 were positive, while 11 countries witnessed steep decline in their exports to US.[7]

Merchandise exports from India to US grew by +21.4 per cent in 2002 compared to 2001, rising from $9.74 billion to $11.82 billion. This robust performance reflects the highest annual percentage growth in Indian exports to US over the past decade. It was particularly noteworthy as it had occurred against a backdrop of lackluster growth in worldwide exports to US in 2002, and despite concerns over trading with India due to heightened tensions in the Indian subcontinent and travel advisories against visiting India that were briefly in place during mid 2002 due to crisis over Kashmir, acts of domestic terrorism in India and resulting tensions with Pakistan.

The good news in terms of US-India trade relations was that India had emerged as the 19th largest merchandise exporter to US in 2002 (up from 22nd position in 2001) with a 1.02 per cent share of total US imports (up from a 0.86% share in 2001). 2002 marks the first year that India had entered the list of top 20 countries exporting to US; it was also the first time that India's exports to the US had exceeded 1 per cent of US merchandise imports. It also marked the first time in recent years that the rate of growth of Indian merchandise exports to US (21.4%) had outpaced the rate of growth in our India's services exports to US (20%).

Growth had been more or less across the board and major Indian export growth sectors in 2002 included diamonds/gold jewellery (+39%), woven apparel (+9%), linen and other textile items (+23%), knit apparel (+13%), fish and seafood (+36%), carpets (+19%), machinery (+23%), iron and steel (+270%), iron and steel products (+15%), and pharmaceuticals (+136%).

As India's largest trading and investment partner, US exports to India for 2000 were $3.7 billion while US imports from India for the same period totaled close to $11 billion. It was worthwhile to note that computer software exports itself accounted for another US$ 4 billion. After the visit made by Robert Zoellick, US Trade Representative under the Bush Administration, India was taking proactive steps to reduce tariff and take other necessary measures so as to attract more potential investors in to its lucrative market. US Administration, in particular, appreciated very much the passing of the Insurance Regulatory and Development Authority Bill by the Indian Parliament which would open India's insurance industry to foreign private insurers. Needless to say, President Bush's proclamation issued on September 22, 2001, the status quo ante as of May 1998 was restored and all economic sanctions imposed pursuant to Glenn Amendment were lifted forthwith. Lifting of economic sanctions was like an icing on the cake for the ongoing trade relations between US and India. As per the news bulletin issued by the Embassy of India, Washington, DC, March 4, 2003, overall, the bilateral trade picture is as follows:

India-US Trade: Calendar Year 2002 (figures for 2001 are in brackets)

1. Indian merchandise exports to US = $11.8 billion ($9.7 billion)
2. US merchandise exports to India = $ 4.1 billion ($3.8 billion)
3. India-US merchandise trade [1+2] = $15.9 billion ($13.5 billion)
4. Indian IT/software exports to the US = $ 5.7 billion ($4.8 billion)
5. Total Indian exports to the US [1+4] = $17.5 billion ($14.5 billion) *{Merchandise + IT/software exports}*
6. US services exports to India = $ 3.1 billion ($2.8 billion)
7. Total US exports to India [2+6] = $ 7.2 billion ($6.6 billion)

{Merchandise + Services}

8. Total India-US trade [5+7] = $ 24.7 billion ($21.1 billion) *{Merchandise + Indian IT/software exports + US services exports}*
9. Merchandise trade gap [1-2] = +$7.7 billion (+$5.9 billion) *(in India's favour)*
10. Total trade gap [5-7] = +$10.3 billion (+$7.9 billion)

Defense and Military Cooperation

Both India and the United States had also embarked upon a sustained defence cooperation. Although there were outstanding non-proliferation measures, both sides remained committed to explore further avenues of cooperation within the framework of new strategic look for South Asia in which India was to play a vital role. In particular, there was broad agreement to broaden relation in civilian space and nuclear cooperation as well as over the issues on export controls for dual-use items, materials and technologies.[8]

One of the significant aspects of the emerging US policy of engagement towards India was reflected in the growing military ties between the two nations. In February 2001, the US Navy participated in the international fleet review sponsored by the Indian Navy off the coast from Mumbai in the Arabian Sea. It was the first such occasion for US Navy to take part in military exercise in Indian territorial waters. Navies of two countries also cooperated in securing the maritime trade routes between the Suez Canal and the Strait of Malacca for maintaining economic and strategic stability, preventing acts of piracy in the high seas, interdicting narcotics smuggling among the littoral states in the areas surrounding the Indian Ocean. Indo-US joint military exercise took place in Agra, India, in May 2002 with air paratroopers from both countries participating. In Alaska, USA, under sub-zero temperature, US Army 1st Batallion 501st Para Infantry Regiment and India's 50(1) Para Brigade took part in joint training exercise in September 2002 as well. As a follow up to Agra exercise, on September 8, 2003, special forces from India and the United States as part of an ongoing interaction began joint exercises in the strategically important Ladakh region of Jammu and Kashmir. With an aim to bolster cooperative security and stability, US and Indian military delegations took part in the June 2003 Multinational Ballistic Missile Defence conference held in Koyo, Japan, to be followed up by other related conference to be held in Berlin in July 2004 and in Roving Sands in 2005.

It was expected that the newly created Indo-US Defence Policy Group (DPG) would be fully operational for enhancing the level of military cooperation between the two countries for the foreseeable future.

With the approval to sell Phalcon radar that was long pending between India and Israel subject to US approval, a new sense of pragmatic realism had dawned upon both India and the United States to cement their strategic ties which have been on the upswing since 2000.

Washington was also believed to be giving the nod to the proposed sale of Israeli Arrow anti-missile system as well as its own, Patriot Advanced Capability-3 or PAC-3 system to India. During Israeli Prime Minister, Ariel Sharon's visit to New Delhi in September 2003, there were widespread media buzz about the possibility of a strategic axis emerging between three pluralist, vibrant democracies namely, US, India and Israel, each of which had to endure repeated acts of terrorism of varying degrees in its soil.[9]

The acquisition of these fresh assortment of strategic weapons are likely to bolster India militarily as it fine tunes the induction of the Phalcons twin AWACS radar, the Greenpine as well as the Aerostat low level baloon radars it received in 2002 to give Indian Air Force a definite edge in its capability to track down incoming missiles and other mobile targets. The Phalcons can pick up aircraft, including at low altitude, hundreds of kilometers away in any weather, day or night. It can also intercept and decode radio transmissions, anticipating in many cases the weaponry an enemy might employ.

The Arrow System, capable of defending against short and medium range missiles, was developed by Israel in collaboration with United States and needed Washington's approval for sale to third countries. The internal debate in Washington on Arrow sales to India had remained unfinished as deep divisions within the Bush administration had stalled an early decision. While the White House and the Pentagon were said to view favourably the transfer of the Arrow system to India, the State Department and the non-proliferation lobby in Washington were opposed to the deal. The opponents of the deal had marshaled four arguments.

First, the sale would further destabilize the already tense military relations between India and Pakistan. Second, India's acquisition of missile defence capabilities might lead to an escalating arms race with Pakistan which might either expand its offensive nuclear capabilities or seek to buy defensive systems of its own. Third, it was argued that the sale of Arrow might violate the Missile Technology Control Regime that limits the transfer of missiles and associated technologies. Fourth, it was being suggested that such a sale could set a precedent for missile sales by other countries resulting in increasing proliferation risks all around.

The PAC-3, India was seeking, had been under discussion at a number of bilateral exchanges including the one concluded in Washington in June 2003 where India's National Security Advisor, Brajesh Mishra met his

US counterpart, Ms. Condoleezza Rice and US Deputy Secretary of State, Richard Armitage.

The PAC-3 or the Patriot System has usually been doled out by the US Administration to its close strategic partners as was evidenced in the April 2003 war over Iraq when Patriot missiles were placed under US command and control in countries such as Kuwait and Israel and with close monitoring of the system from the newly created the US Central Command in Doha, Qatar.

Indian strategic planners, based on the country's solid credentials on non-proliferation, commitment towards resumption of meaningful dialogue as was envisioned by Indian Prime Minister Vajpayee's call to Prime Minister Jamali of Pakistan, steadfast in its (India) pledge made in 1998 on the no-first-use of nuclear weapons, India was counting upon a positive response from the Bush Administration to reward India with PAC-3. By doing so, the Indian strategists thought the US could signal to a new proactive, long term strategic relationship with a country that had stood by it (US) in its relentless pursuit against international terrorism as well as in showing exemplary restraint amidst repeated, provocative acts of cross-border terrorism on the part of Pakistan.

The interceptor missile, PAC-3 will suit Indian military really well as it has a hit-to-kill system with an eight-round launcher and a range of 15 km. As the system has single-stage and short-range, PAC-3 can be used ideally under Indian conditions with low to high altitude capability and with a maximum speed that is five times the speed of sound thus bolstering other comparable arsenals India has at the present time.

The evolution of the present accelerated phase of Indo-US defense cooperation began in 2000 when the outgoing Clinton Administration removed various sanctions imposed on India in the aftermath of the 1998 Pokhran II nuclear tests. The process of engaging India took further impetus when President Bush came to the White House and he further waived sanctions from the 'Entity List' thus allowing the US business houses to undertake long rang defense supply relationship with India. As an immediate positive fall out of this executive measure from President Bush, India was able to lease several US Fire-finding, weapon locating radars, Sea King helicopters, Special Forces equipment including protective gears for use as chemical and biological weapons, target drones for the Indian Navy, etc.

India's vital contribution in the post-war reconstruction of Afghanistan was noteworthy. In particular, in India's strategic interest in enhancing the security environment inside Afghanistan including the building of the Afghan National Army through intensive training was applauded by the Bush Administration thus synchronizing the security objectives of the world's largest and the oldest democracies.

India's offer to be a part of the UN efforts in the rebuilding of post-war Iraq and its infrastructure had received favourable attention by the US-British occupation forces including its leaders, Jay Garner and Paul Bremmer.

However, it needed to be remembered that as friends, the US and India would continue to have differences as well both over style and substance while trying to cement areas of cooperation, be it strategic or military, within the framework of a shared partnership.

Let it be understood by both sides that it takes two to tango and the threads of cooperation be viewed and rewarded in its totality and not being seen in isolation to the detriment of one or the other partner as both countries charted a new level of understanding keeping in view the core national interests of one another.

The United States had put India's request for border sensors and equipment for its special forces on a high priority basis and had also given the go ahead to the sale of GE engines and advanced avionics for India's indigenous Light Combat Aircraft and leasing of the US fire-locating, weapon-locating radars.

Concluding Observations

A seven-point engagement, as Karl F. Inderfurth suggested in a seminal article agenda[10], can be considered as a baseline for upward swing in the bilateral relations between India and the United States.

First, strengthen strategic ties. A strong India is vital for balance of power purposes in Asia and for providing stability in the strategically important Indian Ocean littoral area. India is in a strong position to safeguard sea-lanes that are used to transport more than half the world's oil and gas. The navies of the United States and India have begun to conduct joint exercises aimed against specific threats to maritime commerce.

There has been a huge jump in the US-India defence ties in the past several years — with joint military exercises, the signing of a 10-year defence framework agreement, and enhanced interest in defence procurement and collaboration between defence industries. These ties should be accelerated to a higher level.

Another arena for greater strategic cooperation is in the field of counter-terrorism. India has been a potent target of terrorist attacks longer than the United States. Expanding counter-terrorism cooperation requires increased information sharing and building tighter liaison bonds between the US and the Indian intelligence and security services.

Second, realise economic potential. Underpinning the strategic partnership should be a concerted effort to fulfill the full economic potential of the US-India relationship. Steps need to be taken to deepen commercial ties, identify and remove impediments and irritants on both sides and clear the way for a new era of trade cooperation and investment. Deeper economic ties will also have the added advantage of providing needed boost to the overall relationship when political differences arise.

Third, pursue a broader nuclear dialogue. It has long been a strategic goal of the United States to engage India as a partner in global efforts to check and control the spread of nuclear weapons.

But for more than a quarter of a century, the two countries have been on the opposite side of the nuclear divide — unable to reconcile India's overt nuclear weapons programme and its security compulsions with the nuclear non-proliferation concerns and official policies of the United States.

The US-India civilian nuclear agreement announced in 2005 launched a major effort to bridge that divide. With that announcement, the United States explicitly recognised India's status as a full-fledged overt nuclear power, and committed itself to a partnership in the realm of civilian nuclear energy. The decision of the 45-member Nuclear Supplies Group to approve access by India to nuclear fuel and advanced technology is a major step forward in this regard. It brings to an end India's decades-long isolation from the nuclear group.

Fourth, highlight higher education. A 2005 policy report by a high-level panel of US and Indian experts states Higher education as among the most significant foundations of the budding partnership between India and the United States. The benefits for India of higher education collaboration with the United States are likely to increase the quality of its higher education opportunities, retaining good talent within the country, and reaping the benefits of foreign investment for India's higher education sector. For the United States, there will be greater opportunities for educational exchanges and to learn and collaborate in cutting edge fields of increasing importance to both countries — including science, public health, and information technology.

Fifth, support India's United Nations bid. Enhanced US-India cooperation should also extend to the institutions of global governance in a positive way. It is time for the United States to publicly support India's bid for a permanent seat on the UN Security Council and to work actively with India (and others) to accomplish the goal of Security Council expansion. With its thriving democracy, its billion plus population, its expanding economy, and its longstanding contributions to the UN peacekeeping on a sustained basis, the case for a permanent Indian seat has been quite strong.

Sixth, collaborate in the neighbourhood. Another area for greater collaboration should be at the regional level, in South Asia itself. Both

India and the United States want a South Asia that is prosperous, stable and democratic. Already, the United States and India are working together in Nepal as it pursues a permanent peace and a new political dispensation in the post-monarchy environment. India and the United States should cooperate in trying to stabilise Sri Lanka and Bangladesh, both of which face significant internal political difficulties in nation building. India and the United States also have a shared interest in a secure and stable Afghanistan and one that is at peace with all its neighbours including India and Pakistan.

Seventh, promote a cooperative triangle. Along with the much-improved US-India relationship has at times raised questions about the underlying motivations for this new direction in American foreign policy, specifically whether it represents a hedge by Washington against a rising China, India's most consequential neighbour. These manipulative temptations should be resisted. Strengthened US ties with India have their own strategic logic and imperatives and should not be part of a China containment strategy, something Indian officials would strongly oppose.

It is hoped that the policy of accommodation and mutual appreciation of views on both sides will take the relationship between the two countries to a more matured phase. If engaging India is the new focus in Washington, this apparent 'paradigm shift' in Indo-US relations is likely to usher in more far reaching changes with both nations continuing their rendezvous while keeping their national interest intact.[11] Being multiethnic and multicultural societies in this new information age in the new millennium, despite generic problems, both the United States and India have opted in favour of democratic path of free and open dialogue and discourse in bridging the cultural divide and in exploring newer avenues toward a synergized US-India relations well in to the future.

REFERENCES

1. For a general overview of Franklin D. Roosevelt's response to India's independence, see, Hess, Gary R. (1971). *America Encounters India.* Baltimore: Johns Hopkins Press (pp. 83-84); Foreign Relations of the United States, 1942, President Roosevelt to Prime Minister Churchill, p. 615; Report of American Public Opinion published in *The Hindu*, Madras, India, 1 April 1942, p. 20; Alam, Mohammed B "In The Shadow of World War II: US Role In India's Quest for Independence", *Comparative Culture*, Miyazaki, Japan, Vol. 4, 1998, pp. 68-76; also, see, Kux, Dennis (1994). *Estranged Democracies. India and the United States.* New Delhi; Sage Publications (p. 451); Gould Harold and Ganguly, Sumit (1992). (Eds). *The Hope and The Reality: US-India Relations from Roosevelt to Reagan.*

Boulder: Westview Press. Also, see, Mohammed Badrul Alam, "Between Engagement and Estrangement: Bush administration and US-India Relations", *Evaluation of the Bush Administration*, Small World Monograph Series, ArchiTect Press, Tokyo, Japan, 2003, see, "Analysing Indo-US Relations during Bush Presidency", *Area Studies: A Journal of International Studies and Analyses*, Tirupati, India, Vol.3, No.1, January-March 2009

2. See, Pillai, R. "Indo-US Relations in the Bush White House", *Strategic Analysis*, New Delhi: India, Vol. XXV, No.4, 2001, pp. 545-556. *Also see*, Alam, Mohammed B. "US-India Relations: New Dimensions", Institute of Peace and Conflict Studies ON Line Publication, New Delhi, No. 936, December 14, 2002, available at http://www.ipcs.org/ipcs.index.htm
3. *Ibid*, Pillai, p. 546; also see, George W. Bush, "A Distinctly American Internationalism", Foreign Policy Speech at the Ronald Reagan Presidential library, November 19, 1999, available at http://www.reagan.utexas.edu
4. 'President Bush and India's Nuclear Programme", *Global Issues*, SAPRA India, New Delhi, available at http://www.subcontinent.com/sapra/nuclear/nuclear20010305&c.html, also see, Alam, Mohammed B. "Bush Presidency: An Early Assessment", *Third Concept*, September 2001, New Delhi, India.
5. *Ibid*, "President Bush and India's Nuclear Programme", as above; also see, Alam, Mohammed B. "Indo-US Relations during Bush administration", (Oriya language article), *The Sambad*, Bhubaneswar, India, February 18, 2003, p. 4.
6. *Ibid*, Pillai, p. 546; Colin Powell, Opening Statement before the US Senate Foreign Relations Committee, January 17, 2001, available at http://www.access.gpo.gov/congress/senate/senate11.html
7. For more detailed analysis, see, "India-US Trade Relations", Embassy of India, Washington, DC, Archives, 2002, available at http://www.indianembassy.org; Speech made by Robert D. Blackwill, US Ambassador to India, New Delhi, January 28, 2002, available at http://www.usembassy.state.gov/posts/in1/wwwhmain.html; 'Indo-US Trade Zooms in 2002", available at http://www.rediff.com; Timberg, Thomas. "The Impact of Indian Economic Liberalization on US-India Relations", *SAIS Review*, Winter-Spring 1998, Vol. XVIII, No.1, Washington DC, pp. 123-136; India-US Trade Statistics, Information from the US Census Bureau, available at http://www. indian embassy.org/industrial/2002/trade/india_U_S_trade.htm
8. For a fuller description of US-India military and defence cooperation, see, Alam, Mohammed B. "Tectonic Shift: Indo-US Defence Cooperation", *National Herald*, New Delhi, June 19, 2003, p. 4; Alam, Mohammed B. "Re-Discovery of India: Glenn Amendment and After", *National Herald*, New Delhi, January 5, 2003, p. 4; "Rumsfield tells India that US wants to extend military ties", New York Ties, November 5, 2001, available at http://www.indianembassy.org
9. See, "US-Israel-India: Strategic Axis", BBC World News, available at http://www.news.bbc.co.uk/2/hi/south_asia/3092726.stm; "US hails Indo-Israeli

friendship", *The Hindustan Times*, New Delhi, September 9, 2003, p. 1; "Power of three will combat terror: Israel", *The Times of India*, New Delhi, September 10, 2003, available at, http:www.timesofindia.indiatimes.com; "Indo-Israel-US axis may emerge", *The Tribune*, New Delhi, September 9, 2003, available at http://www.tribuneindia.com; "India discusses Orion deal with US", *The Hindu*, Chennai, September 10, 2003, available at http://www.hinduonline.com, ; For an overview, see, P.R. Kumaraswamy, *India and Israel: Evolving Strategic Partnership, Security, and Policy Studies*, No.40, Ramargan, Israel, Begin and Sadat Centre for Strategic Studies, 1998; Farah Naaz, "Indo-Israel Military Cooperation", *Strategic Analysis*, New Delhi, Vol. XXIV, No.5, August 2000, pp. 969-986; Bidanda Chengappa, "Indo-Israel Relations: The Great Leap Forward", *India Defence Review*, New Delhi, 1993, p. 108; Address by Shri Brajesh Mishra, India's National Security Advisor at the American Jewish Committee Annual Dinner, Washington, DC, May 8, 2003, available at http://www.indianembassy.org

10. Karl F.Inderfurth. "The US and India expanding agenda", *The Hindu*, Chennai, September 10, 2008
11. *Ibid*, "India-US Relations Promoting Synergy", p. 41-43; *Ibid*, "The Future of US-India Relations" Ambassador Robert Blackwill, p. 1-7; "India: World Power", *The Washington Times*, September 5, 2001; "Breaking Ice in South Asia", *The Christian Science Monitor*, May 8, 2003; Speech, "India, United States and the New World Order", made by Mr. Brajesh Mishra, National Security Advisor of India, at the Council of Foreign Relations, New York, May 7, 2003 available at http://www.indianembassy.org; "India: America's New Partner", *The Mercury News*, July 24, 2003, available at http://www.bayarea.com/mid/mercurynews; "New Dimension in US-Indian Relations", Richard Boucher, US Department of State at the India Business Council Meeting, Washington, DC June 19, 2001, available at http://www.state.gov/p/sa/; Alam, Mohammed B. "Indo-US Relations Today", *National Herald*, New Delhi, January 16, 2002, p. 4; The following are from the US-India Friendship Association web site, http://www.usindia-friendship.net/links.html. "Time to woo India", *National Security Outlook*, December 2002, American Enterprise Institute of Public Policy Research; "Indo-US Relations Have Reached the Highest Point Ever", Interview of India's Ambassador to US, Mr. Lalit Mansingh, *India Abroad*, New York, January 3, 2003; "India and the US: Meeting the Challenges of the 21st Century together", September 10, 2002, Remarks by India's External Affairs Minister, Mr. Yashwant Sinha; "Indo-US Ties all about Cooperation; not Carping", Address by Richard N. Haas, Deputy Policy Planning Staff, US Department of State, at the Chamber of Indian Industry Partnership Summit, Hyderabad, India, January 7, 2003.

2

India-USA Relationship: From Estrangement to Engagement

B.V. Muralidhar and *M.Vishnu Prakash*

The considerable progress achieved in bilateral relations following the visits by Prime Minister Dr. Manmohan Singh to the United States in 2009 and President Mr. Barak Obama to India in 2010, the strategic partnership between India and the United States for meaningful dialogue, cooperation, and engagement have launched a new phase in this partnership.[1] The two leaders acknowledged the immense possibilities for further collaboration between the two countries given the inherent dynamism, emerging challenges, and numerous exciting opportunities available for sharing and growing together.

India and US have moved from being "estranged democracies" to "engaged democracies". The relations between the two nations are getting thicker due to changing international scenario. The bilateral relation is taking a new dimension which was not visible earlier. However it takes time to strengthen their mutual confidence in various conditions under myriad situations. America's new strategical shift towards south Asia, south-east Asia, and especially India, made their relations to look in new light.

The volatile situation in south Asia like territorial skirmishes, nuclear issues, terrorism, ethnic disputes, further contributed to drift its cold-war strategy to new adjustment to suit the changing situations.

By the time of the 1990 India-Pakistan crisis, many in Washington felt that south Asia was out of control. The assumption was that conflict over Kashmir could lead to a conventional war, which in turn could ignite a nuclear conflagration. When India tested five nuclear devices in May 1998, there were predictions that Washington and New Delhi were on a collision course. Indian strategists talked of defying the US, joining with Russia or China in an alliance to counter American power and developing a nuclear capability could reach American territory. Reconciliation between Washington and New Delhi seemed unlikely. The nuclear tests appeared to have erected a barrier to a more normal relationship between these two countries. New Delhi and Washington held eight rounds of talks between June 1998 and February 1999, the longest extended strategic dialogue between the two. The talks proved to be surprisingly valuable in the summer of 1999 when India was confronted by the Pakistani move across the line of control at Kargil.

While nuclear issues remains at the center of US policy towards New Delhi, there also grew the realization that direct pressure might counter-productive, and a more subtle, long-term strategy was called for to make New Delhi adopt tighter restraints on its nuclear program. Such a strategy had been outlined in a number of non-governmental and think-tank reports like the Brookings Institution, the Carnegie Endowment for International Peace, and the Council on Foreign Relations and these observed that south-Asia was under-appreciated and that India's economic and strategic potential was not given enough weight in American policy. This has created a situation, despite the nuclear tests, wherein the well known points of disagreements are fading and several important areas of agreement are emerging.

The image of India has been transformed, acquiring a new face. India has a visible and tangible presence in the US through the 1.5 million strong Indian-American community. The influence of the community on American images of India, and Indian images of the United States, has been generally positive and likely to have an enduring impact on the bilateral relationship. Indian-Americans have been spectacular high achievers in a few important fields. There are approximately three hundred Indian-American entrepreneurs with a personal net worth of at least $5 million. Nearly forty per cent of start-up companies in the Silicon Valley and Washington areas are Indian or Indian-American owned, and there are at least 774 India-American companies in the Silicon Valley alone. Overall, the community is extremely prosperous, and its per capita income of over $50,000 places it at the top of hyphenated-Americans. The Indian-American community has also begun to organize itself along political lines and has become an important source of funding in several Congressional and Senate races.

'India-US relations: A Vision for the 21st Century', the Indo-US relationship was termed a 'continuous, constructive in political area, and beneficial in economic arena'; a joint communiqué declared during March 2000, when President Bill Clinton visited India is one such significant step. From then the bilateral relations are undergoing structural changes[2], though not at the expected pace.

India's swift offer of full support for the US led counter-terrorism operations after September 2001 was widely viewed as a reflective change.

Mr. George Bush calls India a "natural partner" of the United Sates and his administration seeks to assist India's rise as a major power in the new century. In July 2005, President George Bush and Indian Prime Minister Singh issued a Joint Statement resolving to establish a US-India "Global Partnership" on a wide range of issues. Mr. Bush administration dubbed India "a responsible state with advanced nuclear technology" and seeks to achieve "full civilian nuclear energy co-operation".

Mr. Robert Blake, Assistant Secretary of State for south and central Asia described Mr. Obama's visit to India as "a defining moment in the history of our bilateral relations" and further pointed out that the Obama administration realized that "everyone had a stake in India's emergence as a global power".[3]

A joint statement issued at the end of the conclusion of second India-US Economic and Financial Partnership in June, 2011 the US Treasury Secretary Timothy Geithner and Finance Minister Pranab Mukherjee said, "Through stronger collaboration and coordination amongst our economic and financial policymakers, this Partnership has sought to deepen US-India bilateral and multilateral engagement in order to fully capitalize on the wealth of economic opportunities between our two nations".[4] Thanks to the deeper links between the USA and India, that the two states find their economies and their populations coming into closer alignment.

An article published in *Washington Times*, [5] quoting the Executive Director of US-India Commercial Committee, Michael Clark, stated that, for an American company, the most important thing was not the rising of the Indian middle class, but undoubtedly the information technology corporations in India, which have extraordinary potential.

India is in the midst of a massive military modernization effort, and is expected to spend $80 billion over the coming years. Strategically, these purchases will bolster India's strategic military capabilities, and increase opportunities for bilateral training and exchanges between Indian and US forces. Economically, further defense sales will provide a much needed boost to American exports. The US defense industry has greatly benefited from this expansion as India's defense orders have topped $8 billion over the past decade. India's Ministry of Defense has purchased six Lockheed Martin C-130J Super Hercules cargo planes, and has quickly become the largest international customer of Boeing's C-17 Globemaster III airlifters.

Indeed the two sides finalized a deal worth nearly $4 billion for the US to provide India with enough C-17 aircraft to give India the second-largest C-17 fleet in the world. Enhancing Indo-US cooperation in maritime security in the Indian Ocean region is also an area of mutual interest that is ripe for new initiatives.

In an effort aimed at expanding high technology trade and forging closer strategic relations with India, on January 25, 2011, the US Department of Commerce's Bureau of Industry and Security (BIS) issued a final rule amending the Export Administration Regulations (EAR), which removed nine Indian defense and space companies from the Entity List (EL).

The amendment further adds India to the country group A: 2 in the EAR, which consists of members of the Missile Technology Control Regime, thus recognizing and communicating India's adherence to the regime, the Indo-US strategic partnership, and India's global non-proliferation credentials. In addition, it also supports India's efforts to join four multilateral export-control regimes, i.e. Nuclear Suppliers Group (NSG), Missile Technology Control Regime (MTCR), Australia Group (AG), and Wassenaar Arrangement (WA), which require the US to revise its own export restrictions.

Though the Indo-US technological cooperation resumed after a Memorandum of Understanding (MoU)[6] for technology transfers was signed in 1984 and especially after the end of the Cold War, the problems and doubts still remained as to the reliability of the United States as a supply partner and its reluctance to release dual-use technology. However, the 'strategic dialogue' [7] led by then Deputy Secretary of State Strobe Talbott and External Affairs Minister Jaswant Singh built confidence and trust and created the ground for Clinton's March 2000 visit to India. The signing of the "Vision Statement" during this visit provided a framework for closer cooperation in the future and a guideline for subsequent governments in both countries.

It was only after George Bush came to power that bilateral defense and technological cooperation started to move forward steadily. The stated objectives of recent efforts of Mr. Barak Obama administration in reforming the EAR are to realign US export policy towards India to reflect India's status as a strategic partner, effectively treating India like other close US allies and partners.

The September 11, 2001 attack and the war on terrorism that followed provided a chance for the US and India to forge an even closer strategic cooperation. India has condemned the two Pakistan-based groups, the Lashkar-e-Toiba and Jaish-e-Mohammed, that led the terrorist attack on India's Parliament on December 13, 2001, and that are also responsible for cross-border terrorist activities.

Terrorism has become a turning point in the Indo-US security relationship. Most Indians have trouble accepting the principle of humanitarian interventions and fear that the US would extend the principle to south Asia—which means the United States would support the principle of 'self-determination' and press for a plebiscite in Kashmir. Similarly, the United States is unwilling to accept the Indian demand for a UN

Security Council seat. Some Americans would regard it as a 'reward' for India's nuclear programme, and fear that this would further accelerate the trend towards nuclear weapons. But the two countries together implemented a co-operative framework of relationships based on three dimensions: democracy, economy, and security.

The US recognizes India as the largest democracy in the world. India's economy increased by six per cent annually in the 1990's and it also has a growing information technology industry. The United States is India's largest trading partner, its biggest investor and its biggest provider of advanced technology. Besides, Indian Americans are playing an important role in shaping the United States' South Asia policy. Compared with Pakistan, which experiences economical trouble and political turbulence and has only one-seventh of India's territory, Washington regards New Delhi as a potentially important economic partner.

In the security field, felt that India, as a de-facto nuclear state, had co-operative potential with the US on the proliferation issue. India actively supported the US missile defence plan as well as that on counter-terrorism. India and the US have discussed several measures for improving military-to-military cooperation between the two countries, including the holding of joint exercises and a "multi-pronged proactive approach" of the security forces to counter infiltration. The US has changed its strategy from 'focusing on India and reducing Pakistan' during the Clinton administration to 'raising India and curbing Pakistan'.

Nevertheless, the United States is unlikely to discard its Cold War ally – Pakistan. Contrarily, it needs Pakistani support and co-operation as an Islamic 'frontline state' in the war against terrorism. But Osama bin Laden's death confirmed that one can't rely on Pakistan to take out prominent terrorists on its soil.

India and the United States are each groping for a strategy to cope with the emergence of China as a major world power. The United States is especially concerned about China's challenge to its world leadership, while India is especially concerned about China's future relationship with Pakistan. The United States and India both have substantive interests in China. Both within the United States and India, there are significant numbers of people that believe that China is a 'threat' to the interests of the two countries. India and the Indian Ocean are expected to play an important role in a geo-strategy. In the closing days of the Clinton administration, the containment of China gradually increased in importance as a factor influencing America's Asia-Pacific strategy. In addition to causing trouble on the Taiwan issue, the strategy of containment included reliance on Japanese and Indian Forces, and especially on the trend of enhancing India's capabilities to contain China.

The three points demonstrate the growing convergence of the US-India regional interests and ideals. Regionally, both nations seek to eliminate terrorist safe havens in Afghanistan, the peaceful and democratic rise of China, free access to the global commons, and regional maritime security. And while traditional allies – Australia, Japan and South Korea – will remain the cornerstone of America's Pacific strategy, the United States will increasingly need India to be a critical regional partner. Mr. Obama echoed this sentiment last November, when he proclaimed that relations between the United States and India will be one of "the defining partnerships of the 21st century."

India has taken a substantial role in reconstruction efforts in Afghanistan having provided $750 million to the cause, as well as contributing personnel and opening consulates. Support includes $111 million power station, $84 million road-building project, a $77 million project dam, and construction of a $67 million parliament building to be finished in 2010. Earlier this year, India announced a $100 million increase in Indian aid to Afghanistan. A team of army doctors and para-medics, including three medical officers and three nursing assistants, have been sent to Afghanistan to provide humanitarian assistance.

The changing US-Indian security relations will have a great impact on China's security's environment. These can be viewed in three perspectives: the emergence of a Sino-US-India strategic triangle; the complicated security situation in south Asia; and the America factor in Sino-India relations.

Giving the fact that counter-terrorism has became the primary issue in American strategy; the United States intends to use the war on terrorism to implement its military strategy in the Asia-Pacific region in addition to strengthening homeland security. The US military strategy in the Asia-Pacific region, consequently, includes securing influence and location in central Asia; the limiting of western Asia's development; and a return to South East Asia. Within this context, India and the Indian Ocean constitute the bridge for the United States in its regional military strategy.

India has the world's fifth largest navy. It already has one aircraft carrier and is striving to put into place three carriers by 2020 as a part of its naval expansion and a desire to project power throughout the Indian Ocean. Difficulties in defense procurement and deficiencies in its own shipbuilding sector, however, could stall India's progress in developing its naval capabilities. India has also carefully cultivated ties with the countries of the Indian Ocean rim, including Mauritius, Maldives, Seychelles, and Madagascar, providing these countries with naval support, such as offshore naval patrol vessels and staff and training.

India has prioritized strengthening relations with Japan through increasing military contacts, maritime cooperation, and trade and investment ties. Tokyo has pledged $4.5 billion in soft loans for the Delhi-Mumbai railway freight corridor, and the two sides inked a joint security declaration in 2008, calling their partnership[8] "an essential pillar for the future architecture of the region." In 2007 and 2009, Japan participated in the Malabar naval exercises in the Indian Ocean. In a significant turnaround from its past tough stance toward India's nuclear program, Tokyo is currently negotiating a civil nuclear deal with New Delhi.

Canberra[9] has summarily removed the only block on putting together a US-led containment strategy toward China that includes India and Australia (aside Japan and others). The unleashing of the nuclear business ensures that the US-India relationship is not stuck in a groove.

The United States and India have mutual interests, but different policies, in terms the nature of their future dealings with a rising China. There are essential divergences on issues such as Taiwan and human rights between China and the United States. There are also basic differences on issues including border problems and non-proliferation between China and India. Washington fears most is the possibility of China and India, with Russia, forming an alliance based on a common understanding and interests of a new international political and economical order and a multi-polar world.

China and India are among what Brzezinski described as "five geo-strategic players", what Henry Kissinger listed as the "six big powers", and what Samuel Huntington pointed out are "core states of seven civilizations." China is a big power in east Asia while India is a big power in south Asia. Each has advantages and influence in their respective regions. However, they are not world powers that have global influence. In terms of institution and comprehensive strength, they cannot even be ranked as strong powers. For America, China and India, at one end, are two emerging markets offering economic benefits and developing opportunities. At the other end, China and India are also two transitional countries demonstrating uncertainty, from the United States' strategic point of view.

The US-India Higher Education Summit in Washington, DC will bring hundreds of educational institutes together from both countries, and could foster linkages that ease the ability of American students to participate in India's venerable educational system, while further extending the number of Indians studying in the United States and bringing higher education institutional ties between the two countries to a new level. President Mr. Barak Obama and Prime Minister Singh announced expansion of Fulbright-Nehru Scholarship on November 24, 2009. In a joint statement on higher education cooperation released at the conclusion of the summit, Secretary of State Hillary Clinton and Minister for Human

Resources Development Kapil Sibal agreed to make the higher education dialogue an annual bilateral event to "map out strategies for partnership in the field of education"[10] between the two countries.

The two leaders also expressed their support for the Indo-US Science and Technology Forum, which provides fresh impetus to academic collaboration in the cutting-edge areas of scientific research and technology development.

The two leaders lauded the continuing efforts by both sides to explore new avenues for collaboration such as the Indo-US Engineering Education Conclave, held in January 2011 in New Delhi, for strengthening higher educational institutions in the fields of engineering and technology and expressed the hope that more such opportunities for engagement would emerge in the future in other fields. India announced its intention to set up an India-US higher education platform as a means to pursue these goals. But the recent incident, mockery on innocent Indian students who went to pursue higher education in United States have lost lakhs of rupees they paid as fees and returned home without getting the degree they sought to attain is real cause for concern.

Jobs are always a sensitive issue in India, but they were not making headlines in Delhi as they were in Washington. Mr. Obama has often contended that outsourcing work to Bangalore was stealing jobs from the US workers. [11] However, one of the early announcements made during his visit was that, 20 deals worth US$10 billion had been signed between Indian and the US companies. It was emphasized that this would create 50,000 plus jobs in the US

Some businessmen from the US showed up in Mumbai to listen to Mr. Obama and network with their Indian counterparts. They included Jeff Immelt of GE, Indra Nooyi of PepsiCo and David Cote of Honeywell.[12] "Obama is coming to India as a salesman, not a statesman", *The Washington Times* had reported before the India sojourn, "This is a business trip."[12]

However, both sides today realize that there is much to be gained from working with each other. "If there is acceptance of the business capabilities of India and that, because of its vibrant and emerging market, it can help create jobs back in the US, then that itself would be a very interesting development," says Parekh of E&Y. "That puts us on a very different pedestal altogether. From a business perspective both these markets need each others' support. There is so much of complementing possibilities. It can be a win-win situation."

In Parliament, where he addressed a joint session of the two houses, Mr. Obama reiterated the employment issue.[13] "Together, we can create the high-tech, high-wage jobs of the future. With my visit, we are now ready to begin implementing our civil nuclear agreement. This will help meet India's growing energy needs and create thousands of jobs in both our countries.... We can pursue joint research and development to create green jobs."

The details given for the deals highlight the emphasis on jobs. A US$4.1 billion agreement with Boeing will result in 22,160 jobs. A US$822 million accord for light combat aircraft engines with General Electric: 2,220 jobs. A US$2.7 billion Boeing deal with SpiceJet: 12,970 jobs. A US$750 million gas turbine sale by General Electric to Reliance Power: 2,650 jobs.

"The deals are real and trackable," says Rajan Mittal, president of apex chamber, the Federation of Indian Chambers of Commerce and Industry (FICCI). "In fact the number of jobs to be created is understated at times. For example, Boeing alone will be selling US$28 billion worth of aircraft to Air India, Spice Jet and Jet Airways. This will create 280,000 jobs in the US."

Mittal is responding to skepticism about the number of jobs. Others tend to agree with him. Says Ashok Soota, executive chairman of IT Company MindTree Ltd: "All increased trade does lead to increased jobs. The numbers may be real because every direct job created also has an indirect multiplier effect." If you create a job at McDonald's in India, it doesn't stop there, says Gulabchand of HCC. "This results in the creation of another job at McDonald's in the US Yes, all these jobs they are talking about will be there. But it won't happen overnight."

There were agreements at the government level that should pay rich dividends. Mittal of FICCI sums up: Indo-US deals were signed in the areas of military aviation, energy cooperation and research, nuclear partnership, defense (Indian companies have been removed from the Entities List—a list of organizations to which export of sensitive technologies are restricted), nuclear non-proliferation, and infrastructure (where a US$10 billion joint debt fund has been set up). "The main thrust of the [new] relationship will come from removal of Indian organizations from the Entities List and the relaxation of export controls," adds Mittal.

"Job creation must be the first priority in both countries," says a report by the United States India Business Council (USIBC), titled *Partners in Prosperity: Business leading the way*. "Without jobs, weak consumer confidence, protectionism, and trade barriers will impede America's desire to lead in a truly global economy. And in India, the ideal of inclusive growth will remain elusive without jobs to fuel it."[14]

In his address to the Parliament, Mr. Obama said: "I look forward to a reformed UN Security Council that includes India as a permanent member." And again, "We welcome India as it prepares to take its seat on the UN Security Council." Obama officials later clarified that this was no feel-good sound bite; the US would actively work towards getting India to the high table. Mr. Obama echoed the sentiment last November, when he proclaimed that relations between the United States and India will be one of "the defining partnerships of the 21st century".[15]

Not everybody is so positive. "Obama has given India a ticket to Mars," writes economist and commentator Swaminathan S. Ankleswar Aiyar in a column in the *Sunday Times* of Mumbai. "The US has no power to give anybody a permanent Security Council seat.... Obama's support is like a ticket for the first commercial flight to Mars, a favour no doubt, but one so far off in the future that most of us will be dead before it happens."

"US support of India's permanent seat in the UN Security Council has wide-ranging implications," says Chakrabarti of ISB. "India has benefited diplomatically. The US support to India may also be seen as creating a regional counterweight to China in the long run." The USIBC *Partners in Prosperity* report underscores this. "The U.N. Security Council remains the clearest symbol of decision-making in world security matters," it says. "The US-India business community strongly feels that our partnership should begin here. President Mr. Obama calling for a renewal of the U.N. Security Council and the inclusion of India as one of its new permanent members will galvanize both societies, laying the groundwork for deeper collaboration at every level."[16] Adds FICCI chief Mittal: "This political relationship will also impact the economies of both countries in a positive manner."

The task of expanding this important relationship won't be easy. Some leaders in New Delhi remain skeptical of increasing ties with Washington. India remains cautious about developing operational co-operation with US because of the political implications in terms of India's domestic and international politics. India wants to develop broad-based mutually beneficial relations with various global power centers, rather than be seen as leaning towards one power center. After all, in the recent decades, the United States has closely engaged with Indian regional rivals in China and Pakistan.

India's non-aligned tradition continues to carry weight within much of New Delhi's diplomatic establishment. [17] But if the United States is "making a strategic bet on India's future," as Secretary of State Hillary Clinton recently wrote in *Foreign Policy* magazine, the administration must take the lead in prioritizing and moving this important relationship forward. The maxim that there are no permanent friends, only interests can be invoked? [18] or expect positive engagement from both the sides.

Nevertheless, leveraging their combined knowledge, experience, and shared interests, the two sides have to create a robust agenda for the coming years that includes deeper engagement and strategic co-operation.

REFERENCES

1. http://www.thehindu.com/news/resources/article2537074.ece
2. http://dspace.cigilibrary.org/jspui/bitstream/123456789/18255/1/India%20and%20America%20An%20Emerging%20Relationship.pdf?1
3. http://articles.economictimes.indiatimes.com/2010-09-28/news/27613311_1_obamas-visit-president-barack-obama-reciprocal-visit
4. http://www.firstpost.com/world/india-us-look-to-enhance-economic-partnership-33365.html/2
5. Jasmin Fischer, "After Cold War, India, US find common ground", *The Washington Times*, August 7, 1999.
6. http://www.idsa.in/idsacomments/IndiaUSHighTechnology Cooperation Moving Forward_sbishoyi_160211
7. http://www.idsa.in/idsacomments/IndiaUSHighTechnology Cooperation Moving Forward_sbishoyi_160211
8. http://nehu.academia.edu/BiswajitMohapatra/Papers/1285216/Australia_-_India_Relations_and_the_Asia_Pacific_A_Strategic_Shift_or_A_Long_Term_Policy_Goal
9. http://blogs.rediff.com/mkbhadrakumar/2011/11/17/india-delivers-its-obamas-turn-now/
10. http://articles.economictimes.indiatimes.com/2011-10-14/news/30279373.
11. http://knowledge.wharton.upenn.edu/india/article.cfm?articleid=4546
12. http://www.washingtontimes.com/news/2010/nov/4/india-expects-less-mythical-obama/
13. http://www.idsa.in/idsacomments/IndiaUSHighTechnologyCooperation MovingForward_sbishoyi_160211
14. http://knowledge.wharton.upenn.edu/india/article.cfm?articleid=4546#
15. http://www.idsa.in/idsacomments/IndiaUSHighTechnologyCooperation MovingForward_sbishoyi_160211
16. http://knowledge.wharton.upenn.edu/india/article.cfm?articleid=4546
17. http://the-diplomat.com/flashpoints-blog/2011/12/01/avoiding-u-s-india-drift/
18. Morganthau, Hans•J., *Politics Among Nations: The struggle for power and peace*, 6th ed., Mc-Graw Hill, 1985.

3

Indo-US Defence Relations: Challenges and Prospects

Uma Purushothaman

There has undoubtedly been a transformational change in the Indo-US relations, in terms of quality as well as the quantity of exchanges, since the end of the Cold War. India and the US have moved forward from being "estranged democracies" at one time to "engaged democracies".

India and the US today recognise their importance to each other. This transformational change can be attributed to the changing balance of power in world politics (particularly in Asia), increased recognition of common interests and shared values, India's economic growth and the increased influence of the Indian American lobby in the US. India is one of the few countries which has been mentioned in the US strategic defense guidelines as a long-term strategic partner which can "serve as a regional economic anchor and provider of security in the broader Indian Ocean region". Hillary Clinton's article in *Foreign Policy* titled 'America's Pacific Century' announced the US 'pivot to Asia' talks about deepening ties with India. Similarly, US Defense Secretary Leon Panetta recently described India as the linchpin of the US rebalancing towards the Asia Pacific. Clearly, both the State and the Defense Departments agree on the importance of India for the US in the coming years.

For India, the US is an important partner in its inexorable rise towards great power status. India also sees the US as an important force for stability in Asia. Economically too, the US is an important trading partner and is one of the top sources of foreign investment in India. India's growing national capabilities, especially its large and professional military, give it more tools to pursue its national interests to the benefit of the United States.[1] Thus, the need to build closer relations is mutual and has bipartisan support in the US and support from all the major political parties in India.

This paper looks at the history of Indo-US defence relations, the

---

The paper is partially based on an Occasional Paper titled 'Indo-US Defence Relations: In Search of a Direction', published by the Observer Research Foundation and co-authored by Deba R Mohanty and me.

current state of play in defence relations, the reasons why the two countries are now engaged more than ever in defence cooperation, prospects for greater cooperation and the hurdles and obstacles to further engagement on this front.

Defence relations constitute one of the most important areas of the US-India bilateral relationship. The importance of Indo-US defence relations lies in the fact that both countries face similar challenges today and in the future: terrorism, proliferation of WMDs and the security challenges emanating from the rise of China. They therefore share a need to have similar strategic doctrines and operations to meet these challenges. The India-US defence relationship as it exists today has, to a large extent, been propelled by the increased trust between the two countries. This is evident from the large number of high-level visits between defence officials of the two countries and the number of joint military exercises. The aim of the defence ties is to develop capabilities and confidence, jointly tackle multilateral security issues like protecting sea lanes of communication and energy supplies, conduct peacekeeping, and fight terrorism and piracy.[2] However, the picture was not so rosy during the Cold War as can be understand from the following sections:

Defence Relations during the Cold War

In the years immediately after India gained independence, the Indo-US defence relations were limited, because of the need to develop a degree of mutual trust.[3] Defence relations between India and America can be traced to the 1950s when they engaged in joint exercises with the UK and Australia. Arms sales from the US to India date back to 1951 when the US gave India five T-6 Texan Trainer aircrafts. In 1952, India asked for a large number of tanks and aircraft to modernize its armed forces. The request for 200 Sherman tanks worth $19 million, was approved quickly though a request by India to sell its 200 jet aircraft was not approved.[4] However, the US acceded to India's request to sell its 54 C-119 aircraft. In 1954, Nehru refused to accept President Eisenhower's offer of military assistance. In May 1960, the US delivered the US C-119 aircraft bought by India. Again, in 1962, the US rushed in emergency military assistance during the Sino-India war though this would have hampered its ties with Pakistan.

It is notable that at this time, India's close friend at the time i.e. the USSR first adopted a position of neutrality and then almost supported the Chinese suggesting that India and China talk was based on Chinese proposals to solve the border issue, and even stopped MIG-21 deliveries to India temporarily.[5] Even India's non-aligned friends, other than Nasser and Tito, did not come out in support of India. However, the US only sent in equipment like light arms, communications equipment and ammunition that would be more useful in mountain warfare against the Chinese than against the Pakistanis.[6] It also promised military assistance in the future to India.

In December 1962, President Kennedy approved an emergency military aid programme for India worth $60 million. Shocked by its defeat by the Chinese, India asked for air defence against Chinese attacks.[7] The US and India even held joint air defence exercises in September 1963, but this became a one-off incident and the idea did not catch on after that. Dennis Kux claims that President Kennedy was on the verge of approving a five year military package for India when he was tragically assassinated.[8]

The Johnson administration approved a five year military aid package to India, though it refused to provide the F-104s that India wanted, as the Pentagon felt that these would not really be useful against the Chinese and would cause strains in US-Pakistan relations.[9] After the 1965 Indo-Pak war, the US stopped all arms exports and military assistance to India. In 1969, India received ten Hughes-300/TH-55 Light helicopters from the US which were delivered in 1971-1972. But again, on 2 December 1971 during the Bangladesh War, Washington announced a suspension of military sales to India (of which the most important was a $70 million communications system designed to improve air defense capabilities).[10] Nixon's tilt to Pakistan and his support for the country during the 1971 war saw relations plummeting to their lowest ever.

During the Reagan administration, the US approved some high technology cooperation with India's defence industry and eased barriers to technology transfer and a MOU on transfer of technology was signed in 1984.[11]

This allowed items that were on the US government's export control lists to be transferred to India, showing Washington's willingness to develop closer ties with New Delhi. On its part, India assured the US that it would not use the equipment supplied by it to inappropriate end-uses and that it would not be re-exported to the USSR.[12] The MOU further established a forum where non-proliferation issues—one of the major reasons for Washington's misgivings with India—could be raised and addressed. Essentially, the MOU was 'designed to reconcile India's weapons procurement politics with American technology transfer conditions, and thereby expand military links'.[13] The most significant cooperation in defence in the late 1980s was the collaboration with the US Air Force in India's Light Combat Aircraft project and India received F-404 engines for use in the project. The Reagan administration also offered to India advanced military equipment and weaponry including surveillance and fighter aircraft.[14] But this proposal fell through because of Rajiv Gandhi's unease over continued US support for Pakistan's military modernisation programmes.

Thus, arms sales and consequently defence and bilateral relations during the Cold war were hampered by India's fears about the US' reliability as an arms supplier and sensitiveness to the terms of US government agreements as the US had unilaterally stopped arms sales after the 1965 war and was reluctant to carry out the Tarapur contract. This fear continues to cast a long shadow over the Indo-US defence relations. Another reason for the limited defence cooperation was the absence of an overlapping strategic concern. India's status as a recipient of arms from the Soviet Union also reduced the US' enthusiasm in providing military aid to India while India's concerns about its strategic autonomy being affected if it got arms from the US made it also less than enthusiastic about the US arms. Likewise, the US' alliance with Pakistan was another impeding factor. Moreover, India simply could not afford to buy American weapons systems; the Soviet weapons that India got were sold to India on a concessionary basis and they were paid for in soft currency with low interest rates and long-term repayment schedules.[15] The end of the Cold War, however, changed the scenario due to a variety of reasons.

The Post Cold War Era

The end of the Cold War began auspiciously for the Indo-US defence relations as India gave the US refuelling rights during the first Gulf War. The Indo-US defence cooperation was strengthened by the Kicklighter proposals which recommended that Indo-US defence cooperation and military-to-military ties could be promoted through joint seminars, training, etc. and mooted the idea of expanding the defence cooperation framework. Executive Steering Groups were established in both India and the US so as to deepen military-to-military cooperation.

In 1991, as the US government was not able to confirm that Pakistan was not developing nuclear weapons, under the Pressler amendment, the US had to stop all economic and military aid to India.[16] The While US-Pakistan relations deteriorated, this inversely improved US-India relations.[17] Nevertheless, in 1992, the Indo-Russian agreement to collaborate on the Agni missile programme made Washington suspicious about New Delhi's commitment to arms control. So it threatened to suspend military and technology transfer programmes to India and imposed a two-year ban on 'sensitive' technology exports to India.[18] In February 1992, Indian and the US army and Air Force paratroopers held their first joint training exercise codenamed 'Teak Iroquios' followed by another exercise in October 1993.[19] Subsequently, the Indian and the American navies conducted joint exercises in the Indian Ocean in May 1992 and September 1995 and 1996 in keeping with the US policy of cooperative engagement with friendly militaries.[20] In 1995, India and the US signed the Agreed Minute of Defense Relations, which became the foundation of defence relations between New Delhi and Washington till the New Framework for the India-US Defense Relationship was signed in 2005.

As per the 1995 agreement, bilateral cooperation was sought to be achieved through multi-level interactions: ministerial level, service-to-service levels, defence research and production and at the level of senior officers form the Ministry of defence and the Office of the Secretary of Defense.[21] Three groups were created to aid discussion and improve interaction. These were:[22]

- Joint Defence Policy Group (DPG) of the Ministries of Defence for tackling issues of defence cooperation. It was meant to review issues of joint concern such as post-Cold War security planning and policy perspectives on both sides, to provide policy guidance to the Joint Technical Group and Joint Steering Committee. The joint Indo-US Defence Ministry-Department of Defence Group also tackled sensitive issues like the Comprehensive Test Ban Treaty (CTBT) and Kashmir.
- Joint Technical Group (JTG), for discussing issues related to defence research and production cooperation which was to develop the scope and content of further expansion of cooperative defence research and production activities. However, this was to be within the laws, policies and treaty commitments of each country.
- Joint Steering Committee (JSC), to increase the frequency and scope of Service-to-Service cooperation. It was agreed that the emphasis of such cooperation would be on professional contacts and functional cooperation, high level exchanges, presence of observers at each other's military exercises, attendance at seminars on subjects of mutual professional interest, professional/technical training and joint exercises at progressively higher levels of scale and sophistication.

The Agreed Minute promoted greater mutual understanding and facilitated greater interaction, identification of issues of mutual concern and led to high-level visits, more joint exercises, etc. However, the US stressed that arms sales and transfer of technology were not part of the agreement and that no arms/technology transfer would be done at the expense of Pakistan.[23] The DPG is even today the prime mechanism to guide the Indo-US defence relations.

Overall bilateral relations and therefore defence relations took a turn for the worse when India conducted nuclear tests in 1998. Soon after the nuclear tests, the US imposed sanctions on it under the provisions of the Arms Export Control Act, which (among other things) terminated military sales to India and withdrew product support for the F-404 engines in India's LCA project. Many of these sanctions were lifted between 1998-2000 by President Clinton and the rest were lifted by President Bush on 22 September 2001. This change in America's policy was propelled by India's quick response to the 9/11 attacks and its support for the US war on terrorism. The lifting of sanctions paved the way for a major improvement in defence relations and subsequently led to major arms purchases by India from the US. The India-US Defence Policy Group, which was stalled after the 1998 nuclear tests, was revived in 2001 and now meets every year. In 2000, sanctions imposed on India were revoked and since then defence cooperation between India and the US has reached a new high.

Defence sales, joint military exercises, subject matter expert exchanges, high-level visits and seminars and conferences are the important components of the new Indo-US defence relationship. The first major arms sale to India was in 2002, when India bought 12 counter-battery radar sets ("Firefinder" radars) worth $190 million.[24] In 2003, India became eligible for Excess Defense Articles (EDA) on grant basis under the US Foreign Assistance Act. This was meant to support the war on terrorism, promote interoperability of systems and to modernise previously sold equipment.[25] This was followed in 2005 by a momentous development: the Next Steps in Strategic Partnership (NSSP) agreement which was signed in January 2004. The NSSP sought to expand cooperation on nuclear and civilian space technology, missile defence and dual use high-technology trade. Another agreement on High Technology Trade resulted in the removal of ISRO from the US' Entity List.

Later, during the tsunami of 2004, the armed forces of the two countries worked along with those of Japan and Australia in a multilateral disaster management effort, showing that cooperation in the military field was no longer constrained by bureaucratic formalities.[26] The next big breakthrough came with the ten year 'New Framework in the India-US Defence Relationship' signed on 28 June 2005, which charts a course for defence relations in the coming years as a key component of the burgeoning Indo-US strategic partnership.[27] This replaced the Agreed Minute of 1995 and seeks to remove mutual suspicion of the past and replaces it with an active agenda for military cooperation.[28] The Agreement aimed at advancing "shared security interests", namely[29]:

- Maintaining security and stability;
- defeating terrorism and violent religious extremism;
- preventing the spread of weapons of mass destruction and associated materials, data, and technologies; and
- protecting the free flow of commerce via land, air and sea lanes.

In pursuit of these interests, India and US agreed to:

a) Conduct joint and combined exercises and exchanges;
b) Collaborate in multinational operations if it is in common interest;
c) Strengthen capabilities of militaries to promote security and defeat terrorism;
d) Promote regional and global peace and stability;
e) Enhance capabilities to combat the proliferation of weapons of mass destruction;
f) Increase opportunities for technology transfer, collaboration, co-production, and research and development;
g) Expand collaboration relating to missile defence;
h) Strengthen abilities of the Armed Forces to respond quickly to disasters, including in combined operations;
i) Conduct successful peacekeeping operations;
j) Conduct and increase exchanges of intelligence.

Under this framework, the institutionalized framework for cooperation was further strengthened with the creation of the Defence Procurement and Production Group and the Joint Working Group on Defence, under the comprehensive bilateral mechanism of the Defence Policy Group.[30]

Recent Trends in Defence Cooperation

In 2006, India bought the USS Trenton, a decommissioned American amphibious transport dock, for $44 million. This was later named the INS Jalashwa. Subsequently, India spent another $39 million on six Sikorsky UH-3H Sea King helicopters. In 2008, India decided to buy six C-130J Hercules military transport aircrafts worth nearly $1 billion from the US. The same year, the Indo-US civil nuclear deal was signed, showing the growing trust between the two countries. In 2009, it agreed to buy eight P-8I maritime surveillance aircraft worth $2.1 billion, six C-1301J transport aircraft worth $1 billion and 99 jet engines for the Tejas LCA worth around $800 from General Electric.

During his visit to India, President Obama announced that Washington would sell to New Delhi US military equipment worth $5 billion to India, including ten C-17 Globemaster III military transport aircraft and 100 F-414 fighter aircraft. The Security Cooperation Act of 2010 (P.L. 111-266) authorized the President to transfer to India two Osprey-class coastal minehunter ships as Excess Defense Articles. Obama also removed as many as nine Indian defence and space-related companies from the Entity List. Yet, the US lost out on by far the most lucrative potential sale i.e. the bid for 126 new medium, multi-role combat aircraft (MMCA) worth some $11 billion. However, this should not affect defence ties between the two countries as it was a decision based purely on technical evaluation.

The strength of Indo-US relations can be seen from the fact that despite its disappointment over not getting the deal, the Pentagon has said that it will continue to defence cooperation with India. In the months since the MMRCA fracas, India has agreed to buy 145 Howitzer guns worth $560 million from the US-based BAE system. There are more deals in the offing as India has announced a military modernisation for which it will spend around $100 billion over the next decade and thus India is a lucrative market for American weapons manufacturers.

Aims of Indo-US Defence Cooperation

Interoperability is a key aim of the Indo-US defence relationship, if not openly for India, at least for the US. Interoperability is possible only when the armed forces of both countries are familiar with each other's procedures, systems and methodologies and when there is trust between them. Interoperability also depends on compatibility of equipment.

Joint exercises are one way of enhancing interoperability. They are therefore the key component of Indo-US defence relations. Since early 2002, India and the US have held several substantive joint military exercises. The Indian and US navies have annually held joint exercises called the Malabar Exercises. These are held to reinforce maritime tactics, techniques, and procedures (TTPs) of both nations.[31] In some years, these were also held as multilateral exercises with the navies of Japan, Singapore and Australia joining in. The Indian and American navies conduct three other exercises annually i.e. Habu Nag (naval aspects of amphibious operations), Spitting Cobra (explosive ordnance destruction focus), and Salvex (diving and salvage).[32] Moreover, the Indian and American navies have cooperated operationally on four separate occasions: security by the Indian Navy for US ships transiting the Strait of Malacca after 9/11;

disaster relief efforts after the Indian Ocean tsunami in 2004-2005; non-combatant evacuation operations in Lebanon in 2006; and counter-piracy operations in the Gulf of Aden since 2008.[33] The US Coast Guard also conducts exercises with the Indian Coast Guard.

The US and the Indian armies have been conducting the 'Yudh Abhyas' exercises annually since 2004. Similarly, the US marines and Indian Army hold a joint exercise called 'Shatrujeet' which focuses on amphibious operations. The Air Forces have held the bi-annual 'Cope India' air exercises. Special Forces of both countries have held joint exercises called the 'Vajra Prahar' which focus on advanced rifle marksmanship, combat marksmanship, close-quarters combat, helicopter insertion, medical evacuation, combined mission planning, and scenario-based missions.[34] The Indian Air Force is also all set to join the 'Red Flag' combat aviation exercise hosted by the US Air Force in 2013, having participated in it in 2008 as well. Hundreds of Special Forces soldiers from the US have attended courses in India's Counter-Insurgency Jungle Warfare School and India has allowed US Special Forces to conduct joint manoeuvres in the mountainous regions of Kashmir. Over the last ten years, Indian and American forces have participated in over sixty joint exercises and military-to-military training.[35] These exercises have helped to improve interoperability between US and Indian armed forces.

Another major aim for both countries is of course India's need to buy superior weapons and technology from the US. India is poised to spend over $100 billion on military modernisation over the next ten years. So, it needs to find reliable suppliers who can provide it with state of the art weapons systems and technology. This makes it a huge market for the US' military-industrial complex's need at a time when Pentagon's budget is coming under severe fiscal constraints due to the US' domestic travails and accumulated debts. This would also create a large number of jobs in the US.

A major imperative for closer defence cooperation without doubt is the fact that New Delhi and Washington share similar concerns about the rapidly-changing geo-strategic situation in Asia. Washington has already announced that its focus in the coming years is going to be on Asia, through its announcement of the "pivot to Asia". India is also wary of the situation in Asia and is boosting its defences and going in for modernisation of its military. So, clearly there is a convergence of aims related to defence and security.

Obstacles in Defence Relations

The main obstacles in India-US defence relations are American laws.

India wants access to technology and the manufacturing process when it buys equipment. But US laws prevent the transfer of sensitive defence technologies to countries that have not signed certain agreements with the US. Examples of such restrictive and intrusive defence cooperation agreements are the Basic Exchange and Cooperation Agreement for geo-spatial cooperation (BECA), Logistics Support Agreement (LSA), Communication Interoperability and Security Memorandum of Agreement (CISMOA) and End User Monitoring Agreement (EUMA).

While India believes that the LSA compromises on its strategic autonomy as it could be dragged into US conflicts in the Middle East and Asia, CISMOA and BECA could imperil its operational autonomy.[36] India signed the EUMA in 2009. This allows American representatives to regularly check and transfer inventory items to India. But there has been no forward movement on the CISMOA, LSA and BECA so far. Both countries need to make political concessions and adopt a policy of give and take to get around these laws. In fact, US Defense Secretary Leon Panetta, during his visit to India in June 2012, said that "not signing these agreements is no barrier to furthering bilateral military relations", adding that the US is committed to providing the best defence technology to India.[37] This statement reflects a major change in US policy. So, there seems to be some room of hope on the issue of the foundational agreements.

Another hurdle is India's procurement system, which is perceived to be non-transparent, corrupt and lacks legitimacy by some scholars.[38] An additional problem is Indian laws (offset policy) which require foreign suppliers to source components and invest in R&D in India, but prevent them from establishing wholly-owned or majority-owned subsidiaries in India.[39] Though meant to ensure that foreign technology is eventually transferred to Indian companies, the Americans will not agree to it till the US law on transfer of technology are amended and India guarantees the protection of IPRs.[40] India's nuclear liability bill has also put off American companies. Other structural obstacles include India's long-standing defence procurement relationship with Russia and American military aid to Pakistan.[41] With the current downturn in US-Pakistan relations, reduction in aid to Pakistan and the US' interest in a role for India in Afghanistan, this last hurdle is showing signs of gradually being crossed.

Conclusion: The Way Forward

The India-US strategic partnership, which now has the glue of strategic convergence on many issues, would be meaningless without more defence cooperation and military-to-military ties. Indo-US defence relations over the years have mirrored the state of overall relations between the two countries: when relations were bad, defence relations never took off and today when relations are at their best, defence cooperation too has gained support in both countries. Defence cooperation is the litmus test in any bilateral relationship and the state of the Indo-US defence cooperation buttresses the Indo-US strategic partnership, though there is much room for more cooperation. Given the fact that both countries face similar challenges and share long-term strategic convergence, it is important that they cooperate in defence and have interoperability.

But defence cooperation, despite having increased exponentially since 2001, has not realised its full potential. This is because of mutual suspicion and non-understanding of each others' concerns, particularly because of India's distrust of America's domestic laws that have a bearing on defence trade and cooperation. One way of getting around American and Indian laws would be for India and the US to pursue joint projects for technology development.[42] India's highly-skilled personnel can make significant contributions in this and also learn from the Americans. Joint ventures would also reduce unpredictability in future military cooperation and sales.

The US suspension of military sales in during the 1965 and 1971 war continues to cast a long shadow in the minds of Indian policymakers about the reliability of the US as a weapons supplier and as a strategic partner. This mutual suspicion can only be reduced through greater interaction and more joint exercises. New Delhi and Washington should move away from a buyer-seller relationship in arms transfers and lay the foundation for more defence industrial collaboration, co-production of weapons systems and joint research in advanced areas.[43] In fact, New Delhi and Washington have already moved forward in this direction as is seen in the joint statement issued after the Annual Strategic Dialogue in 2012 in which both sides agreed to "strengthen defense cooperation through increased technology transfer, collaborative joint research and development, and co-production of defense items".[44] This is a good sign and holds immense opportunities for Indo-US defence cooperation in the future. The Indo-US defence cooperation is in the long-term mutual interest of both countries and therefore must be enhanced in the future.

Annexure

The Tables below show US Military Assistance and Sales to India from 1950-2009.

Table 3.1: US Military Assistance and Sales to India from 1950–2009

Years	*Total Sales Agreements*	*Total Sales Deliveries*	*FMS Agreements*	*FMS Deliveries*	*Foreign Mil Fin Waived*	*Foreign Mil Fin Direct*	*Commercial Exports Deliveries*
50–69	58,267	56,745	58,267	56,745	–	27,310	–
70	911	1,931	911	1,931	–	–	–
71	856	1,072	856	1,072	–	–	2,277
72	46	254	46	254	–	–	3,591
73	*	77	*	77	–	–	22
74	1,941	81	1,941	81	–	–	659
75	2,559	2,370	2,559	2,370	–	–	219
76	2,933	3,134	2,933	3,134	–	–	6,169
77	1,366	1,410	1,366	1,410	–	–	9,132
78	1,145	1,168	1,145	1,168	–	–	9,456
79	6,184	1,272	6,184	1,272	–	–	9,887
80	1,019	6,224	1,019	6,224	–	–	2,833
81	184	509	184	509	–	–	4,643
82	675	581	675	581	–	–	5,000
83	10	904	10	904	–	–	2,389
84	446	548	446	548	–	–	12,454
85	1	144	1	144	–	–	19,395
86	53	21	53	21	–	–	48,088
87	–	126	–	126	–	–	88,256
88	3,751	14	3,751	14	–	–	11,643
89	35	675	35	675	–	–	43,357

Years	Total Sales Agreements	Total Sales Deliveries	FMS Agreements	FMS Deliveries	Foreign Mil Fin Waived	Foreign Mil Fin Direct	Commercial Exports Deliveries
90	4	40	4	40	–	–	17,389
91	2,000	359	2,000	359	–	–	62,210
92	–	36	–	36	–	–	4,503
93	4	12	4	12	–	–	10,440
94	–	31	–	31	–	–	97,367
95	*	24	*	24	–	–	–
96	–	4,497	–	4,497	–	–	–
97	297	*	297	*	–	–	–
98	–	171	–	171	–	–	–
99	–	–	–	–	–	–	–
0	–	–	–	–	–	–	–
1	–	–	–	–	–	–	–
2	140,002	38	140,002	38	800	–	–
3	60,640	20,507	60,640	20,507	–	–	5,651
4	946	6,567	946	6,567	–	–	15,516
5	76,885	100,328	76,885	100,328	–	–	31,891
6	25	48,576	25	48,576	–	–	39,673
7	92,340	91,999	92,340	91,999	–	–	27,784
8	1,020,944	40,108	1,020,944	40,108	–	–	129,516
9	10,401	15,004	10,401	15,004	–	–	–
10	142,501	31,607	142,501	31, 607			
TOTAL	1,625,968	439,006	1,625,968	439,006	800	27,310	721,409

Years	MAP Program (Emergency Drawdowns)	MAP DELS (Emergency Drawdowns)	Excess MAP/MASF Programme	Excess MAP/MASF Deliveries	IMET Program (Emergency Drawdowns)	Number of Students Trained (IMET,MASF Emergency Drawdowns)
50-69	90,017	86,677	21,995	21,990	4,773	477
70	–	630	*	4	78	19
71	–	754	–	–	151	26
72	–	369	–	–	27	10
73	–	493	–	–	–	–
74	28	214	–	–	196	25
75	39	219	–	–	57	6
76	116	511	–	–	133	17
77	35	76	–	–	165	13
78	9	230	–	–	300	21
79	10	68	–	–	444	31
80	–	7	–	–	263	26
81	1	2	–	–	4	–
82	–	6	–	–	82	9
83	–	1	–	–	139	27
84	–	*	–	–	129	19
85	–	–	–	–	293	35
86	–	–	–	–	303	44
87	–	–	–	–	194	18
88	–	–	–	–	261	24
89	–	–	–	–	297	29
90	–	–	–	–	263	30
91	–	–	–	–	226	20
92	–	–	–	–	310	31
93	–	–	–	–	362	42
94	–	–	–	–	152	8
95	–	–	–	–	208	10

Years	MAP Program (Emergency Drawdowns)	MAP DELS (Emergency Drawdowns)	Excess MAP/MASF Programme	Excess MAP/MASF Deliveries	IMET Program (Emergency Drawdowns)	Number of Students Trained (IMET,MASF Emergency Drawdowns)
96	–	–	–	–	357	21
97	–	–	–	–	404	18
98	–	–	–	–	177	13
99	–	–	–	–	241	6
0	–	–	–	–	489	18
1	–	–	–	–	498	24
2	–	–	–	–	1,012	78
3	–	–	–	–	1,000	36
4	–	–	–	–	1,354	101
5	6,842	–	–	–	1,462	86
6	–	6,842	–	–	1,217	48
7	–	–	–	–	1,427	55
8	–	–	–	–	1,353	82
9	–	–	–	–	1,361	56
10					1269	32
TOTAL	97,098	97,098	21,995	21,995	23,541	1,691

Source: Fiscal Year Series, Defense Security Cooperation Agency, Ministry of Defense. (Latest Data available) http://www.dsca.mil/programs/biz-ops/factsbook/FiscalYearSeries-2010.pdf.

Table 3.2: US Arms Sales to India

Supplier	*No. ordered*	*Weapon designation*	*Weapon description*	*Year of order/ license*	*Year(s) of deliveries*	*No. delivered/ produced*	*Comments*
USA R: India	200	M-4 Sherman	Tank	1951	1952	200	Ex-US; $19 m deal
	5	T-6 Texan	Trainer aircraft	1951	1951	5	Ex-US; probably modernized to T-6G before delivery
	6	S-55/H-19 Chickasaw	Helicopter	1952	1954	6	S-55C version
	26	C-119G Packet	Transport aircraft	1954	1954-1955	26	'MDAP' aid
	30	T-6 Texan	Trainer aircraft	1955	1956	30	Ex-US; T-6G version
	4	Bell-47/OH-13	Light helicopter	1956	1957	4	Bell-47G-2 version
	2	S-55/H-19 Chickasaw	Helicopter	1956	1957	2	
	12	Bell-47/OH-13	Light helicopter	1960	1961-1962	12	
	28	C-119G Packet	Transport aircraft	1960	1961	28	Ex-US
	2	S-62A	Helicopter	1960	1960	2	For evaluation and VIP transport
	24	C-119G Packet	Transport aircraft	1962	1963	24	Ex-US; aid during border war with China
	2	DHC-4 Caribou	Transport aircraft	1962	1963	2	Originally ordered for US armed forecs but transferred to India as aid during border war with China
	10	Hughes-300/TH-55	Light helicopter	1969	1971-1972	10	
	112	TPE-331	Turboprop	1983	1986-2010	112	For 61 Do-228 MP aircraft from

Supplier	No. ordered	Weapon designation	Weapon description	Year of order/ license	Year(s) of deliveries	No. delivered/ produced	Comments
							FRG
	2	Gulfstream-3	Transport aircraft	1987	1988	2	Incl for reconnaissance role
	2	AN/TPQ-37 Firefinder	Arty locating radar	1990	1992	2	$22 m deal
	315	Paveway	Guided bomb	1993	1994	315	Paveway-2 version
	6	LM-2500	Gas turbine	1999	2010	2	For 3 Shivalik (Project-17) frigates produced in India; possibly from Italian production line
	8	AN/TPQ-37 Firefinder	Arty locating radar	2002	2006	8	Part of $142-190 m deal; orginally planned for 1998 but embargoed by USA after Indian nuclear tests in 1998; AN/TPQ-37(V)3 version
	4	AN/TPQ-37 Firefinder	Arty locating radar	2003	2006-2007	4	Part of $142-190 m deal; AN/TPQ-37(V)3 version
	4	LM-2500	Gas turbine	2003			For 1 IAC (ADS) aircraft carrier produced in India; from Italian production line
	17	F-404	Turbofan	2004			$105 m deal; for Tejas (LCA) combat aircraft produced in India; F404-GE-IN20 version; ordered after Indian Kaveri engine delayed
	1	Austin	AALS	2006	2007	1	Ex-US; INR2.2 b ($48 m) deal (incl modernization); Indian designation Jalashwa
	6	S-61/H-3A Sea King	Helicopter	2006	2007	6	Ex-US; $39 m deal; UH-3H version

Supplier	*No. ordered*	*Weapon designation*	*Weapon description*	*Year of order/ license*	*Year(s) of deliveries*	*No. delivered/ produced*	*Comments*
	24	F-404	Turbofan	2007			$100 m deal; for Tejas (LCA) combat aircraft produced in India; F-404-GE-F2J3 version
	6	C-130J Hercules-2	Transport aircraft	2008	2010	1	$1 b deal (incl $596 m for aircraft and $400 m for special equipment); C-130J-30 version; for special forces; delivery 2010-2011
	10	C-17A Globemaster-3	Transport aircraft	2010			$4.1-5.8 b deal; contract not yet signed
	512	CBU-97 SFW	Guided bomb	2010			$258 m deal; CBU-105 version
	20	RGM-84L Harpoon-2	Anti-ship missile	2010			$170 m deal; AGM-84L version
	6	C-130J-30 Hercules	Transport aircraft	2011			For special forces; contract not yet signed
	10	C-17A Globemaster-3	Transport aircraft	2011			$4.1 b deal; delivery 2013-2014/2015
	32	Mk-54 MAKO	ASW torpedo	2011			$86 m deal; contract not yet signed
L: India	8	P-8A Poseidon	ASW aircraft				$2 b deal (offsets 30% incl production of components in India); P-8I version; delivery by 2015
	99	F-414	Turbofan				For Tejas (LCA) combat aircraft produced in India; F-414INS-6 version

Source: SIPRI trade registers (Information generated: 31 May 2012)

REFERENES

1. Robert D. Blackwill, Naresh Chandra and Christopher Clary, 'The United States and India: A Shared Strategic Future', Joint Study Group Report, September 2011, http://www.cfr.org/india/united-states-india-shared-strategic-future/p25740, p. 3.
2. *People, Progress, Partnership: the Transformation of US-India Relations*: Defense Relations: Shared Strategic Future' (New Delhi: US Embassy, undated), 38.
3. David J Louscher *et al.* "Military Relations between the US and India: Assessment and Prospects", in Ashok Kapur*et al.* (ed.) *India and the United States in a Changing World* (New Delhi: Sage Publications, 2002), 304.
4. Dennis Kux, *India and the United States: Estranged Democracies, 1941–1991*, (Washington D.C.: National Defense University Press, 1992), 86.
5. Kux, 205.
6. Kux, 206.
7. Kux, 224.
8. Kux, 213–218.
9. Kux, 229–231.
10. Kux, 302.
11. Kux, 417.
12. Louscher *et al.*, 308–09.
13. quoted in Louscher *et al.*, 309.
14. Louscher *et al.*, 309.
15. Louscher *et al.*, 300.
16. Louscher *et al.*, 311.
17. Louscher *et al.*,311.
18. Louscher *et al.*, 311–312.
19. V.P. Malik, 'Indo-US Defense and Military Relations: From "Estrangement" to "Strategic Partnership"', in Sumit Ganguly, Brian Shoup, *et al.* (ed.) *US-India Strategic Cooperation Into the 21st Century: More Than Words*, (London: Routledge, 2006), 84.
20. Malik, 84.
21. Malik, 84.
22. Ashok Sharma, *Indo-US Strategic Convergence: An Overview of Defence and Military Cooperation*, (New Delhi: Centre for Land Warfare Studies, 2008), 12.
23. Malik, 85.
24. K. Alan Kronstadt *et al. CRS Report*, 27 October 2010, available at http://fpc.state.gov/documents/organization/150780.pdf, 55.
25. Rajesh Kadian, *Concise Enclyopedia of United States South Asia Relations* (New Delhi: Vision Books, 2009), 127.
26. Malik, 93.
27. 'India-US Defence Relations', http://www.indianembassy.org/india-us-defense-relations.php.
28. Malik, 96.

29. 'India-US Defence Relations', *op. cit.*
30. 'India-US Defence Relations', *op. cit.*
31. 'Report to Congress on US-India Security Cooperation', US Department of Defense, November 2011, http://www.defense.gov/pubs/pdfs/20111101_NDAA_Report_on_US_India_Security_Cooperation.pdf, p. 3.
32. Report to Congress on US-India Security Cooperation, op. cit.
33. Report to Congress on US-India Security Cooperation, *op. cit.*, p. 4.
34. Report to Congress on US-India Security Cooperation, op. cit., p. 4.
35. Tim Sullivan and Michael Mazza, 'Shaping the Future of US-India Defense Cooperation', *CDS Strategic Briefing No.*1, 27 September 2010, 2.
36. Rahul Bedi, "India-US strategic dialogue to strengthen ties", http://www.bbc.co.uk/news/world-asia-india-18406453, accessed 13 June 2012.
37. Bedi.
38. Sunil Dasgupta and Stephen P. Cohen, 'Arms Sales for India: How Military Trade could Energize US-India Relations', *Foreign Affairs*, March/April 2011.
39. Dasgupta and Cohen.
40. Dasgupta and Cohen.
41. 'The India-US Defense Relationship: An Update for President Obama's State Visit to India, November 2010', *NBR Workshop Report*, November 2010, p. 7.
42. Dasgupta and Cohen.
43. C Raja Mohan, *The Indian Express*, 06 June 2012.
44. 'Joint Statement', 2012 US-India Strategic Dialogue, *op. cit.*

BIBLIOGRAPHY

Bedi, Rahul. "India-US strategic dialogue to strengthen ties", http://www.bbc.co.uk/news/world-asia-india-18406453, accessed 13 June 2012.

Blackwill, Robert D., Naresh Chandra and Christopher Clary, 'The United States and India: A Shared Strategic Future', *Joint Study Group Report*, September 2011, http://www.cfr.org/india/united-states-india-shared-strategic-future/p25740.

Dasgupta, Sunil and Stephen P. Cohen. 'Arms Sales for India: How Military Trade could Energize US-India Relations', *Foreign Affairs*, March/April 2011.

'India-US Defence Relations', http://www.indianembassy.org/india-us-defense-relations.php.

'Joint Statement', '2012 US-India Strategic Dialogue', 13 June 2012, available at http://meaindia.nic.in/mystart.php?id=190019618, accessed on 14 June 2012.

Kadian, Rajesh. *Concise Enclyopedia of United States South Asia Relations*. New Delhi: Vision Books, 2009.

Kronstadt, K. Alan, Paul K. Kerr, Michael F. Martin and Bruce Vaughn. "India-US Relations", 27 October 2010, *CRS Report*, available at http://fpc.state.gov/documents/organization/150780.pdf.

Kux, Dennis. *India and the United States: Estranged Democracies, 1941–1991.* Washington D.C.: National Defense University Press, 1992.

Louscher, David J., Alethia H. Cook and Victoria D. Barto. 'Military Relations between the US and India: Assessment and Prospects', in Ashok Kapur, Y.K. Malik, Harold A. Gould and Arthur G. Rubinoff (ed.). *India and the United States in a Changing World.* New Delhi: Sage Publications, 2002.

Malik, V.P. 'Indo-US Defense and Military Relations: From "Estrangement" to "Strategic Partnership", in Ganguly, Sumit, Brian Shoup and Andrew Scobell (ed.). *US-India Strategic Cooperation Into the 21st Century: More Than Words*. London: Routledge, 2006.

Mohan, C Raja. "Let's get real", *The Indian Express*, 06 June 2012.

"People, Progress, Partnership: the Transformation of US-India Relations," *Defense Relations: Shared Strategic Future*, published by the Public Affairs Sections of the US Embassy in India, undated.

"Report to Congress on US-India Security Cooperation", US Department of Defense, November 2011, http://www.defense.gov/pubs/pdfs/20111101_NDAA_Report_on_US_India_Security_Cooperation.pdf.

Sharma, Ashok. *Indo-US Strategic Convergence: An Overview of Defence and Military Cooperation*. New Delhi: Centre for Land Warfare Studies, 2008.

Sullivan, Tim and Michael Mazza. 'Shaping the Future of US-India Defense Cooperation', *CDS Strategic Briefing No.*1, 27 September 2010.

'The India-US Defense Relationship: An Update for President Obama's State Visit to India, November 2010', *NBR Workshop Report*, November 2010.

4

Indo-US Civil Nuclear Deal: Heralding a New Era in Indo-US Relations

Muzaffar Ahemad Ganaie

The relations between India and the United States had not always been so cosy and cordial as one finds them today; but for a long period of time, their relations remained cold, and the most important factor responsible for their cold and strained relationship was the "nuclear factor" which impaired cooperation even in the areas not related to nuclear field any way. In the initial years of her nuclear programme, India received support and cooperation from US to exploit atom for peaceful purposes under "Atoms for Peace" plan which was designed to reach out to countries with minimal research capabilities in nuclear field. In 1956, the US Atomic Energy Commission signed an agreement with India under which US agreed to supply heavy water for a Canadian supplied 40 MW research reactor CIRUS. In 1963, the two sides signed an agreement for the construction of two Boiling Water Reactors (BWRs) at Tarapur and under a contract signed on May 17, 1966 it was also agreed upon that US will supply fuel for these twin reactors throughout their life time[1]. However, trouble in their relations started in 1968 when India refused to join Nuclear Non-Proliferation Treaty (NPT) because of its discriminatory nature which reached to culmination in 1974 when India carried out a Peaceful Nuclear Explosion (PNE) at Pokhran. With this PNE, US ceased all nuclear cooperation with India and put brakes on the supply of fuel to Tarapur reactors. This act was in clear violation of 1963 agreement under which it was obligatory upon US to supply fuel for Tarapur reactors as the agreement did not prohibit any type of PNE. Though India protested against this act of non-compliance but failed to restore fuel supply and in 1980 US completely stopped the fuel supply and thus left the agreement dead [2].

The decade of 1980s witnessed no process of rapprochement and relations virtually remained cold. In this period, besides the issue of non-proliferation, Indian policy of non alignment with soviet tilt greatly impaired the relations. To quote S. Paul Kapur and Summit Ganguly,

> 'India's non-aligned foreign policy thus became a source of considerable irritation to the US. Not only did India refused to assist US in containing Soviet power, but they also cooperated with Soviet Union in significant ways'.[3]

However with the disintegration of USSR and end of cold war "which greatly altered the strategic calculus of India and forced Indian policy makers to recalculate their strategic options"[4] the seeds of engagement were sown as both the sides found enough reasons to redefine their relationship. India on her part realised the potential of US as sole super power of the world and US realised the strategic importance of India and found India's large untapped market quite appealing. The decade of 1990s witnessed many developments towards rapprochement. In 1992, first meeting of the Indo-US Army Steering Committee was called which helped to resume strategic dialogue. After this, the meetings of the Steering Committees of Air force and Navy followed and all this paved the way for Indo-US Military Cooperation Agreement of 1995.[5] But the process of normalisation could not lost long and ruptured in 1998 when India conducted five nuclear tests at Pokhran desert site. The tests were not less than a shock to non-proliferation priests in US and sent a clear message to them that the US policy of "non-proliferation" and "isolation" vis-à-vis India had resulted in an utter failure. So in order to bring India close to non-proliferation regime and to give a new direction to torn Indo-US relations, Strobe Talbot, the then US Deputy Secretary of State, started a series of talks with Indian External Affairs Minister Jaswant Singh. The two officials met around fourteen times in different parts of the world [6] and discussed diverse issues but "nuclear issue" remained the focus of talks. Strobe-Jaswant spirit could not cut much ice on this issue but facilitated the visit of President Bill Clinton to India in 2000.This was the time when a US president was visiting India after a gap of twenty two years. But Clinton's visit could not do much to repair the damaged Indo-US relations as he came to India with a "non-proliferation" agenda which greatly limited the scope to explore the potential of full cooperation between two sides. In his address to the joint session of Indian parliament, he said:

> 'Nuclear future is not a secure future and most of the world is moving towards the elimination of nuclear weapons. That goal is not advanced if any country in any in region moves in other direction.'[7]

During his visit, Clinton also discussed the scope of cooperation in economic field, counter terrorism and regional stability but showed no signs to break the dead lock on nuclear issue which for decades had dogged the relations between the two countries. After the visit of Clinton, John Holum, a senior adviser of Clinton on non-proliferation announced that "full potential of Indo-US relations couldn't be realised until India joined NPT".[8]

A paradigm shift in Indo-US relations came in 2000 when George W. Bush came to power in US. After assuming the office of the President of US, he reversed the policy of "isolation" and put emphasis on the policy of "engagement" vis-à-vis India because it was a long term objective of Bush to engage world's largest democracy, often telling his advisers that one can't ignore one billion strong democracy and one has to find ways of engaging with it. Bush was keen on improving relations with India became evident even before his presidency as Condoleezza Rice, who served as National Security Adviser during Bush's first term indicated during 2000 presidential campaign that a future Bush Administration would take a fresh approach to India. In the same year, she wrote in *Foreign Affairs* journal that:

> 'the United States should pay closer attention to India's role in the regional balance. ... India is an element in China's calculation and id should be in America's too. India is not a great power yet, but it has a great potential to emerge as one'.[9]

Robert Blackwill, who served as US ambassador to India from September 2001 to July 2003, while speaking at the Indo-American Chamber of Commerce on September 6, 2001 also said that Bush administration was determined to 'transform fundamentally the very essence of bilateral relationship'.[10] Within these developments erupted September 11, 2001 crisis which was a defining moment in the bilateral relationship between two countries. The 9/11 crisis made Bush administration shift its focus from non-proliferation to terrorism which was a common enemy to both the countries. In its fight against terrorism, India extended full support and cooperation to Bush administration. It supported US in operation "Enduring Freedom" by escorting US warships through Malacca strait. It also supported US in Iraq war by sending its combat troops to Iraq [11] and also granted permission to FBI to set up its office in New Delhi and also offered ports and air port facilities to US.[12]

In order to take the process of cooperation forward and to widen its scope, President Bush and Indian Prime Minister Atal Behari Vajpayee announced Next Steps in Strategic Partnership (NSSP) in January 2004 which turned out to be a milestone in emerging Indo-US relations. Under

NSSP, both the sides agreed to take reciprocal measures to facilitate cooperation in technology transfers. US agreed to ease restrictions on the transfer of technology to India in three crucial areas, civil nuclear technology, civilian space and dual use technology goods. India on its part agreed to tighten the control on the export of sensitive technology and not to divert technology received from US towards military Purposes.[13] First phase of NSSP was concluded in September 2004 when Indian Foreign Secretary Shyam Saran and US Under Secretary of State Kenneth Juster sealed an agreement under which Indian Space Research Organisation (ISRO) was removed from Entity List and licence requirements for exporting low level dual use items to Indian research organisations were also eased.[14] After this land mark initiative, several other positive developments took place which greatly helped to transform Indo-US relations, most significant being the visit of US Secretary of State Condoleezza Rice to India. Rice visited India in March 2005 and expressed the willingness of Bush administration to cooperate with India in the field of civil nuclear energy. Indians were highly surprised by this offer and lost no time in seizing the opportunity and immediately after her visit, the two sides started negotiations to chalk out contours for this broad cooperation. After some high profile talks and delegation level meetings Indian Prime Minister Manmohan Singh and US President George Bush issued a joint statement on 18 July, 2005 which set a framework for Indo-US Civil Nuclear Agreement. With this initiative, Bush not only reversed decades old US policy on non-proliferation but also removed a biggest obstacle which for years had clouded the relations between two countries. In the joint statement, President Bush described India as a responsible state with highly advanced nuclear related technology and stated that it "should acquire same benefits and advantages as other such states". Bush also stated that "he will work to achieve full civil nuclear energy cooperation with India as it realizes its goals of promoting nuclear power and achieving energy security".[15] Indian Prime Minister on his part stated that India would assume the same responsibilities and safety practices and derive the same benefits and advantages as other leading countries and would work towards:

- Splitting its nuclear facilities into military and civil ones and placing the latter under IAEA (International Atomic Energy Agency) safeguards.
- Continuing its unilateral moratorium on nuclear testing.
- Early conclusion of Fissile Material Cut off Treaty.
- Ensuring strict control on the transfer of sensitive nuclear technology to states that do not have such technology.[16]

Process of Negotiation

Indo-US civil nuclear deal was a very complex deal by nature as it had to go through several complex stages to see the light of the day which included:

1. Separation of Indian nuclear facilities.
2. Amending US domestic law.
3. Negotiating a bilateral 123 Agreement.
4. Negotiating a safeguards agreement with IAEA.
5. Amendment of the guide lines of Nuclear Suppliers Group (NSG).

After the July 18, 2005 statement, India started negotiations with US interlocutors to split its nuclear facilities into civil and military ones called "separation plan". US position on separation plan was very clear that it should be very comprehensive from non-proliferation standpoint and Bush urged India "to produce a credible, transparent and defensible plan to separate its civilian and military nuclear programmes under the same international safeguards that govern nuclear power programmes in other countries".[17] During negotiations, US negotiators insisted India to place maximum number of nuclear reactors along with breeder programme under civilian list. But Indian position was to place minimum number of reactors under the civilian list and also to keep breeder programme outside the list. After much bargaining, it was finally agreed upon that India will place its 14 out of 22 reactors under operation and construction in the civilian list which will be placed under IAEA safeguards. The separation will be completed by the end of 2014. It was also agreed that breeder programme will remain outside safeguards, [18] a great strategic win for India.

After separation plan was finalised, Bush administration passed Henry J. Hyde United States-India peaceful Atomic Energy Cooperation Act also called Hyde Act after the name of outgoing chairman of House International Relations Committee Henry J. Hyde on 18 December, 2006. The Act provides legal basis for nuclear cooperation between India and the United States. It was necessary for Bush administration to pass this Act as it waives some of the requirements of US Atomic Energy Act of 1954. These requirements are:

- A country should have full scope safeguards in place.
- A country should not have exploded a nuclear device in past (after March 10 1978).
- A country should not be involved in activities leading to the production of nuclear explosive devices.[19]

A country is eligible for nuclear cooperation with US only if it fulfils these requirements. As India did not fulfil any of these requirements, so Hyde Act was passed which waived these requirements and thereby allowed US to engage India in civil nuclear energy cooperation. However, the Act was drafted in such a way that it created serious concerns among Indian political and scientific establishments. The Act contains a number of provisions which are not only contrary to the July 18 2005 statement but are also against the assurances given by Indian Prime Minister to Parliament. The Act faced such a stiff opposition in India that at one time it appeared that the deal would fall. The stiff opposition in India made the task for Indian negotiators very difficult as they had to negotiate such a deal which could address their concerns caused by the passage of Hyde Act and which they could sell in India. After some nine rounds of tough and hectic negotiations, Indian interlocutors were in a position to strike an agreement which they could have ever negotiated. Inter alia the agreement gives India reprocessing rights which only few countries in the world have, provides for fuel supply assurances and more importantly doesn't interfere with India's strategic nuclear programme. The agreement was settled on 20 July 2007 and the text of the agreement was released on 3 august 2007. In their joint statement Indian External Affairs Minister, Pranab Mukherjeee and US Secretary of State Condoleezza Rice termed the agreement 'a historic mile stone in [the] strategic partnership between two countries'.[20] while expressing satisfaction over the agreement then Indian Atomic Energy Commission chairman Anil Kakodkar termed the agreement satisfactory and said that "This Agreement gives advance consent rights for us [India] to reprocess spent fuel and recover material in a national safeguarded facility". On fuel supply assurances Kakodkar said that, "the fuel supply assurances built into March 2006 statement and in this final draft are entirely consistent. The Agreement also allows the country to continue its domestic programme...".[21]

After finalising the 123 Agreement, India negotiated a safeguards agreement with IAEA in August 2008 under which it was agreed that India will place its civilian reactors under the surveillance of IAEA and in the same year NSG amended its guidelines thereby allowing India to engage in nuclear trade and commerce with rest of the world. Thereafter, the 123 Agreement was sent to US congress for approval. After much debate and discussion, the House of Representatives passed it on September 28, 2008 with 298 members voted in favour and 117 voted against it. The Senate passed it on 1st October 2008 with 86-13 margin. US President signed it on 8 October 2008 now known as "United States-India Nuclear cooperation Approval and Non-proliferation Enhancement Act". At the signing ceremony, Bush said that 'the legislation makes no changes to the terms of the 123 agreement as I sent to Congress'. He also said that the legislation does not change the fuel supply commitments that the US government has made to the government of India as recorded in the 123 agreement'. Bush also underlined that 'the agreement also grants India "advance consent to reprocessing" which brought in to effect upon the conclusion of arrangements and procedures for a dedicated reprocessing facility under safeguards'.[22] The agreement was formally inked by Indian External affairs Minister, Pranab Mukherjee and his counterpart US Secretary of State Condoleezza Rice on 10 October, 2008.

Benefits of the Deal

The Indo-US civil nuclear deal is not only about cooperation between India and United States in the field of nuclear energy but it is more than that. It is a gateway to a broader strategic cooperation between two countries as was laid down by Condoleezza Rice at the agreement signing ceremony:

> 'Let no one assume that our work is finalised. Indeed what is most valuable about this agreement is that it unlocks a new and a far broader world of potential for our strategic partnership in 21st century, not just on nuclear cooperation but on every area of national endeavour'.[23]

The deal has the potential to advance energy security, protect environment, boost economic and technological development in both the countries, strengthen non-proliferation regime and international security and to create balance of power in Asian region. The deal is a win-win situation for the two countries and provides huge benefits to both the countries.

Benefits to India

The deal puts an end to India's decades old nuclear isolation and technology denial regimes. Right after 1974, India was subjected to severe international sanctions because of her nuclear test conducted in 1974 which left India isolated in the international environment. Export of nuclear technology and material was highly restricted to India. Such was the state of affairs that India was not allowed to purchase a super computer for weather forecasting because of its dual use. Indian nuclear scientists were denied visas by US and were not allowed to visit nuclear laboratories in US. All these restrictions greatly hindered the development of India's power programme. In mid 1990s, its power reactors had some of the world's lowest capacity factor, telling the story of country's nuclear isolation. Nuclear deal puts an end to this nuclear segregation and technology denial regimes. The agreement gives India access to nuclear material, equipment and dual use technology. According to US Department of Commerce, more than 87 per cent of dual use trade to India no longer requires license and less than 0.5 per cent of US exports to India now require a dual use export licernse.[24] All this has become possible because of the civil nuclear initiative. The cooperation will not only benefit the nuclear sector but space and defense sectors are also likely to get huge benefits. Indian space industry now can cooperate with US companies for developing and marketing US commercial satellites. In the same way Indian defense industry can get latest military equipments and hardware from US.

The civil nuclear deal will help India to meet its growing energy needs. India is one of the fast growing economies of the world with burgeoning energy requirements. In the period between 1980-2001, India witnessed 208 per cent increase in the demand of energy, in contrast to this China only saw 130 per cent increase in the same period.[25] Its energy requirements are expected to increase by four times in the next twenty-five years. Currently, India is fifth largest consumer of energy in the world and is expected to come to third rank in the middle of century.[26] So, in order to meet its growing energy needs, India has to exploit every possible source of energy bur here India has limited options. Coal, oil and hydro power are three main contributors to India's energy mix. India is world's third largest producer of coal but most of the Indian coal is inefficient with high ash content. That is why India has to import a huge quantity of coal every year. In 2010-2011 it imported 82 billion tonnes of coal and this figure is likely to increase in future. Experts believe that by 2032 India will import coal worth $ 200-250 billion.[27] Besides this, coal has a very harmful effect on our environment as it generates a huge amount of green house gases. India's emission of green house gases increased by 61 per cent between 1990-2001 and as per the estimates of Department of Atomic Energy India's carbon emissions will increase by 3 per cent annually between 2001 and 2025.[28] Hydro power is a clean source of energy and India has a vast potential of Hydro power but problem with the exploitation of this source is that the hydro power projects cause damage to environment and displacement of large sections of population. Oil is a significant contributor to India's energy basket. It accounts for nearly 33 per cent of India's energy consumption but India has very meagre reserves of oil and it imports about 70 per cent of its oil from west Asian and Middle East countries. India wants to free itself from heavy reliance on oil imports because of instability of oil prices in international market.

So, in order to meet these challenges nuclear energy is the best option. It is a robust source of energy. 1 kg of uranium generates 4000000 kwh of electricity and if this uranium is recycled then it can generate 7000000 kwh of electricity.[29] Besides this, it is a clean source of energy and does not produce green house gases. According to Nuclear Energy Institute, US nuclear power plants in 2004 "prevented 3.43 million tonnes of sulphur dioxide, 1.11 million tonnes of nitrogen oxide, 696.6 million metric tonnes of carbon dioxide from entering earth's atmosphere".[30] Nuclear power in India can also bring same benefits and it has been estimated that 10 per cent increase in India's nuclear power generating capacity would decrease India's carbon dioxide emission by 130 million tonnes annually.[31] So the civil nuclear initiative does not only ensure energy security to India but will also help it to reduce its heavy dependence on coal and oil and will also help it to reduce its emission of green house gases and it is for this reason Condoleezza Rice called it "one of the greenest parts of India's new Green Revolution."[32]

Another benefit which nuclear deal provides to India is that it will get fuel to feed its starving nuclear power programme. Among developing countries, India has the largest and unique nuclear programme, but shortage of fuel has been a main constraint for its nuclear power programme. India has very limited reserves of uranium (61,000 tonnes) which is used as fuel in nuclear reactors and access to foreign fuel was restricted to by technology denial regimes in the wake of her 1974 nuclear test. There has been a big gap between demand and supply for instance in 2006 the demand for uranium was 475 tonnes per year but production was only 300 tonnes.[33] The shortage of fuel was a main factor responsible for low capacity factor of its nuclear reactors. In 2000-2003, its Pressurised Heavy Water Reactors were operating at 90 per cent capacity factor. But it dropped to 81 per cent in 2003-2004 and worsened in 2004-2005 when it reached to 76 per cent.[34] By signing this historic deal, India will get fuel for its nuclear reactors not only from US but from other suppliers as well and in this way a biggest impediment of its nuclear programme stands removed. After nuclear deal was signed an Indian official told BBC that "If this agreement had not come through we might have as well closed down our nuclear reactors and by extension our nuclear programme" because of shortage of fuel.[35]

Benefits to America

Like India, the deal is also of great importance for United States as it also provides huge benefits to it ranging from economic to strategic. In the first place, the deal has a great potential to boost economic fortunes of United States. The deal will generate a business of $40 billion worldwide in next fifteen years as India plans to build about 24 reactors in next 15 years. It will open new markets for American firms and will generate employment opportunities for Americans. This was confirmed by Jeffery T. Bergner, Assistant Secretary of Legislative Affairs before the House Committee on Foreign affairs:

> 'of the 15 or so reactors India plans to import, even if the US vendors can win two reactors it could add 3000-5000 direct Jobs and 10,000-15,000 indirect jobs in America for Americans. Furthermore at least 15 US companies including General Electric and Westinghouse will be involved in the process'.[36]

The nuclear deal is a boon for American nuclear sector as it will rejuvenate dormant American nuclear industry which is losing markets in the world and will make it globally more competitive. This was admitted by Condoleezza rice in these words:

> 'At its core our initiative with India is not simply government to government. It was crafted with private sector firmly in mind. Because it will fully open the door to civil nuclear trade and cooperation, this is good for American business'.[37]

Not only the nuclear sector but other sectors like aero space and defense are also likely to reap huge benefits. The order for purchasing commercial air planes worth $ 8 billion from Boeing of Seattle has been placed before it. Likewise American defense industry by selling military equipments and hardware to India could gain billions of dollars. William Cohen, former US Defense Secretary, claimed that "the US defense companies could gain purchases from India worth $ 30 billion in the period 2007-2012".[38]

Secondly, the initiative will help US to balance the rising power of China. The US policy has always been to remain engaged in every part of globe and not to allow any particular power to dominate any particular region. This was confirmed by US Defense Planning Guidance (DPG) document published in 1992: "To prevent the re-emergence of new rival is the primary objective of the country and not to allow any hostile power to dominate a region and generate global power".[39] The rise of China as a regional power after the disintegration of USSR created serious apprehensions for US as it started viewing China as a serious security threat. Bush administration directly dubbed China as "future military adversary" and an important "strategic issue" facing US.[40] The rise of China as a great economic and military power in the region has not only created an imbalance in the region but has also greatly limited the chances of US engagement in the region, thus posing a direct challenge to US. To quote Kapil Sibal, "If US is facing a challenge in the 21st century, it will not be from India, somebody from its neighbourhood".[41] So in order to face this challenge US has offered nuclear deal to India by which it not only wants to balance the rising power of China but also wants to make its presence felt in the region from which it has been excluded from decades. According to Ferguson, science and technology fellow at Council on Foreign Relation, 'The United States is trying to cement its relationship with the largest democracy in order to counter balance China'.[42] Bill Emmott, editor in chief of *The Economist*, also writes that, "The basic reason to make India an exception and to bring it closer to US is the desire to balance rising power of China in Asia".[43]

Third important strategic achievement for the US is that the nuclear deal brings India close to Nuclear Non-Proliferation (NPT) regime which past US policies has failed to achieve. The US policy of isolation vis-à-vis India not only kept India outside the NPT regime but also provoked her to accelerate her weapons programme. So it was a big foreign policy challenge for US to bring India within the ambit of NPT regime and this challenge has been met by this civil nuclear cooperation initiative as US Security Advisor Hedely stated that:

> 'this [civil nuclear deal] is actually a way to bring India within non-proliferation framework. It will be adopting the kind of non-proliferation protection that we do. It is to bring India on the same page as we, so they can be global partner in the proliferation issue as well.......... This is actually the vehicle to bring India on to our page in terms of proliferation policy'.[44]

Under the agreement, India has agreed to divide its nuclear programme into military and civilian ones and has also committed to place its 14 reactors under the IAEA safeguards. This will make India to open 65 per cent of its reactors for IAEA inspections so that nuclear material and technology is not diverted. This figure could rise to 90 per cent in future. Prior to the agreement, only 9 per cent of India's nuclear reactors were open for inspections. Besides this, India has also committed to continue its unilateral moratorium on nuclear testing, negotiate a multilateral Fissile Material Cut Off Treaty and not to transfer sensitive nuclear technology to other countries. All these steps bring India close to NPT regime. To quote Dr. Elbaradi, former Director of IAEA

> 'the nuclear deal would bring India closer as an important Partner in the non-proliferation and which would be a milestone, timely for on going efforts to consolidate the non-proliferation regime, combat terrorism and strengthen nuclear safety'.[45]

Deal and the Opposition

In spite of its great strategic importance the nuclear deal was met with stiff opposition in both the countries. In US the deal faced stiff opposition from non-proliferation lobby on the grounds that the deal undermines NPT, would lead to increase in India's nuclear arsenal and would lead to arms race in the region. Non-proliferation priests held that the deal is a violation of NPT. According to Hennery Sokoloski, 'the violation is hardly a "pretty canard", it's a real problem – one which as the US and its allies plead their case against Iran and North Korea – is only likely to become more of a headache. The US will be joining the ranks of North Korea and Iran as NPT violaters'.[46] Senator Byron Dorgan termed the deal a "grievous mistake" that would reward the rogue behaviour. Daryll Kimball Executive Director of the Arms Control association called it a "non-proliferation disaster".[47]

NPT requires that assistance in the field of civil nuclear energy should only be provided to those States that join the treaty and work towards strengthen the regime. As India has not signed the treaty and has a weapons programme in operation but still will receive assistance from the US and other countries of the world like NPT signatories. It has been claimed that this could encourage other countries to offer similar assistance to NPT outsiders and this could weaken the NPT regime. According to George Perkovich, 'the deal would set a precedent for China, a major nuclear exporter and an alleged source of Pakistan's nuclear technology, to seek similar rule changes or exceptions.'[48] Leonard S. Specter, Deputy Director of Centre for Non-Proliferation, International Relations and Security Network also holds the same argument: "If you allow India to achieve same facilities as legitimate nuclear states signed the Nuclear Non-Proliferation treaty (NPT), many other nations are likely to tread through it. China is before now believing of selling other reactors to Pakistan".[49] According to Aston B. Carter, the nuclear deal "would create a serious blow to non-proliferation regime and could set a dangerous precedent for rogue countries like Iran, North Korea and other aspiring nuclear powers.....The deal has given a message that forgiveness comes to proliferators who wait long and that the nuclear aspirants could bypass the NPT if they waited long enough".[50]

The deal was also criticised on the ground that it does not place any restrictions on India's weapons programme nor does it cap its production of fissile material. The deal gives India right to import fuel for its civilian reactors from international market and this could free her indigenous reserves of uranium which could be diverted towards the production of nuclear weapons and this could led to arms race in the region and could destabilise it. This made Senator Richard Lugar to say:

> "In pursuing a nuclear relationship with India, we must deal with some fundamental facts. India has not signed the Nuclear Non-Proliferation treaty, it has built and tested nuclear weapons and it has declared its intention to continue its nuclear weapons programme and the production of fissile material. Although the US-India Civil Nuclear Agreement would move India into a closer relationship with International Atomic Energy Agency and would put more Indian reactors under safeguards, it would not prevent India from expanding its nuclear arsenal'.[51]

The claim the that deal would lead to increase in India's nuclear arsenal and it undermines NPT is not justified. The fact is that it strengthens it. It is because of the agreement that for the first time in history, India has separated it civil nuclear facilities from military ones and has agreed to place its entire civilian programme under the IAEA safeguards. This will not only lead to greater transparency in its nuclear establishment but will also help to reduce the production of fissile material and thereby nuclear weapons. Because of the separation plan India's plutonium production will come down from 2000 kg/year in 2007 to around 1,250 kg/year after 2014 when plan will be fully implemented. So there will be a 1/3rd reduction in its plutonium production.[52] Moreover India has also committed to work towards the negotiation of multilateral Fissile Material Cut Off treaty and exercise a strict control over the transfer of sensitive nuclear technology and material. All these efforts rally promote NPT regime. It may also be noted that in spite of being outside NPT, India has maintained an impeccable non-proliferation record and has always behaved like a responsible nuclear weapon state and the nuclear deal is obviously a reward for such a record. The deal has sent a message that in ultimate analysis responsible states with good non-proliferation rerecord are rewarded by international community and not the rogue states.[53]

In India the deal faced stiff opposition from political establishments. Bhartiya Janta Party (BJP), the main opposition party in parliament and the left parties were mainly involved in the opposition. BJP criticised the deal on the grounds that it compromises India's strategic programme and sovereignty. In a memorandum submitted to the President on 21 June 2006, senior BJP leaders stressed as follows: "The government must be restrained from dismantling India's nuclear programme.......... The deal will bind India in future and it was worse than CTBT.'[54] In his address to India Conclave, leader of the opposition in Lok Sabha, L.K. Advani said that nuclear deal was a "treaty between unequals" and it takes away India's right to test in future". He further said:

> "We are opposed to any agreement which says Indira Gandhi may have done Pokhran I, Atal Behari Vajpayee may have done Pokhran II, but here after no government must do Pokhran III. This we can't accept. If this is the price to be paid in the name of nuclear energy our party is not in favour".[55]

During a debate on nuclear deal in Lok Sabha, Advani went on to say that it undermines India's long term interests and BJP would renegotiate the deal if it came to power.[56] BJP was also upset with the passage of the Hyde Act on the grounds that it has far-reaching consequences for India's foreign policy and it jeopardises India's strategic objectives.[56] The Act has been passed as Advani said with this objective to 'cap, rollback and ultimately eliminate India's nuclear weapons capability'[57]

The BJP's opposition to the nuclear deal was only to score political gains. Claim of the BJP that the agreement undermines India's strategic programme is wrong because the agreement fully protects it. India has agreed to open only 14 reactors for IAEA inspections and the remaining 8 reactors will serve its strategic purposes. Besides this India is not obliged to place its future reactors under IAEA safeguards. The agreement also does not take away India's "right to test". India can conduct a nuclear test in future if her security interests are jeopardisd.[58] BJP's opposition to the nuclear deal on the grounds of Hyde Act is also short sighted as the Hyde Act is a US domestic law and is applicable to US only. It does not bind India. This was declared by Indian External Affairs Minister in Parliament: 'India's rights and obligations on civil nuclear cooperation with US arise only from 123 agreement that we have agreed upon, where as the Hyde act is a piece of America's domestic legislation'.[59] This was also confirmed by US Assistant Secretary Richard Boucher:

> "the Hyde Act was a domestic legislation of the United States the main function of which is to allow the kind of co-operation in the civil nuclear field which India envisaged under the nuclear agreement between the two countries. While the Hyde Act binds US government, it has nothing to do with India".[60]

Left parties criticised the deal for the reasons that it is a part of a larger and wider strategic cooperation between India and United States which could have serious implications on India's independent foreign policy and strategic autonomy. They highly criticised India's vote against Iran at IAEA and viewed it not an independent decision but one exercised under US pressure. Also, they challenged the logic that the deal is vital for India's energy security because of poor performance of India's nuclear sector in the past and argued that even if government succeeds to generate 20,000 MWe through nuclear means by 2020 which is too ambitious, it is not going to make a huge difference to India's energy mix because the contribution of nuclear power to its energy mix will only rise to 7 per cent from current 3 per cent. Besides this nuclear power is not cost competitive when compared with power generated from coal power plants. The cost of power generated from imported nuclear reactors will be twice that of coal fired plants.[61]

Left parties also expressed serious concerns regarding various provisions of Hyde Act. It was claimed that the Act runs contrary to the assurances given by Indian Prime Minister to the Parliament. The Act denies full civil nuclear cooperation to India as laid down in July18 statement because under the Act, dual use items and sensitive nuclear technology will not be transferred to India. The Act also denies "fuel supply assurances" as mentioned in March 2006 separation plan as it calls up on the US administration to stop fuel supply to India and also to encourage other suppliers to do so if the agreement is terminated. Besides this the Act contains a number of provisions which could have serious implications on India's foreign policy and her strategic nuclear programme.[62]

It is true that deal is a part of a broad strategic cooperation with US, but what is wrong in having a strategic cooperation with US. There are a number of countries which are having such cooperation with US. For instance China is having a strategic cooperation with US since a long time and it has earned her huge benefits. Today, China imports more than 10 times dual use technology from the US than India imports. When such an engagement has not made China Subservient to US how can it make India which is world's largest democracy. History bears testimony that India has never compromised her independent foreign policy and decision making whenever it was tested. Whether it was UN resolution on Kashmir, 1971 resolution on Bangladesh, NPT or CTBT. On all these international issues India never succumbed to foreign pressure and acted like an independent and responsible State upholding her national interests. So it is mere an exaggeration to claim that because of the deal India will lose her right of independent decision making and will become a US satellite State as claimed by the left.

It has been argued that the nuclear deal, if fully implemented, cannot make a huge difference to India's energy mix because nuclear power contributes very little to India's electricity generation (3%) and can exceed to 7 per cent if India succeeds in generating 20,000 MW by 2020 which will be an insignificant contribution. Keeping in view India's fast growing energy requirements the demand for electricity, in India would be around 4,48,000 MW by 2020 and by 2030 it will be between 8,00,000 to 10,00,000 MW. In this demand of electricity the share of nuclear power at 7 per cent rate will be between 56,000 to 70,000 MW which will be a significant contribution,[63] as the present contribution is only 4,385 MW. Besides this the civil nuclear agreement brings in other benefits. Because of the agreement Western technology will flow to India and from this Indian companies will benefit a lot. "A number of Indian companies could become a manufacturing hub for making nuclear related parts and export them to US and other countries". India can also collaborate with other countries with great expertise in the field of nuclear technology and can truly become a "global nuclear power".[64]

Nuclear power is also cost competitive with coal power. Power from coal fired plants is cheap only when they are near to coal pith head which is not the case in India. According to Nuclear Power Cooperation of India if a coal plant is more than 1000 km away from coal pith head then nuclear power may be a cheaper than coal power.[65] When comparison between coal fired thermal power and nuclear power is made an important fact is neglected which is how much damage coal power plants cause to our environment and how much economic loss they cause. On an average, a 1000 MW coal plant annually consumes 2.86 million tonnes of coal and in this process it generates 8.37 million tonnes of carbon dioxide annually. Due to this emission of carbon dioxide 401 persons die every year (362 due to air pollution and 39 due to climate change mitigation) and economic loss caused due to climate change is $ 83.7 million per year. In comparison to this a nuclear power plant of the same capacity only consumes 52 tonnes of natural uranium annually.[66] Since nuclear energy is a clean source of energy and does not emit green house gases thus by replacina coal power with nuclear power, we can annually save millions of dollars and hundreds of human lives.

As already point out, the Hyde Act which was the main concern of left parties does not apply to India. It is only the 123 agreement which binds India. Under the agreement "sensitive nuclear technology, heavy water production technology, sensitive nuclear facilities, heavy water production facilities and major critical components of such facilities may be transferred pursuant to an amend to the agreement" (Art. 5.2). The agreement also does not bar the transfer of dual use items to India, besides that such items can also be imported from other countries as NSG waiver given to India does not prohibit such transfers. The Agreement also gives India reprocessing rights and also guarantees fuel for civilian reactors for life time. Besides this, the US will also help India to develop "strategic reserve" of fuel to guard against any disruption of fuel in future. [Art. 5.6 (b) (iii)][67]. So the full civil nuclear cooperation and fuel supply assurances are fully guaranteed under the agreement.

Conclusion

Indo-US civil nuclear agreement is a win-win situation for both the countries. For India it has put an end to decades old nuclear apartheid and has given her a passport to import latest dual use technology from world suppliers. It ensures energy security for India and has a great potential to make her a dominant player in the region. What is more important it recognizes India as a Nuclear Weapon State as it allows it to reap same benefits of civil nuclear technology as other nuclear powers do. The deal also serves broad economic and strategic objectives of United States. More importantly, it has buried the past animosities and has opened a new chapter in Indo-US strategic partnership. Today, the two countries have forged a closer cooperation in a number of vital areas like fight against terrorism, preventing nuclear proliferation, protecting environment, promoting democracy and energy security, protecting vital sea lanes etc. All this can have a positive impact on world system. Thanks to this historic Indo-US civil nuclear deal that has made all this possible.

REFERENCES

1. A.G. Noorani, April 1981, "Indo-US Nuclear Relations", *Asian Survey*, Vol. 21, No.4, p. 401.
2. Paul F. Power, June 1979, "the Indo-American Nuclear Controversy", *Asian Survey*, Vol. 19, No. 9, pp. 582, 596.
3. Harsh V. Pant, 2011, *The US-India Nuclear Pact: Policy Process and Great Power Politics*, Oxford University Press, New Delhi, p. 38.
4. S. Paul Kapur and Summit Ganguly, 2007, "The Transformation of US-India Relations: An Explanation of Rapprochement and Prospects for Future", *Asian Survey*, Vol. 47, No. 4, p. 647.
5. Sadia Tasleem, 2008, "Indo-US Civil Nuclear Cooperation: Altering Strategic Positioning and Balance of Power in South Asia", RSS Policy Studies 44, pp. 22-23.
6. K. Alan Kronstadt, August 12, 2008, "Indo-US Relations", CRS Report for Congress.
7. Ajai K. Rai, 2009, *India's Nuclear Diplomacy after Pokhran II*, Darling

Kindersley, Delhi, p. 22.

8. *Ibid.* p. 21.
9. Glenn Kessler, April 4, 2006, "India's Nuclear Deal May face Hard Sell", The Washington Post. Available at http // www.washingtonpost.com/wpdyun/content/article/2006/04/02/Ar2006040201315.html?referrer=email&referrer=email. Accessed on 22/4/2008.
10. Dhruva Jaishankar, "Chronicle of a Deal Foretold: Washington's Perspective on Negotiating the Indo-US Nuclear Deal" in P.R. Chari (ed.), 2009, *Indo-US civil Nuclear Deal: Seeking Synergy in Bilateralism*, Routledge, New Delhi, p. 103.
11. P.R. Lawy, January/February, 2007, "Indian in 2006: A New Emphasis on Engagement", *Asian Survey*, Vol. 47, No. 1, p. 115.
12. Tasleem, *op. cit.* p. 23.
13. Rai, *op. cit.* pp. 43-44.
14. Dinshaw Mistry, September/October, 2006, "Diplomacy, Domestic Politics and US-India Nuclear Agreement", *Asian survey*, Vol. 46, No. 5, pp. 681-682.
15. "Indo-US Joint Statement" Available at http//www.meaindia mic.in mystart.php?id=53019889. Accessed on 5/6/2012.
16. *Ibid.*
17. John Cherian, March 10,2006, "On a Mission to India", *Frontline*, Vol. 23, Issue 4.
18. M.R. Srinivasan, May 25, 2006, "Indo-US Nuclear Agreement: Expectation and Concerns", *Current Science*, Vol. 90, No.10, p. 1318.
19. Paul K. Kerr, December 15, 2011, "US Nuclear Cooperation with India: Issues for Congress, CRS Report for Congress, pp. 22-23.
20. Sidarath Vardarajan, August 28, 2007, Nuclear Deal Satisfactory: Kakodkar", *The Hindu.*
21. Sidarath Vardarajan, July 28, 2007, "Kakodkar Supports Nuclear Deal", *The Hindu.*
22. "Bush Signs Nuclear Deal into Law", October 10, 2008, *The Hindu.*
23. Rai, *op. cit.* p. 63
24. Ajay Lele and Archana Mishra, December, 2010, "Indo-US Strategic Partnership: Beyond the Nuclear Deal", *Asia Pacific Journal of Social Science*, Special Issue No. 1, p. 102.
25. "Remarks of Secretary of State Condoleezza Rice at the Senate Foreign Relations Committee on the US-India Civil Nuclear Cooperation Initiative", Wednesday, April 5, 2005, p. 7. Available at http//www.carnegieendowment.org/static/npp/reports/rice_4-5-06.pdf.
26. K. Alan, *op. cit.* p. 60.
27. A.P.J. Abdul Kalam and Srijan Pal Singh, November 6, 2011, "Nuclear Power is Our Gateway to a Prosperous Future", *The Hindu.*
28. Remarks of Rice, *op. cit.* p. 8.
29. Richard Rhodes and Dennis Beller, January/February 2000, "The Need for Nuclear Power", *Foreign Affairs*, Vol. 79, No. 1, p. 31.
30. K.R. Gupta, "Indo-US Nuclear Cooperation" in Rahul Bhonsle *et al.* (eds.),

2007, *Indo-US Nuclear Deal*, Vol. II, Atlantic Publishers, New Delhi, p. 165.

31. Sudesh Rani, 2010, "Indo-US Nuclear Agreement: A Critical Study", *Punjab Journal of Politics*, Vol. XXXIV, Nos. 1-2, p. 77.
32. "Remarks of Rice", *op. cit.* p. 9.
33. John Stephenson and Peter Tyman, "Will the US-India Civil Nuclear Cooperation Initiative Light India" in Henry Sokoloski (ed.), March 2007, *Gauging US-India Strategic Partnership*, p. 22. Report published by Strategic Studies Institute. Available at http//www.strategicstudies institute.army.mil.Accessed on 5/4/2012.
34. "Uranium Crises", December 21-January 13, *Frontline* Vol. 22, Issue 27.
35. Zia Mian *et al.*, "Plutonium Production in India and US-India Nuclear Deal", in Sokoloski, *op. cit.* p. 107.
36. Prashant Hosur, Spring 2010, "The Indo-US Civilian Nuclear Agreement: What's the Big deal", *International Journal*, p. 439.
37. Dr. Tom Sauer, May 2010, "Drivers Behind the Nuclear Deal with India: US Domestic Politics or Geostrategic Concerns", p. 8. Available at www.suc.kiley-ven-be/web/files/11/72wi6-115.pdf. accessed on 25/5/2012. Accessed on 5/4/2012.
38. *Ibid.* p. 16.
39. John Cherian, February 25-March 10, 2006, "The China Factor", *Frontline*, Vol. 23, Issue 04.
40. *Ibid.*
41. Jabin T. Jacob, March 2006, "Indo-US Civil Nuclear Deal: The China Factor", IPCS Special Report 14, p. 12.
42. Jayshree Pajaria and Ether Pan, November 5, 2012, "The US-India Nuclear Deal". Available at http//www.crf.org/india/us-india-nucleardeal/19663. Accessed on 24/2/2012.
43. Tom Sauer, *op. cit.* p. 8.
44. Sudesh Rani, *op. cit.* p. 78.
45. Annapurna Nautiyal, September 2008, "Indo-US Civil Nuclear Deal: What is There", *Strategic Insight*, Vol. VII, Issue 4.
46. Aadil Sultan Mohammad, July 2006, "Indo-US Civilian Nuclear Agreement: Implications on South Asian Security Environment", p. 5. Available at http//www.stimson.org/images/uploads/research-pdfs/ AdilSultan.pdf. Accessed on 3/3/2012.
47. Prashant Hosur, *op. cit.* p. 437.
48. Pant, *op. cit.* p. 95.
49. Mohammed Ishaque Fani, "The Indo-US Strategic Partnership in Post 9/ 11: Implications for Pakistan", *Pakistan Vision*, Vol. 10, No. 2, p. 143.
50. Nantiyal, *op. cit.*
51. K.R. Gupta, *op. cit.* p. 181.
52. Zia Mian, *op. cit.* p. 115.
53. T.V. Paul and Mahesh Shankar, Winter 2007-2008, "Why the US-India Nuclear Accord is a Good Deal", *Survival*, Vol. 49, No. 4, p. 119.
54. Col. Ved Prakash, "Indo-US Nuclear Deal" in Rahul Bhonsle *et al.*, *op. cit.* p. 101.

55. "Left told Deal Will not be Pursued: Advani", March 5, 2008, *The Hindu.*
56. "123 Agreement with US is Unacceptable to us: Advani, November 29, 2007, *The Hindu.*
57. Sudesh Rani, *op. cit.* p. 81.
58. Sidarath Vardarajan, August 4, 2007, "A Guide to the Provisions of 123 Agreement", *The Hindu.*
59. Sudesh Rani, *op. cit.* pp. 78-79.
60. *Ibid.* p. 79.
61. Prakash Karat, July/September, 2007, "The Indo-US Civil Nuclear Deal: Struggle to Defend National Sovereignty, *Marxist*, Vol. XXIII, No. 3.
62. Prakash Karat, August 20, 2007, "Why the CPI (M) and the Left Oppose Nuclear Deal, *The Hindu.*
63. Kapil Sibal, September 5, 2007, "The Left is not Right on Nuclear Deal". *The Indian Express.*
64. Srinivas Laxman, September 12, 2008, "N-Trade: It's a $40 Billion Opportunity", *The Times of India.*
65. K.R. Gupta, *op. cit.* p. 165.
66. Kalam, *op. cit.*
67. See the text of "Agreement for Cooperation Between the Government of India and the Government of United States of America Concerning Peaceful Uses of Nuclear Energy", pp. 9-10. Available at http//www.hindu.com/nic/123agreement.pdf. Accessed on1/6/2012.

5

Environmental Security in Indian Ocean Region: US Policy in Parlance and Practice

Narottam Gaan

The state centric and military perspective of security has lost both its practical relevance and intellectual credibility in the context of a number of historic forces and events in the contemporary age. Those include the end of the cold war, global integration of national economies, erosion of national identities, and cultures, the shift in priority from military rivalry to economic competition and diminishing role of state as the dominant actor in international politics. On the other hand, there have emerged diverse new issues raging from poverty to refugee crises, information privacy to cyber-terrorism, environmental problems to natural disasters- which require not-state and non-military policies and strategies. These newly emerging security concerns have been characterized as non-traditional, and are now considered a major equipment of what is christened as comprehensive Security. Environmental security considered a major component of non-traditional security concepts has been broad based, discursively shifting away from State towards the comprehension of security threats from the causes and consequence of environmental degradation. Recent years have witnessed a rediscovery of interest in the interconnection between the environment and security in international relations thought and practice. This attention has been reinforced by disasters, such as Indian Ocean Tsunami of 2004, Hurricane Katrina and its aftermath in 2005, European heat waves in 2003 and 2006 and the Gulf of Mexico Oil Spill of 2010. It has also been developed through global political interventions, ranging from the 2005 entry into force of the Kyoto protocol, the 2006 Stern Review and the 2007 IPCC report. The environment-security relationship reached its apogee in 2007 with UN Security Council discussions of the strategic implications of climate change and direct attempts to link conflict in Darfur to climate change by both the UNEP and the UN Secretary-General Ban Ki-Moon. All these developments have reinforced the global concern about environmental change and its effects which come as greater threat to human kind than the State centric threats. A strong argument can be adduced for linking certain resources and environmental problems with prospects for political evictions and tensions as even war and peace. At the centre of ongoing debate is the assertion that resource scarcity and certain forms of environmental degradation are important amplifying factors contributing to political instability or violent conflict at the local, regional and inter-state levels. The most vulnerable to the stresses and strains of environmental change are and would be the poor, and marginalized of the developing world. While the dominant minority and richest few of the developed world be concerned with threats from environmental change to their luxurious and inordinate way of life, the poor majority of developing world is concerned with damages and threats to their very survival needs—food, water, land, shelter and health. In addition, the exploitation of non-renewable resources in the process of development has further exacerbated the renewable resources affecting the lives of human beings.

Establishing an environmental security agenda for the Indian Ocean Region (IOR) is significant in that it addresses basic survival issues which affect most of the inhabitants of the region, approximately one third of the globe's population. The Indian Ocean has been rightly described as the "heart of the third world" or the "Ocean of the South" with low per capita income and low level of development in the majority of countries.

A concept of environmental security which is more inclusive of the interest of the poor majority of people in the Indian Ocean states both littoral and non littoral is one that shifts away from viewing environmental stress as an additional threat within the traditional conflictual statist framework, to placing environmental change at the gravamen of global security with accent on non-military approaches. This will be premised on an increased understanding of the environment not as an external enemy force, but as a diverse nature which is inclusive of people, a nature which has the potential to provide secure access to individual citizens of all countries in the Indian Ocean region to basic nutrition, adequate access to healthy environments, appropriate shelter, and a security to practice a diverse range of livelihoods which are both culturally and ecologically determined.

The hiatus between the literature on environmental security and Indian Ocean Region is enormous. While a plethora of academic works and research has been made on environmental security, very little substantial work has been done in regard to the applicability of the concept "environmental security" in the Indian Ocean Region.

The Indian Ocean rim region, the home to one third of the world's populations, assumes a geo-strategic significance in that nearly half of the world's container traffic and 70 per cent of the total traffic of petroleum products is accounted for by the Indian Ocean and 60,000 ships transit through it each year. Extensively discussed in strategic affairs is its geo-strategic significance but little attention has been paid to the environmental challenges facing the Indian Ocean and the rim countries.

Key Environmental Issues

Ocean Resources

The Indian Ocean possesses a range of valuable natural resources including sea minerals and coral reefs. Coral reefs are under the threat of depletion due to global climate change, direct human pressures and inadequate governance, awareness and political will (Laipson,2009). Degradation of coastal ecosystems can have negative impacts on national economic as ecosystems and recreational services provided by them play an important role in tourism, fisheries and livelihoods of coastal communities. This region is also replete with economically valuable natural, mineral and energy resources which remain less exploited. Utilization of these resources needs to the done collaboratively by the rim countries keeping in mind the deleterious impacts on marine environment. With regard to usage and conservation of natural resources in the Indian Ocean region the rim countries have enmeshed in political and traditional concerns.

Climate Change

The Indian Ocean region is highly vulnerable to the impacts of climate change, and the majority of its population are poor and marginalized. The rim countries have varying but limited capacity to cope with the impacts of climate changes which can come in the forms of extreme weather events, sea level rise, storms—to name but a few. Climate change coupled with other regional environmental issues, loss of biodiversity—for instance can have serious negative economic impacts on the development in the region.

Bio Security

Marine bio security refers to the protection of marine environments from non-indigenous species, and this has direct implications on biodiversity in the marine ecological systems in the Indian Ocean. It has been found that invasive alien species (I.A.S.) are becoming a significant threat to marine biodiversity. Where ballast water is viewed as a major cause of their proliferation, comprehensive studies on bio-security are rarely found in this region and it is increasingly becoming important to assess the marine bio security risks for Indian Ocean rim countries. It needs cooperative efforts of a range of actors including scientists and policy makers to asses the threats thereto.

Marine Pollution

The Indian Ocean Region is also vulnerable to high levels of pollution caused by ocean dumping, waste disposal and oil spills as a significant amount of international trade takes place in the region's waters. The wastes pose threats to the survival of marine organisms and consequently on the marine ecosystem on which millions of livelihoods depend. In addition being bordered by fast growing economies such as India and China, as well as East Asian economies, there is a high possibility of more industrial waste disposed to the ocean. Eutrophication of near shore environments due to pollution from land based sources and their run off has impacted economic activities such as fisheries and tourism, and also affected fragile ecosystems.

Role of External Powers

Diego Garcia

The chief natural glory of the Diego Garcia atoll is its unique coral reef with well over 100 species of coral, part of one of the richest stores of biodiversity in the Indian Ocean. It has now turned out to be an environmental black hole by the American and British activities. The construction work undertaken at the military base over the years inevitably has left its mark on the atoll starting with the elimination of much of the tree vegetation. Massive reef blasting, coral mining, dredging and relocating sites for coral harvestings, draining and filling of large swamp/ wetland areas as part of development of harbour and air field construction by the US have made Diageo Garcia look more reminiscent of the Florida keys than of the Indian ocean with all the facilities of a small American town. The US Navy's own legal black hole doctrine being located overseas, the US Environmental Protection Agency (EPA) regulations do not apply to Diego Garcia. It is most surprising therefore that the US Naval facilities Engineering Command / Pacific apparently did not prepare formal environmental impact statements, reviews or studies prior to the multi million dollar dredging and landfill projects undertaken at all in the Diego Garcia at all which in retrospect were found to have had a potential to cause deleterious, long term impacts, including increased beach and shoreline erosion and adverse impacts on marine life.

The introduction of invasive alien plant species from overseas- including tangan-tangan (*Leucaena leucocephala*) considered one of the ten 100 worst invasive species of the world with the massive impacts of aggregate landfill material from Singapore/ Malaysia and by seeds introduced with Navy equipment has been ruinous to the marine environment. It has turned out to be an ecological time bomb that should be defused.

Nuclear Issues as Environmental Security

Recognizing its inherent, long term environmental dangers, nuclear energy cannot be relied upon as an environmentally sustained source of energy. The Indian Ocean Region is now undergoing rapid nuclearization. Issues of nuclear waste, its safe transport and its final disposal have not been high on their environmental or nuclear agendas. Nations are still persistent in their efforts to encapsulate nuclear issues into the realm of mainstream traditional 'hard security or defense'. Almost centered on identities of nation states, nuclear energy still demands priority from the angle of weaponry and arms proliferation. What remains most devastating to the marine environment and the livelihood of the people in Indian Ocean Region is the problem of nuclear waste, its production, transport and its storage.

Nuclearization has normally been a characteristic of industrialization. But most importantly, the dangers of nuclear accidents—whether they occur during plutonium production or during the handling and storage of waste products are often regarded by majority world governments as constituting acceptable levels of environmental risk. Moreover, such environmental risks are often regarded as luxury concerns.

Within the Indian Ocean Region, there are two key areas of concern. The first relates to radioactive waste being transported by sea from international reprocessing units in Europe. The second area relates to transport of waste by land. This may include waste which emerges from the mining process as well as the more toxic substances which evolve after the process of nuclear reaction.

Transport and Storages of Nuclear Waste

The key problem for the globe in relation to waste has been waste disposal after atomic reaction. But because most countries in IOR have infant nuclear programmes, this problem has not yet reached its future magnitude. But what is already pressing in these less affluent countries are issues of primary waste management which relate directly to the mining process itself.

The management of these wastes through the utilization of tailing dams is usually based on adequate levels of technology, although there are still dangerous leakages reported at intervals. In the poorer parts of the region, these basic storage issues pertaining to tailing dams are further exacerbated by the increased levels of environmental risk.

For example, in the three stage nuclear energy programme India needs mining of low grade Uranium stocks on an extremely large scale. The hazards of Jaduguda mining and dumping of liquid waste from the mine in tailing dams and diverted into Subarnarekha river upon the villagers are to be taken note of. Thus environmental security issues relating to Uranium mining and nuclear energy will be magnified in less affluent world. The Indian Ocean as a nuclear ocean will exhibit levels of environmental degradation which can be scarcely understood in West imagination. The lives of people are more expendable in political terms. In the majority world and this in turn, has a devastating impact on their environments.

It is not just waste that is generated within the region but also the ever increasing waste which passes through the region. It is very difficult to know just how many of these shipments carrying MOX fuel (Plutonium mixed with Uranium) are being made due to high levels of secrecy which enshroud them.

Apart from dismissively being regarded as simply en route states for the international trade in waste reprocessing, countries of Indian Ocean Region are also increasingly being looked at as possible repositories for international waste as a nuclear dumping ground. Indian Ocean has already been affected by the waste product of nuclear energy with high levels of radioactivity.

Because spent nuclear fuel can be reprocessed to produce both weapons of mass destruction—as well as energy, the placement of such waste dumps is highly politicized. With US increasingly involved in decisions as to who can and who cannot store and reprocess spent nuclear fuel.

In May and June 2008 Diego Garcia also served as transit point for 550 tonnes of low grade uranium from Iraq, which the US Department of Defense flew out of Baghdad in 37 cargo plane loads for trans-shipments to Canada by sea in a $ 70 million operative code named McCall. The volume of nuclear material and nuclear weaponry regularly transiting the Diego Garcia base poses considerable risks of radioactive contamination, especially to the waters of the lagoon.

Fuel Spills

Another serious and continuous environmental problem for Diego Garcia has been the chronic pollution by fuel spills from Petroleum, Oil and lubricant storage tanks on the island which hold 1.34 million barrels of jet fuel and diesel oil. Major oil spills in 1980, 1991, 1997 and1998 can illustrate the magnitude of environmental pollution.

Environmental Security in Discourse Not in Practice

When the environment challenges are regional in nature, national level policies and strategies of individual countries alone are insufficient to meet the onslaught of the fury of nature. Future actions and strategic measures have to take cognizance of the fact that these environmental challenges are inherently interrelated and complex and entwined with the global course of action to deal with environmental challenges and climate change. There needs to be a regional level cooperation to deal with the environmental challenges which are common to all Indian Ocean rim countries. As of now such challenges are not adequately addressed through regional policies, laws, multilateral agreements or in the least regional collaboration by scientists and experts.

Since the causes and consequence of environmental degradation are trans-boundary and need to be addressed globally, the minority rich industrialized countries like US and Western Europe owe a great historical responsibility in ensuring environmental and human security throughout the world in general and in Indian Ocean Region in particular by taking exemplary steps in reducing emission of CO_2 to the atmosphere. Instead of accepting the differential responsibility in mitigating environmental change including climate change, the US and Western Europe countries have been insistent on involving developing countries like India, China etc in the talks, negotiation and conventions on environment. This dilutes their historical responsibility by sharing the burden of cleansing the dirt of atmosphere with the developing world whose contribution to polluting the atmosphere is minimal. In the State centric and military predominance definition of national security the dominant players like, US in world politics are yet to accord environment that peremptory place in the security and defense realm, though there have been more rhetoric analysis, and discourse than practice and implementation. For example: the US Navy's own 'legal black hole' doctrine being located overseas, the US Environmental Protection Agency (EPA) regulations do not apply to Diego Garcia. It is most surprising that the US Naval facilities Engineering Command/Pacific apparently did not prepare formal environmental impact statement, reviews or studies prior to the multi million dollar dredging and landfill projects undertaken in the Diego Garcia atoll which in retrospect were found to have had a potential to cause deleterious long term impacts including increased beach and shoreline erosion and adverse impacts on marine life.

The Indian Ocean is first becoming the nuclear ocean. Because of its status as ocean of the South, the environmental security focus on nuclear power has not been sufficiently explored, as the possibilities of nuclear accidents whether in the mining of Uranium, power generation, reprocessing, transport and storage are seen as risks which are going to affect the less affluent. With its increased nuclear profile, it is critical that environmental security concerns are included alongside the more traditional concerns of weapons proliferation and possible nuclear war.

In the Unites States, the discourse on the security implications of environmental change, including climate change, has clearly been overshadowed by the highly controversial debate over the anthropogenic nature of climate change. During the Bush presidency climate change was a "dirty word" in official publications. The 2006 Quadrennial Defense Review by the US Department of Defense (DOD), for instance contains no reference to it. Humanitarian and environmental disasters are however seen as a task for the armed forces. The 2008 Defense Review, still under the Bush Administration's watch but after the intensive debates of 2007, includes climate change, but only as a factor increasing the negative effects of population growth. On relevant policies it is stated that "The Department will invest in hedging against the loss of disruption of our traditional advantages, not only through developing mitigation strategies, but also by developing alternative or parallel means to the same end. Further, the Department is examining its own energy demands and is taking action to reduce fuel demand where it will not negatively affect operational capability. Such efforts will reduce DOD fuel costs and assist wider US Government energy security and environmental objectives" (United States 2008, p. 22).

Meanwhile, opponents to the Bush administrations' view on climate change took up the public debate on security implications and attempted to put pressure on the administration to change its policies in general, and also to start looking into implications for US security policy. For instance, in 2007 Member of the House of Representative Markey and 13 co-sponsors (one of them Republican) introduced the "Global Climate Change Security Act", which among other measures also asked for a major assessment of the implication of climate change for security. While the act never went beyond the initial legislative steps a provision for a major national security assessment is contained in the 2008 National Defense Authorization Act. More, however, was difficult to achieve in the US Parliament, where there was little overlap between parliamentarians with concern about climate change and those which focused their work on security issues ((Richart 2009, p. 8-9).

The Obama administration came to power with climate change as one of its major issues, However, not much of that has, at least so far, translated into defense planning.

The 2010 Quadrennial Defense Review, as the major recent document, contains numerous references to climate change. Climate change is depicted as a problem for global security as well as national security. Allusions are made to the environmental security, the environmental conflict and the environmental threat discourse. But the document is vague on actual policies.

The emphasis is on mitigation strategies by the armed forces, on assessment and general improvements in preparedness. In continuation of measures already adopted earlier, the military is to reduce its energy consumption and carbon footprint. In addition to the studies already initiated in the intelligence community and the military, more assessments are announced, for instance on the effects of climate change on the US military basis, noting that "in 2008, the National Intelligence Council judged that more than 30 US military installations were already facing elevated levels of risk from rising sea levels". In addition to that, the documents states that "as climate science advances, the Department will regularly re-evaluate climate change risks and opportunities in order to develop policies and plans to manage its effects on the Department's operating environment, missions and facilities".

The volume of nuclear material and nuclear weaponry regularly transiting the Diego Garcia base poses considerable risks of radioactive contamination, especially to the waters of the lagoon. Curiously, however, neither the US Navy's 1997 and 2005 Natural Resources Management Plans for neither Diego Garcia nor the BIOT Conservation Management Plan (2003) make any reference to the need for radiation monitoring. Even though US nuclear-powered submarines are well-known to have experienced radiation leakages elsewhere (e.g. in Japan, 2006-08) the BIOT Administration has never taken radiation measurements in the Diego Garcia lagoon."

Indisputable is the fact that environmental change has become an element of the security discourse. But despite major attempts to change the framing of the discourse, environmental security remains dominant—the understanding that environmental change i.e. the climate change is particularly a problem for the life and livelihoods of people in certain areas like the Indian Ocean Region, and not one of armed conflict or threats to national security. The question remains nagging as to how the nuclear presence of major powers like US, China, and India will ensure security to the people living in the region against the threats from environmental change? Can the nuclear weapons stem the tide of storms and cyclones caused by global warming and sea level rise? Rather the redundancy of nuclear weapons as shield against the hazards of environmental change is exhibited. If the nuclear weapons cannot be used as weapons to settle disputes and protect human beings against the threats stemming from environmental change, the felt imperative is to bust the myth of superiority of these as the ultimate security ossified around the state. Consequences of power generation, reprocessing, transport and storage of nuclear materials on human lives far outweighs the supposed security these weapons are to provide in the State centric imaginations. In the practice and postures of foreign policy planning the US and other major powers is found absence of any focus on environmental security except the disaster management as the prime activity for armed forces to address the consequences of climate change. Because of its status as ocean of the south, the environmental security focus on environmental issues along side nuclear power has not been sufficiently explored by the major powers. It is critical that environmental security concerns are prioritized over and alongside the more traditional concerns of weapons proliferation and possible nuclear war.

REFERENCES

R (Bancoult) v Secretary of State for Foreign and Commonwealth Affairs (No 2) [2008] *UKHL 61*

P Sand, *United States and Britain in Diego Garcia: The Future of a Controversial Base* (Palgrave Macmillan, New York 2009).

R Edis, *Peak of Limuria. The Story of Diego Garcia and the Chagos Archipelago* (2nd rev edn Chagos Conservation Trust, London 2004) 94. See J Thigpen, The Praetorian Starship: The Untold Story of the Combat Talon (Air University Press, Maxwell/Alabama 2001) 212.

R Harkavy, *Bases Abroad: The Global Foreign Military Presence* (Oxford University Press, Oxford 1989) 49, 184, 274, 310. Tsunami' on 26 December 2004; <http://ida.ucsd.edu/SpecialEvents/2004/361/a/DGARunclip.gif> accessed 26 December 2008.

S Winchester, *Outposts: Journeys to the Surviving Relics of the British Empire* (Penguin Books, London 2003) 47.

V Bandjunis, *Diego Garcia: Creation of the Indian Ocean Base* (Writer's Showcase, San José/California 2001) 309; and 50-51 below. 'Terrorist Suspects (Rendition)', statement by Foreign Secretary David Miliband, Hansard HC vol 472 col 547 (21 February 2008); and (Gen) Michael Hayden, 'Director's Statement on the Past Use of Diego Garcia' (US Central Intelligence Agency Press Release, 21 February 2008). On 3 July 2008, Miliband assured Parliament that 'our US allies are agreed on the need to seek our permission for any future renditions through UK territory'; 'Terrorist

Suspects (Rendition)' Hansard HC vol 478, col 58 WS. See also HC Select Committee on Foreign Affairs, Overseas Territories: Seventh Report of Session 2007-08 (Hansard HC 147-II, 6 July 2008) Ev203.

S Maslen, *Commentaries on Arms Control Treaties* (OUP, Oxford 2004) 100.

J Mayer, "The Black Sites" *New Yorker (Vol. 83, no. 24, 13 August 2007).*

J Steyn, "*Guant6namo Bay: The Legal Black Hole" (2004) 53 ICLQ 1; and P Sands, Lawless World: Making and Breaking Global Rules* (Penguin Books, London 2006) 143.

See generally *A Aust,* Modern Treaty Law and Practice (2nd edn Cambridge University Press, Cambridge 2007) 206.

See the comments by P Bridgewater and I Orr, "The Future Conservation of the Chagos" (2008) 31 *Chagos News* 6, 13.

D Proctor and V Fleming (eds.), *Biodiversity: The UK Overseas Territories* (Joint Nature Conservation Committee, London 1999) 38 (emphasis added).

For an overview of current fishery management and control problems, see the presentation by J Pearce at the 2007 Chagos Conservation Trust Conference (n 38) 9; cf M Spalding, 'Partial Recovery of Sharks in the Chagos Archipelago' (2004) 15 Shark News 12.

T Grenier, 'Blowing Holes in the Reef for Fun and Profit' (ibid, posted 17 April 2004), and Y Levi (an Israeli frogman from Oceaneering International), 'Blowing Open the Ship Channel' (ibid, updated 30 April 2007).

R Rais, *The Indian Ocean and the Superpowers: Economic, Political and Strategic Perspectives* (Barnes & Noble, Towota/New Jersey 1987) 84. Diego Garcia boasts the world's longest slipform-paved runway built on crushed coral (12,000 feet = 3.6 kilometres, designated as an emergency landing site for the US space shuttle).

C Menzie and others, Environmental Survey of Construction and Dredging Related Activities on Diego Garcia, Indian Ocean (EG&G Environmental Consultants Inc., Waltham/Massachusetts July 1980

Naval Support Facility on Diego Garcia: Agreement Supplementing the Agreement of 30 December 1966, concluded in Washington/DC by exchange of notes on 13 December 1982; 2001 UNTS 397. Cf the written answer by Baroness Symons, FCO Parliamentary Undersecretary of State, Hansard HL vol 600 col 2 (26 April 1999 W): 'The American authorities on Diego Garcia had been involved in dumping, dredging and coral reef blasting prior to the 1982 UK/US Supplemental Agreement concerning the US Navy Support Facility on Diego Garcia. No estimate of any damage done was made at that point.'

On the 'overseas reach' of US law on environmental impact assessment, see L Schiffer, 'The National Environmental Policy Act Today, with an Emphasis on Its Application Across US Borders' (2003) 14 Duke Envl L Policy Forum 325.

W. Whistler, 'Botanical Survey of Diego Garcia, Chagos Archipelago, British Indian Ocean Territory' in NRMP Diego Garcia 1997 (4-5, 4-19, S Lowe and others (eds), 100 of the World's Worst Invasive Alien Species: A Selection from the Global Invasive Species Database (IUCN/ISSG, Auckland 2004) 6.

On the problems of the Guam-based submarine USS Houston (SSN-713), see

International Herald Tribune: Asia-Pacific/Associated Press (online, 30 August 2008); and M Yamaguchi, 'Nuclear Sub's Radiation Leak Revealed' Seattle Times (online, 8 August 2008).

See the report by C Sheppard, 'The Evolving Science in Chagos' Chagos News (no 30, 2007) 2, 13.

See M Bezboruah, *US Strategy in the Indian Ocean: The International Response* (Praeger, New York 1977) 200. See P MacAlister-Smith, 'Zones of Peace' in R Bernhardt (ed.), *Encyclopedia of Public International Law* (Vol. 4 Elsevier, Amsterdam 2000) 1621, 1625.

African Nuclear-Weapon-Free-Zone Treaty (Cairo, 11 April 1996), 35 ILM 698; named 'Pelindaba' after the former South African nuclear reactor.

See N Pelzer, 'Nuclear-Free Zones' in R Bernhardt (ed.) Encyclopedia of Public International Law (Vol. 3 Elsevier, Amsterdam 1997) 705, 712. Cf the FCO's Explanatory Memorandum on the Treaty of Pelindaba, presented to Parliament in December 2000 (Cm 3498).

See J Goldblat, 'Nuclear-Weapon-Free Zones: A History and Assessment' (1997) 4 Non-proliferation Rev 18, 26. The US Arms Control and Disarmament Agency considers the treaty map adequate to 'protect US interests because any resolution of the [sovereignty] issue will occur outside the framework of the treaty'; see M Rosen, 'Nuclear-Weapon-Free Zones: Time for a Fresh Look' (1997) 8 Duke J Comp Intl L 29, 48.

See J Paquin, '2004 API Awards for Excellence in Fuels Management' Navy Supply Corps Newsletter (November-December 2004).

For a first-hand description see Morris, 'General Ecology of Diego Garcia: Human Use and Industrial Waste' (last updated 31 March 2008).

See J Hansen, 'Cleanup Plan for Fuel Spills at Air Operations Ramp, Diego Garcia, British Indian Ocean Territory' in Pentagon Report A87824 (US Air Force Center for Environmental Excellence, Brooks City/Texas 25 May 1999); and G Tribble, 'Groundwater Geochemistry at the South Ramp Jet Fuel Leak, Diego Garcia Atoll' in Report SuDoc I 19.42/4:01-4090 (US Geological Survey, Washington/DC 2001).

See also J Hansen and D Kampbell, 'Large-Scale Bioslurping Operations Used for Fuel Recovery' EPA Technology News & Trends no 8 (September 2003) 2; and J Hansen, 'LNAPL Characterization and Recovery at Diego Garcia' in Summary of the Remediation Technologies Development Forum (Non-Aqueous Phase Liquid Cleanup Alliance Meeting, San Antonio/TX 7-8 February 2006)

On a 109,000 gallon (465,000 litres) JP-5 fuel spill at the US Navy's Arraij6n base in Panama in January 1995, see J Lindsay-Poland, Emperors in the Jungle: The Hidden History of the US in Panama (Duke University Press, Durham/North Carolina 2003) 147. On a 100,000 gallon (427,000 litres) JP-5 fuel leakage at Naval Air Station Roosevelt Roads, Cieba/Puerto Rico, in October 1999, see Incident News (n 103 above). On jet fuel spills at Clark Air Base in the Philippines, see T Proechel, 'Solving International Environmental Crimes: The International Environmental Military Base Reconstruction Act, a Proposal, and a Solution' (2007) 29 Loyola Los Angeles Intl Comp L Rev 121, 127.

C Sheppard and M Spalding, Chagos Conservation Management Plan (FCO, London 2003) 28.

'Chagos Annual Average Sea Temperature 1871-2006', showing a dramatic increase of warm periods from 1990 onwards, as compared to the standard reference period 1960-89. C Sheppard, Warming Sea Water and Chagos Reefs (Chagos Conservation Trust Fact sheet, London 2007), and the recent upward revision of global ocean temperature forecasts by C Domingues and others, 'Improved Estimates of Upper-Ocean Warming and Multi-Decadal Sea-Level Rise' 453 Nature no 7198 (19 June 2008) 1090.

See C Sheppard, 'Island Elevations, Reef Condition and Sea Level Rise in Atolls of Chagos, British Indian Ocean Territory' in O Lindйn and others (eds), Coral Reef Degradation in the Indian Ocean (IUCN/Cordio, Kalmar 2002) 26; Turner and others (n 124 below) 25-26; and J Petit (ed.), 'Climate Change and Biodiversity in the European Union Overseas Entities', in Pre-conference Document Vol. 3 (IUCN, Saint-Denis/Rйunion, 7-11 July 2008) 90-93.

See S Rahmstorf, 'A Semi-Empirical Approach to Projecting Future Sea-Level Rise' 315 Science no 5810 (19 January 2007) 368, with technical comments by S Holgate and others, 317 Science no 5846 (28 September 2007) 1866; and W Pfeffer and others, 'Kinematic Constraints on Glacier Contributions to 21st-Century Sea-Level Rise' 321 Science no 584 (5 September 2008) 1340.

See C Bouchard, 'Climate Change, Sea Level Rise, and Development in Small Island States and Territories of the Indian Ocean' in T Doyle and M Risely (eds), Crucible for Survival: Environmental Security and Justice in the Indian Ocean Region (Rutgers University Press, New Brunswick/New Jersey 2008) 258.

J Howell (ed.), *Returning Home: A Proposal for the Resettlement of the Chagos* (UK Chagos Support Association, London 2008), which in turn has been critically reviewed by J Turner and others, An Evaluation of 'Returning Home – A Proposal for the Resettlement of the Chagos Islands' (Howell Report) (Chagos Conservation Trust, London 2008).

Laipson, E. (2009), "The Indian Ocean: A Critical Arena for 21st Century Threats and Challenges" in (ed) Laipson, E and A. Pandya, *The Indian Ocean Resource and Governance Challenge*. The Henry L Stimson Center.

S Goodman (ed), *National Security and the Threat of Climate Change* (Center for Naval Analyses, Alexandria/Virginia 2007) 48; see also C Abbott, An Uncertain Future: Law Enforcement, National Security and Climate Change (Oxford Research Group, London 2008) 10.

A Erickson and others, 'Diego Garcia's Strategic Past, Present and Future' (paper presented at the annual meeting of the American Political Science Association, Boston, 28 August 2008) 27; A Erickson and others, 'The Military Geography of Diego Garcia: Future Implications for US Power Projection in the Indian Ocean' in C Lord and A Erickson (eds), US Basing and Presence in the Asia-Pacific (Naval War College Press, Newport/Rhode Island 2009); S Daggett and others, 'Fiscal Year 2008 Supplemental Appropriations for Global War on Terror Military Operations, International Affairs, and Other Purposes', Congressional Research Service Report RL34278 (US Government Printing Office, Washington/DC 10 December 2007),

See S Dalby, 'Empire's Ecological Tyreprints' (2006) 15 Environmental Politics 1.

For an overview see J Gupta, 'Legal Steps outside the Climate Convention: Litigation as a Tool to Address Climate Change' (2007) 16 Rev Europe Community Intl Envl L 76.

See J Charney, 'Rocks That Cannot Sustain Human Habitation' (1999) 93 AJIL 863; and R Lavalle, 'Not Quite a Sure Thing: The Maritime Areas of Rocks and Low-Tide Elevations Under the UN Law of the Sea Convention' (2004) 19 Intl J Marine Coastal L 43. During the UNCLOS negotiations, the UK had opposed Art 121(3) but was outvoted.

The overlapping exclusive economic zones for the Maldives and the Chagos Archipelago are currently separated by an equidistant median line; map in M Adam, 'Country Review: Maldives' in C De Young (ed.), *Review of the State of World Marine Capture Fisheries Management: Indian Ocean* (FAO Fisheries Technical Report no 488) (Food and Agriculture Organization of the United Nations, Rome 2006).

M. Koskenniemi, *The Gentle Civilizer of Nations: The Rise and Fall of International Law 1870-1960* (CUP, Cambridge 2002) 171.

6

Indo-US Relations Beyond the Nuclear Deal: A Study of Bilateral Strategic Cooperation

Reyaz Ahmad Ganaie

The end of cold war politics has seen tremendous and unprecedented changes at the international level and one of such shifts is the emergence of India and US as strategic allies. The importance and depth of this cooperation can be understood from the fact that US imposed sanctions on India in May 1998 following the successful nuclear tests but a decade later both countries signed the historic Civil Nuclear Cooperation Agreement. The platform for this strategic cooperation has been laid by the emergence of India as a nation with converging interests and principles with those of US. Both countries share and cherish democratic ideals, liberal economy and respect for human rights.

The signing of Indo-US Civil Nuclear Deal marked a tectonic shift, a complete metamorphosis – from political adversaries to strategic partners – in the foreign policy of the world's largest democracy and the world's oldest democracy.[1] The importance of the strategic civil nuclear deal between the two countries has been discussed to such an extent that the debate has almost overshadowed all other important aspects of their bilateral relations. The other dimensions of Indo-US relations including economic growth and trade cooperation, cooperation in high technology, non-proliferation and security, democracy and development and last but not least counter-terrorism cooperation have been given little attention in academic discourse while studying the growing proximity between the two countries. Similar to the signing of the historic nuclear deal, each of these dimensions has played a pivotal role in opening up new vistas for deepening cooperation between the two countries.

Indo-US Counterterrorism Cooperation: A Historical Overview

As India and US seek to build a stronger partnership and fully utilize the diplomatic channels created by the Indo-US Civil Nuclear Deal, one of the areas with great potential and benefit to both sides is counter-terrorism cooperation.[2] Although both countries have had different experiences of terrorism, lately the desire of both countries to put an end to this menace has surely come to converge. While India has suffered numerous terrorist and insurgent movements over the past decades which prominently include Sikh uprising of 1980s in Punjab, a separatist movement in Jammu and Kashmir from 1989 to present and various separatist movements in North-eastern states. To add to this list is the recent leftist extremist movement (Maoist and Naxalite) in the rural areas of Eastern and Central India.[3]

On the other hand, terrorism was not such a big issue for US until the fateful September 11, 2001 attacks on the US World Trade Centre and the Pentagon. These planned and well coordinated attacks on the symbols of US economic supremacy and military strength drew worldwide condemnation and in response US came out with its policy of "War on Terror" – a policy which was to eradicate all threats pointed towards US and its allies. The immediate aim of this policy was to eliminate Al-Qaeda network from Afghanistan and dismantle the Taliban regime which provided safe sanctuary to foreign terrorist networks in that country.

Counter-terrorism cooperation between India and US can be traced back to at least 1981, when India's success in combating Sikh terrorism in Punjab stemmed in part from intelligence shared by US and other countries as well as a US law signed in 1996 that barred fundraising in the US by the Indian separatist groups Babbar Khalsa and Khalistani Liberation Front.[4] Intelligence sharing between India and the US during this period was largely a result of Sikh insurgency in Punjab that was assuming global proportions, primarily due to its links with the Sikh Diaspora in the west.[5]

Similarly in the mid 1990s, US counter-terrorism officials sought and received assistance from Indian counterparts following the abduction of two American tourists in 1995 by a terrorist belonging to Harkat-ul-Ansar operating under the name of Al-Faran. This incident marked the cementing of Indo-US counter-terror cooperation.

However, the momentum began to fade away as US imposed sanctions on India following its successful Nuclear Tests of May 1998. Consequently, the Indo-US counter-terror cooperation suffered a serious setback. Furthermore, the suspension of the US-India Defence Policy Group (DPG) reduced the counter-terror cooperation between the two countries. The US sanctions instead helped spur India's counter-terrorism partnership with, as well as arms purchase from, Israel.

The formal commencement of counter-terrorism cooperation came only in January 2000, when US immediately established a US-India Counterterrorism Joint Working Group (CTJWG) in the aftermath of hijacking of an Indian Airlines flight from Kathmandu to Kandahar

(Afghanistan) by five Pakistani militants. The establishment of the Joint Counter-terrorism Working Group signalled President Clinton's resolve to get bilateral ties back on track and sanctions lifted, as well as a general desire to raise the profile of international counter-terrorism cooperation in the face of a growing terrorist threat.[6]

September 11, Attacks and Indo-US Counter-terror Cooperation

The events of September 11, 2001, marked a complete watershed in the counter-terror cooperation between India and the US. India virtually offered unqualified assistance to the United States in its "Operation Enduring Freedom" in Afghanistan aiming at eliminating Al-Qaeda network and ousting Taliban regime – an objective which came as a reprieve to India for it feared the regime's close liaison with Pakistan's military establishment and the ISI. India offered considerable support to Washington including the use of specific air bases, and later in 2002 Indian Naval Ships (INS Sharda and Sukanya) escorted high value American ships passing through the Strait of Malacca. Despite the generosity of India's offer the United States was not able to accept it given the central role Pakistan played in the coalition. Reportedly, Pakistan made its support for Operation Enduring Freedom in Afghanistan contingent upon the United States not accepting direct military support from India.

Even though US chose Pakistan as an active strategic ally in its War in Afghanistan, Washington never missed a chance to come hard on Islamabad for providing sanctuary to the fleeing insurgents from Afghanistan. However, India has always criticised, US for shying away from calling a spade a spade even when it became clear that most of terrorist attacks that India had to suffer were planned and coordinated from Pakistan especially the armed militant struggle in Kashmir which has now entered into its third decade. But lately, under immense pressure from United States, President Musharraf banned two active terror outfits Lashkar-e-Toiba (LeT) and Jaish-e-Mohammad (JeM), which came as a reprieve to India. Furthermore, in September 2003, Condoleezza Rice said that US president had talked with President Musharraf about "the need to stop cross-border terrorism in Kashmir".[7]

All these factors taken together made it quite evident to the Indian officials that US was not indifferent to India's terrorism concerns and thus acted as a platform for the deepening counter-terrorism cooperation between the two countries. In pursuance of this, the Defence Policy Group was revived in the aftermath of September 11 attacks and its scope was expanded further with an emphasis on counter-terrorism initiatives. Similarly, India and US formally launched the joint initiative on cyber-terrorism in 2002. Furthermore, the two countries signed the New Framework for the US-India Defence Relationship in 2005, which includes the need to strengthen their respective military capabilities to defeat terrorism.[8]

The counter-terror cooperation between the two countries has also witnessed India bringing in institutional changes at domestic level to tackle with the menace of terrorism related activities. These structural changes may include the establishment of a department of Defence Intelligence Agency (DIA) and the Multi Agency Centre (MAC) for collecting and coordinating terrorism related information all over the country. However, the implementation of the schemes remained inadequate and the desired objectives remained elusive.

Post 26/11 Attacks Counter-terrorism Cooperation

The Mumbai attacks of November 26, 2008 came as a rejuvenating cause for the Indo-US counter-terror cooperation. The attacks resulted in the death of at least 173 persons including foreign nationals. The attacks drew widespread condemnation from all quarters and India soon began to attract sympathy from US, for both shared a sense of victimhood as the deceased included a number of Americans as well.

These attacks provided the much needed momentum to the Indo-US counter-terror cooperation. The aftermath of the attacks witnessed America pressurising Pakistan to cooperate on 26/11 investigation and to crack down on militants operating on her soil. The American stance towards Pakistan certainly paid off when Pakistani officials admitted that parts of the Mumbai attacks were planned from Pakistan. Soon after the investigations into the attacks picked up, the American intelligence officials worked overtime with Indian counterparts and tried to act as brokers for information exchange between New Delhi and Islamabad. The exchange of intelligence information between India and Pakistan, however, failed miserably amid mutual recriminations owing largely to the historical legacy of mistrust, thus leaving the communication about the 26/11 cases in the hands of law enforcement personnel on the two sides.[9]

Nevertheless, the attacks marked the dawn of a new phase in Indo-US counter-terrorism cooperation. The Federal Bureau of Investigation (FBI) described as "Unprecedented" the access to 26/11-related evidence and intelligence provided by the Indian Intelligence Bureau and the Mumbai Police. Reciprocally, the Indian officials hailed FBI for a number of breakthroughs reached upon during the process of investigation. The technical assistance that India received from US officials related to the locating of the terrorists through Global Positioning System (GPS) and tracing of an e-mail server which was used by LeT chief for claiming the responsibility for the attacks. Furthermore, Indian and the US intelligence agencies were jointly able to intercept all communications passing between the terrorists who had occupied the two hotels and the Nariman House and their controlling officers in Pakistan.[10] Furthermore, US security experts were invited to advise on upgrades to the security of President's residence, Parliament, and other key facilities in New Delhi which were perceived to be easy targets for terrorists.[11]

Apart from this bilateral cooperation, India viewed these attacks as a serious setback to her security and thus came up with a number of structural and legislative tools to tackle with such security breaches. These measures included the amending of the Unlawful Assembly (Prevention) Act, 1967, and, more importantly the setting up of National Investigative Agency (NIA) by UPA Government in 2009 – meant to facilitate investigations and trials of the accused in terrorism cases. Furthermore, Multi Agency Centre has been made functional with total online connectivity with its thirty subsidiary units in the states. Another important change which was brought in the aftermath of the attacks was the augmentation of the strength of Intelligence Bureau. Similarly, in line falls the idea of Indian Government to stretch the strength of CRPF personnel in North-East, J&K, and the "Red Corridor" in Central India from 267,000 to more than 300,000.[12]

Persistent Obstacles in Indo-US Counter-terror Cooperation

Despite general convergence of American and Indian interests on the need to contain terrorism, the counter-terror cooperation between the two countries has continued to suffer on a number of accounts. Prominent among these issues remains the American stance towards Iran. The continuing pressure from United States on India to cut its fuel imports from Tehran has always acted as an irritant in Indo-US relations. More recently, the American move to impose unilateral sanctions on Iran following its suspicious nuclear programme drew an unexpected response from India when New Delhi refused to act according to US dictate and continued to import oil from Iran. Furthermore, US had earlier opposed a proposed Iran-Pakistan-India gas pipeline, which was viewed by Indian and Pakistani officials as a confidence building measure between the two countries, as well as a solution to their energy needs. In 2005, an unnamed Bush Administration source reportedly stated that "…the last thing US would want to see is Iran getting more revenue to fund its nuclear weapons program".[13]

Another important obstacle which has continuously hampered the deepening counter-terror cooperation between the two countries is the difference over Pakistan-a traditional adversary of India and paradoxically an indispensible strategic ally of US-led "War on Terror" in Afghanistan. India has always shown discomfort over Washington's military and security cooperation with Islamabad. Furthermore, India has also opposed the US military aid flow to Pakistan ever since the days of Soviet invasion of Afghanistan. The Indian opposition to this military aid comes from the fact that New Delhi suspects Pakistan of funnelling this money to Jihadist elements to sustain its proxy war against India. Moreover, India claiming Pakistan as a sponsor of terrorism was never acknowledged by US until recently when Pakistan under immense pressure from US had to ban a couple of terror outfits.

In addition to these differences of opinion over Iran and Pakistan, mistrust runs large among some Indian officials given the US record of withholding vital information relating to Al Qaeda operatives suspected of having ties with Kashmiri militants. The US handling of David Headley case furthered the mistrust of Indian officials. US refusal to extradite Headley who was arrested in October 2009 in Chicago for his involvement in 26/11 attacks was perceived by India as an attempt by US to shield Pakistani involvement in the attacks for Headley was known to have received terrorist training from LeT. It took almost nine months before Indian authorities were given direct access to Headley and allowed to question him. Furthermore, clandestine US attempts to penetrate Indian intelligence agencies have also hurt Indo-US intelligence ties.

Apart from the above discussed issues which are global in nature, there are a number of other factors which are domestic in character but certainly affect the counter-terrorism cooperation. Prime among these factors is the lack of political will and determination on India's part. The vote bank politics and the appeasement policies of different political parties in India have politicised the counter-terrorism efforts. The displeasure shown by some prominent politicians from the Hindu heartland over the banning of SIMI (parent organisation of Indian Mujahedeen) to tap their respective Muslim vote banks is a prime example in this regard.

Fractured opinion or lack of consensus among the different states regarding the functioning of counter-terrorism bodies in India is yet another hurdle. The recent controversy over the establishment and functioning of National Counter Terrorism Centre (NCTC) which was scheduled to be operationalised from March 2012 after getting approval from Cabinet Committee on Security (CCS) manifests the lack of consensus among the Indian Political Parties. The main contentious issues is related to Section 43(a) of Unlawful Activities (Prevention) Act, 1967, which empowers the NCTC "to arrest and detain any person if the body feels that the subject is associated with a terror act" on its own. This provision has been widely criticised by the states primarily non-congress alleging central dominance on state powers and authority.

The virulent spread of home grown separatist or ideologically based groups like Naxalites and Maoists and similar groups in North-East will continue to remain a major focus for New Delhi and will certainly continue to preoccupy the Indian authorities and to absorb national counterterrorism and counter insurgency resources, as well as state and local policing assets[14] thus diluting the focus of Indo-US counter-terrorism efforts.

Recommendations for Improving Counter-terror Cooperation

The differences notwithstanding, India and the US have come a long way forward in tackling jointly the menace of terrorism. To minimize the effect of the above mentioned differences, a number of reformatory measures if taken care of, can prove helpful in this regard. There are a number of unexplored avenues that could be exploited to further the counter-terror cooperation between the two countries. First and foremost among these initiatives is the need to enhance the levels of counter-terrorism intelligence sharing. The two countries should work more closely on their shared interests (e.g., containing Islamic extremism, home grown radicalisation of masses) to bridge the trust deficit that impairs their bilateral relations. This enhanced intelligence sharing can be then put to use in Afghanistan where interests of both countries have come to converge and can be used to minimize the levels of terror activities. To improve the levels of intelligence sharing, there should be routinly discussions between the security officials and intelligence services of both the countries. This may also include increasing the frequency of US-India Counter-terrorism Joint Working Group (CTJWG).

Another imperative to deepen the counter-terrorism cooperation between the two countries can be the US refraining from mediating the Kashmir conundrum – an issue India strictly regards as a bilateral issue between New Delhi and Islamabad. Instead, US should to promote confidence building measures between the two countries and diplomatically press Pakistan to dismantle the terrorist infrastructure operating on its territory.

Furthermore, the equipping of Indian police force with latest weaponry and adequate techniques to deal with terror attacks is yet another area which needs immediate attention. The Mumbai attacks made it manifest that the police personnel were ill equipped and lacked the tactics to deal with terrorist attacks. Therefore, what is needed is to revitalize the police force with latest weaponry and their functioning under a unified chain of command, so that in the event of a terrorist attack, counter-efforts are best organised and resources are employed most effectively.

One more area where the two countries can cooperate is the promotion of Democracy and pluralistic political culture[15]. This will ensure a way to disrupt the recruitment process and support for extremist and terror outfits. This initiative might be of great help in Afghanistan where a lot of people join extremism primarily due to ill functioning of democratic institutions or their complete absence especially in rural areas.

Conclusion

The emergence of India and US as strategic allies in the 21st century marks a complete shift in their respective foreign policies and promises to be a strong alliance given the contours of their shared objectives. These shared interests will certainly act as the bridge to take these countries much closer in the coming decades. The signing of Civil Nuclear Deal, the uphill trajectory of growing trade and commerce, the objective of establishing a robust democratic set-up in Afghanistan and to build its military strength and lastly the counter-terrorism cooperation—all point toward the deepening and widening contours of their bilateral relations.

As far as the venture of counter-terrorism cooperation is concerned, it can said that much has been achieved in the last decade, however, both sides will have to work hard to enhance trust and confidence to strengthen the counter-terrorism efforts. Both sides will have to shun away their differences over particular issues (e.g. Iran, Pakistan) and try to find out ways of mutuality and reciprocity. United States as the leading power will have to ensure that if India is to stand up to the task of fighting terrorism, it certainly would require material and technical assistance from Washington. Washington must be ready to impart technological know-how to India to enhance the counter-terror capability of Indian security set-up.

REFERENCES

1. Ajay Lele and Archana Mishra, December 2010, "Indo-US Strategic Partnership: Beyond the Nuclear Deal", *Asia-Pacific Journal Of Political Science,* special issue no. 1, p. 96
2. Lisa Curtis, December 9, 2008, "After Mumbai: Time to Strengthen US-India Counterterrorism Cooperation", *The Heritage Foundation,* Vol. 2217, p. 1.
3. *Ibid.* p. 2.
4. Polly Nayak, "Prospects for US-India Counterterrorism Cooperation: An American View" in Sumit Ganguly *et al.* (eds.) 2006, *US-Indian Strategic Cooperation into the 21st Century: More than Words,* Routledge, New York, p. 133.

5. Manjeet S. Pardesi, "Counterterrorism Cooperation with United States and Japan: An Indain Perspective", p. 20. Available at: http://www.csis.org/files/media/csis/pubs/090201_bsa_pardesi.pdf. accessed on 23-4-2012.
6. Polly Nayak, "Prospects for US-India Counterterrorism Cooperation: An Historical Perspective" in *Counter-Terrorism in South-Asia,* 2011, KW Publishers, New Delhi.
7. *Ibid.* p. 22.
8. *Op. cit.* No.5. pp. 25-26.
9. *Op. cit.* No. 6. p. 29.
10. *Ibid.* p. 31.
11. *Ibid.*
12. Vikram Sood, March 25, 2011, "Counter Terrorism: The Indian Experience". Available at: http://www.soodvikram.blogspot.in/2011/03/counter-terrorism/indian/experience.html. Accessed on 7-5-2012.
13. *Op. cit.* No. 6, p. 25.
14. *Ibid.* p. 39.
15. Lisa Curtis, December 9, 2008, "After Mumbai: Time to Strengthen US-India Counterterrorism Cooperation", *The Heritage Foundation,* Vol. 2217, p. 10.

7

Model Minority: A Study of the Indian Diaspora in the United States

Mohammed Badrul Alam

> "*The banyan tree has thrust down roots in soil, which is stony, sandy, marshy and has somehow drawn sustenance from diverse unpromising conditions. Yet the banyan tree itself has changed, its similarity to the original growth is still there. But it has changed in response to its different environment.*"[1]

The Indian community in the United States is one among many ethnic communities, which have been increasingly visible in the last four decades. Although the flow of Indians as new ethnics started first as a trickle in 1895, their impact was really felt in the aftermath of the landmark 1965 immigration legislation. This "new immigration" group has begun to attract academic attention and has also been the focus of research by a number of scholars.

The Asian Indians are an interesting group among the cluster of newly formed immigrant communities; their level of educational standard is particularly impressive; the rapidity of consolidation of economic indictor is remarkable; and the internal mobility of the Asian Indian community is very much viable.

To put it within a larger context, one of the most striking features which have caught the attention of most of the scholars today in this age of globalization, is the "transnational movement of people" and the "intensification in the creation of diverse diaspora populations in many locations, who are engaged in complex and intercultural relationships with both their host societies and their societies of origin"[2]

It may be useful to clarify the term 'Asian Indian'. The term 'Indian' has both an ethnic and a political connotation. Ethnically, Asian Indians are people who migrated from the Indian sub-continent (from India, Pakistan, Bangladesh, Sri Lanka) and their progeny—are called Indians irrespective of the country of their domicile.[3] Politically, the citizens of the Republic of India holding Indian national's passport could be regarded as Indians. Thus the term 'Asian Indians' is referred to as the ethnic group and 'Indian' as signifying a specific political status. Asian Indian communities in different parts of the world are more akin to one another than to other communities in their respective countries. A typical Asian Indian community member has generally retained his/her traditional customs, religion, language, forms of worship, food habits, social habits, marriage rites and values. He/she acknowledges his relatives living in India, visits them as often as possible, and returns to them when he/she thinks it is desirable to do so. In terms of blood, emotional attachment and the social value system, he/she is no different from other Indians. It is a rational consideration that differentiates an Asian Indians from the Indian national. The Asian Indian, by conscious and deliberate choice, has opted out of the geographical boundary of India and has transformed his paramount loyalty from the country of origin to the country of domicile.

This chapter analyses and examines the case of Asian Indians living in the United States, in the context of 'cultural pluralism' model. This chapter also addresses and evaluates the Asian Indians' attitudes toward family, education, religion, political participation, ethnic association, media and communication.

To begin with, it is important to understand what an ethnic group is in order to evaluate the position of Indians in the United States. In the *International Encyclopedia of the Social Sciences*, an ethnic group is defined as a "distinct category of the population in a larger society whose culture is usually different from is own."[4] In this sense, the Asian Indian population in the United States does qualify as an ethnic group because its cultural traditions are unique and distinctly different from that of the mainstream United States. However, it should be noted that sub-communities of Indians, for example, Bengalis, Punjabis, Telugus, Oriyas, Tamils, Gujratis, do not form ethnic groups either in India or in the United States. In India, they do not have a distinct culture contrasted from the Indian culture, and in the United States the sub-cultural group or the sub-communities are neither perceived nor recognized for purposes of categorization or interaction. In fact, this line of reasoning is supported by the fact that there is no equivalent word for ethnic group in Hindi or in any of the major languages of India. The regional or linguistic groups of India are called ethnic groups. It is because the term ethnic group, minority group, and sub-culture are often used inter-changeably. Social scientists in general and sociologists in particular have different perspectives on the same phenomenon depending on the issues that interest them.[5]

In the United States, the term ethnic group refers to a number of characteristics, such as differentiation by race, religion, or national origin. In this context, a succinct definition has been put forward by Milton Esman.[6] Ethnic groups have both objective and subjective attributes: objective cultural traits expressed in language, religion, historical experiences, and common institutions and the subjective awareness of identity, belongingness, solidarity, and common interests. Thus, ethnic groups maintain sentimental and material links with land of their origin. Though it has an objective, ethnicity is contextual in its manifestations, boundaries, intensities, and issues for any group may shift over time in response to changing experiences and problems.

Thus, an ethnic group can be defined as collectivity of people who share some common patterns of normative behaviour. They form a part of a larger population, interacting with people from other collectivities within the framework of a social network system. It refers to the degree of conformity by members of the collectivity to these shared norms and practices in the course of social interaction. By normative behaviour, one can refer to the symbolic formations and activities found in such contexts as kinship and marriage, friendship, ritual and other types of ceremonies of social and religious nature. For example, the differences between the Indians and the Vietnamese are national, not ethnic. But when members of these two groups interact in a land that are foreign, these can be referred to as ethnic groups. Ethnicity is thus essentially a form of interaction between culture groups operating within social contexts. Thus, ethnicity is a complex social phenomenon that is inter-locking and involved in cultural, psychological, historical, economic and political realities.

The notion of diaspora is also premised along the above lines. As Cohen points out, "All diasporic communities settled outside their homeland, accept that the old country – an idea often found in language, religion, custom or folklore – always has some claim on their loyalty and emotions. That claim may differ according to circumstances and history, but the member's adherence to a diasporic community is demonstrated by acceptance of an inescapable link with their past migration history and sense of co-ethnicity with others of similar background. In addition to these traits, there are possibilities which are distinctive, creative thus enriching life in tolerant host countries."[7]

Emphasizing on socio-economic, political, and cultural networks to understand transmigration, diaspora, and its role in the globalization of production and the increasing spatial mobility of modern times, Sheffer has given a comprehensive definition of diaspora:

> "An ethno-national diaspora is a social-political formation, created as a result of either voluntary or forced migration, whose

members regard themselves as of the same ethno-national origin and who permanently reside as minorities in one or several host countries. Members of such entities maintain regular or occasional contacts with what they regard as their homelands and with individuals and groups of the same background residing in other host countries. Based on aggregate decisions to settle permanently in host countries, but to maintain a common identity, diasporians identify as such, showing solidarity with their group and their entire nation, and they organize and are active in cultural, social, economic, political spheres. Among their various activities members of such diasporas establish trans-state networks that reflect complex relationships among the diasporas, their host countries, their homelands and international actors."[8]

To place ethnic discourse in the American context, one will notice that American history is the history of ethnic groups. This is increasingly expressed in recent times with regard to the nature and scale of integration of American society. For a long time, observers assumed that immigrants came to America simply to find safe haven from the persecution in home states of Europe. Catholics, Jews, and some Protestants migrated, for example, to avoid religious wars in their respective countries. Others migrated to escape civil and inter-state war, political repression, genocide, ethnic-cleansing, cultural assimilation, and instability, and the abject poverty of their homeland. Many other immigrants chose to migrate to the United States as much because it was considered by many as a land of opportunity and abundance. Whatever their reasons for coming to America, right from the beginning there has been pressure exerted on immigrants to embrace Anglo-American institutions ("Anglo-Conformity"). Despite these pressures, in the case of many groups the "melting pot" syndrome, one of complete assimilation and acculturation which have never materialized. Some scholars have subscribed to the idea of "Cultural Pluralism" or "Salad Bowl" suggesting that the United States is not only a nation of immigrants, but it is a nation of immigrant groups of varied cultures and sub-cultures. The notion of cultural pluralism implies that the immigrants in time would become Americanized, but at the same time that they could also retain much that was distinctive and primordial in their own cultural heritage. The "cultural pluralism" model appears to be the more relevant in the context of Asian Indians in the United States. There is a lack of sufficient empirical data to fully support this "cultural pluralism" model. However, there seems to be good social, historical and psychological evidence to argue that the "cultural pluralism" model has greater validity. Gordon's view that assimilation in the sphere of culture has been successful whereas it has lagged behind in the structural sphere is of particular interest to Asian Indian community living in the United States. Moynihan's and Glazer's view that political and socio-economic power keeps ethnic groups together has greater relevance in contemporary American society. But their suggestion that cultural differences are rapidly declining among ethnic groups is not quite true, certainly not for the Asian Indian group.

As indicated earlier, since about 1965, the phenomena of ethnicity has re-emerged in American life and has permeated its social structure. Often this is referred to as the "new ethnicity". The White European ethnics as well as the Puerto-Ricans, Filipino Americans, Chinese Americans, American Indians, Mexican-Americans, Asian Indians, etc. have come to share the option that their distinctiveness is no longer a social stigma but a matter of ethnic pride. Not all ethnic groups have experienced this change, however. For example, increased pride in ethnic heritage has led to movements toward separatism among some black Americans. For many American blacks, a situation of cultural pluralism in which they are accorded social recognition, equal access to job, equitable income base, and decent housing, remains the desired goal.

Most ethnic minorities pursue cultural pluralism model including a moderate degree of assimilation as the preferred path. But there is still a visible discrepancy between what they would prefer and what options are available to them as ground realities. The critical question is whether strengthening the ethnic minorities will further divide the nation, or if the greater strengths of the disparate parts of the American society can bridge the social divide. The outcome depends on the manner in which the ideology of pluralism is applied. The theories of the "melting pot" and the "multiple melting pot" and the rest of it have simply not worked. Glazer[9] has rightly observed that cultural pluralism seems to have won out, at least temporarily. He further makes the distinction between "weak cultural pluralism" and "strong cultural pluralism". The former represents an attitude which is basically a form of tolerance or the way to an expected acculturation and assimilation, whereas the latter is primarily based on an ideological view of the position of racial and ethnic groups in American life, a view that emphasises the colonial status and the repression of their cultures by Anglo-Americans. These may be seen as two polar extremes of cultural pluralism. Glazer suggests that there may be a middle grand between the two, which he calls "integration", which he explains as follow: "... integration implies on the one hand, an organic relationship. Just as personality may be integrated, so may a society. On the other hand, it (integration) implies that there is still a clear articulation of the parts that is, some degree of identifiability of each part."[10] He further argues that this form of cultural pluralism would be in the interest of both individual groups and of the entire nation. Here the emphasis would be on distinctive nature of various ethnic cultures, which would be integrated in larger sense with the American experience.

The critics of cultural pluralism have opposed the 'integration' model because it can be divisive and has the potential for disintegration and separatism. This is evident in the black power and the emergent black pride movement of the mid-1960s. Earlier challenges to cultural pluralism came from those who were proponents of assimilation and Americanization as the most desirable outcome for multi-ethnic American society.

There is another school called 'pluralists' who argue that a multi-cultural society will of necessity contain conflicts and tensions. Thus, managing these tensions, rather than seeking to avoid them, is in the larger interest of the viability and cohesiveness of any society in the long run.

The United States now seems to be moving toward a pluralistic society. However, for pluralism to work, there must be an open society (in the general sense of the term), one in which people with a diversity of backgrounds and characteristics can compete on an equal basis for societal resources. Also, if pluralism is to become the mode of dealing with ethnic diversity, it must be adopted in the American schools. Under pluralist notion, ethnicity is considered ultimately to be a psychological phenomenon that can be expressed in any identical display. The implication is that ethnicity is a general state of consciousness and identity that is not necessarily obvious, but which can be voluntarily displayed in overt behaviour in a variety of settings.

Varma[11] in his essay on Asian Indians, refers to an "ethnic renaissance" in the United States, and suggests that because of advanced industrialization, there is a tendency among people to seek an escape from machines, tools, and technology. The "new ethnicity" emerges both as result of the standardization of values in America society, as well as of the opening up of the American mainstream which is becoming more receptive as well as sensitive, to the needs and aspirations of minorities and sub-cultural groups.

The Asian Indians in America not only show a clear preference for the cultural pluralism model, but also see it as the most desirable and acceptable from their point of view, as well as its being in the longer interests of American society. A study of the behaviour patterns of the Indian immigrants does suggest their groups' strong inclination to maintain and enrich ethnic Indian culture and traditions.

Asian Indians in United States can be categorized under three headings: *Old Indian Diaspora* (constitutes those migrants migrated between 19th century to early part of the 20th century), *New Indian Diaspora* (constitutes those migrants who migrated after 1965 especially the urban and middle class professionals) and *Second Generation Indians* (constitutes those Indians born and brought up in the United States).[12] Between these three groups, the latter two – the *New Indian Diaspora & Second Generation Indians* – continue to have close contact with the families and relatives back home while few of the older generations have lost their contacts with the motherland. Indians have made successful informing their local, international, formal and informal networks by contacting with their kith and kin around the globe. Their networks are maintained through various mechanisms such as regular communications over telephone, visits and correspondence, remittances, the Internet chat and e-mails, sending and receiving videos on important family events and other celebrations. Although these networks sustain itself through the proximity of *density* and *distance* – which are central to the individual and group interaction – the major stakes by which the transnational networks expand and are established, are through the social, cultural, economic, political and religious spheres.

Attitudes toward India and the United States

Indian immigrants generally maintain their respect for and faith in the Indian value system and institutions, even though they are critical of India in many ways.[13] For example, they talk about poverty, the population explosion, nepotism, casteism and lack of opportunity for professional advancement in India. However, there seldom is criticism of the basic Indian value system which evolves around major social institutions such as marriage, the family, religion, etc. Their attitude toward India is generally considered more favourable and they try to organise activities to reinforce their Indianness both within the family and outside it through ethnic Indian organization. The overwhelming majority of Indians indicate that eventually they wish to return to India.

The attitude of the Indian immigrants toward American society is more favourable in the early stages of their residence than later. Initially, they are impressed by American informality, generosity, openness, flexibility and sense of hospitality. The physical environment and the scientific technological advancement of the United States make a profound impact in a positive way. However, as they start moving into the American mainstream and compete for jobs, professional recognition, and social acceptance, the Asian Indians experience some prejudice and discrimination.

The apparent permissiveness of American society and the lack of respect for the elderly are the most frequently voiced observations made by these immigrants. Interestingly enough, their criticism is not confined to the opportunity structure but is often aimed at basic social institutions such as the family and religion. Many American values, such as the American attitude towards sex and the elderly, are observed as immoral. On the whole, the values of the Indian immigrants are more favourable toward India and Indian institutional arrangements than they are toward American society and its social parameters.

Attitudes toward Family

Among the 1965 wave, most of the Indian immigrants were already married when they immigrated. A good number returned to India for arranged marriages (the bride/groom being selected by the parents).[14] In most cases, the wives have taken up outside employment and the husbands share and assist in the household work. Nevertheless, this has not led to change in their attitudes toward each other in any significant way. The husband generally remains at the apex of the decision-making in the family. The immigrants' commitment to the institution of marriage remains strong and they look at marriage as one of life long commitment. Since most of the couples came to the United States as adults, there did not seem to be significant change in their attitudes after migration. Their attitudes toward their children also remain traditional. Most of the children of the immigrants either came to the United States at a very young age or were born in USA.

The lack of change in the attitude of Indian parents and their expectations based on the traditional Indian value system is one of the major sources of discord among the Indian families residing in the United States. Parent-child relationship is one of the most pressing issues confronting the Indian community. As the children are into adulthood, the community has started experiencing the negative consequences of these conflicts.

Attitudes toward Religion

In general, it has been seen that the attitude of Indian immigrants toward their religion is favourable since immigration. One of the possible explanations may be that religion also serves social and cultural functions in an alien society. Another change that one can observe is that the Indian immigrants tend to look at religion more as an ideology than as a set of strict dogmas and prescriptions. Nevertheless, it does not necessary result in a decrease in religious observation and practice. Most Indian families have a place of worship in their homes. They also visit temples, churches, mosques and gurudwaras and participate in all forms of religious activity.

One can support the hypothesis that religious activity among Indian immigrants has not declined as a result of immigration. On the contrary, there is a greater religious consciousness and a need to practice religious rituals individually as well as communally.

The social life of Hindus in the United States revolves largely around temples, and therefore, construction of temples is called the part and parcel of Hinduism in America.[15] The first Hindu temple in United States goes to the credit of the Vedanta Society that was established in San Francisco in 1906. The Sikh Temple at Stockton in the state of California was built in 1915 followed by the Hollywood Temple in 1938, and the Santa Barbara Temple in 1956 (see www.vedanta.org). Two important temples in the United States today are 'Maha Vallabha Ganapati Devasthanam' in Flushing, New York and the Sri Venkateswara Temple in Pittsburgh, Pennsylvania. Besides these, there are hundreds of Hindu temples that are found in and around the United States and these construction activities by Indian immigrants are on the increase. Presently, there are over 450 Hindu temples in the United States. Hinduism in the United States shows every sign of being a flourishing religion. These temples do make honest efforts in fostering a sense of community among Hindus there.

Attitudes toward Economics

Most of the Indian immigrants have more than average education and professional backgrounds.[16] Because of high educational standards, it has become relatively easier for the Asian Indians to find employment and improve their economic profile in the United States. While the per capita income of Indian immigrants is much higher than that of the average American, their consumption pattern is lower than that of Americans on the comparable income level. This is due to their conservative attitude toward spending. Their savings level is almost two to three times higher than the national average. They put a great premium on savings as well as on investment. Most of the Indians in US are highly qualified persons having 43.6 per cent in professional and managerial positions, 33.2 per cent in the technical, sales and service sectors and the remaining 23.3 per cent are skilled labours. The total per capita income of Indians there today is estimated at US $ 60,093 compared to the average per capita income of US $ 38,885. More than half of the Indian immigrant community own houses. This may be considered as an indication of this ethnic group's intention to settle permanently in the United States. The practice of remitting money to India for parents and other family members is quite evident. This also supports the assumption that the close link and bonding with family members in India is maintained despite migration to the United States. It would be fair to suggest that in the sphere of economics as well as in other areas, one finds the continuation of traditional values and attitudes on the part of Indian immigrants, particularly for those who have migrated in the post-1965 phase.

Attitudes toward Education

Most of the Indian immigrants put heavy premium on academic excellence. Since American society also emphasizes on the importance of education, there is no conflict there with prevailing American norms. But there is a perceptible difference in the attitudes between the Indians and the Americans. The Indians' attitude to higher education is closely tied to a family's prestige and status and strong desire for upward social mobility accrued from it. Children of the Indian immigrants (especially of the first generation) are doing exceedingly well in all aspects of academia. However, in certain quarters, there is some doubt about the children's continued success because of the influence of external factors. It is argued that as the children assimilate in the new society, they become more independent and act more in terms of their own values rather than those of the family-based values which are very strong in India. This provides some basis for suggesting that education is not considered as free an enterprise and as individualistic in nature by the Indian immigrants as it is perceived and practised by the larger segment of the host (American) society.

Attitude toward Political Participation

The Asian Indian group in recent years has taken proactive interest in the political process of the country. During Kennedy's Administration, Dilip Singh Saund, a member of the Indian ethnic community, was successfully elected to the House of Representatives of the US Congress. Since then, a number of persons of Indian origin have contested for various political offices under both party tickets (Democrats and Republicans). This Political participation by Asian Indians and their affiliated groups, is also being reflected in the 2008 Presidential races of Republican John McCain and Democratic contenders in the primaries namely Barack Obama and Hillary Clinton. In a way, it shows the maturity of the Indian ethnic community in the United States and their willingness and determination to participate in the politics of America. A number of organizations, such as India League of America and the Association of Asian Indians in North America have taken leading steps in this direction. In 1994, Kumar Brave and Upendra Chivukula – the first Indian Americans – from Maryland

and New Jersey respectively were elected to their respective state legislatures. In the year 2000, Satveer Choudhary became the first state senator to be elected in Minnesota. He was re-elected in 2006 as well. Iowa State Representative Swati Dandekar, Democrat, also won for the third time. Several Indian-Americans have held the position of mayor as well. They include: Bala K. Srinivas in Hollywood Park, Texas, John Abraham in Teaneck, New Jersey, and Arun Jhaveri in Burien, Washington. Number of Indians has also become prominent at the national level. For instance, during Clinton administration, Dr. Arati Prabhakar was appointed as the Director of National Institute of Standards and Technology, Neil Dhillon as the Deputy Assistant Secretary of Transportation and Dr. Rajen Anand as Executive Director of Centre for Nutrition Policy under USDA. Similarly, Bobby Jindal was appointed as the Assistant Secretary of Health, Gopal Khanna, Chief Technology Officer of Peace Corps while Karan Bhatia was appointed as the Deputy Under Secretary in the Department of Commerce in the George Bush, Jr. administration. During Barack Obama administration that took over on January 20, 2009, it had appointed a number of Indian Americans in key positions including Farah Pandith as US State Department's representative to the muslim world, Rashad Hussain as US envoy to the 57-member Organization of Islamic Countries (OIC), Dr. Islam Siddiqui as US Chief Agricultural Negotiator, Dr Rajiv Shah, as the administrator of the United States Agency for International Development (USAID), etc. In the election held for the US Congress on 6 November 2006, bucking the anti-Republican trend, incumbent Bobby Jindal won a thumping victory and got re-elected to the House of Representatives from Louisiana's 1st District, securing 88 per cent of the vote. Subsequently, Bobby Jindal was also elected as the Governor of Louisiana. Similarly, Nimrata Nikki Randhawa Haley won the 2010 South Carolina gubernatorial election and in the process, became the second person of Indian-American origin and the first woman to serve as Governor of South Carolina. Earlier in the race, Nikki Haley won the party's nomination in a runoff election by garnering 65-percent of the primary vote in the southern state of South Carolina. Haley was born Nimrata Randhawa, daughter of Indian-Americans. These candidates were actively supported by the Asian Indian diaspora residing in the United States. In the past few elections, Asian Indian donors have financed and campaigned for members of both political parties. In some cases, Asian Indian donors are supporting candidates from both the Democratic party and the Republican party in a single Congressional district. It will still take some time before Indians make their presence felt more visible on the political landscape. It is important to note, however, that on matters of importance to India, be it signing Nuclear Non-Proliferation Treaty (NPT) and

Comprehensive Test Ban Treaty (CTBT), Outsourcing of jobs to India, Sale of sophisticated offensive weapon systems to Pakistan that could be used against India, a proactive role for India on the Afghanistan issue, negotiations on climate change and global warming, civilian nuclear deal, etc, Indian diaspora have courted support on both sides of the political aisle for promoting and enhancing India's national interest.

A coalition pattern, in conjunction with other ethnic groups, such as Italian Americans, Greek Americans, Japanese Americans, Mexican Americans, etc, may be an ideal type for the Asian Indians to pursue. At the formative stages of building up a political front, these steps leading towards ethnic solidarity are an interesting proposition.

Attitude toward Media and Communication

While Asian Indians have ventured into almost every field of profession in the United States, one such successful foray by Indians, is in the field of media and communication. Eminent writers, journalists, musicians and filmmakers have made noteworthy contribution in their respective fields. Writers of English with international repute includes Jhumpa Lahiri, whose work *Interpreter of Maladies* won the Pulitzer Prize in 2000. Besides Lahiri, Bharati Mukherji and Anita Desai are included in the list of international writers of Indian origin. Similarly, Fareed Zakaria who earlier became the Editor of the prestigious *Foreign Affairs* is now in charge of the Editorial board of *Newsweek.* The names of Pankaj Mishra and Shashi Tharoor are also widely acclaimed in this field. In Music, the credit goes to Pandit Ravi Shankar, Ali Akbar Khan and Zakir Hussein who have settled in US and yet have brought Indian music into American mainstream by winning critical public acclaim. Zubin Mehta's success in New York Philharmonic Orchestra is also a tribute to the talent of Indian communities in the United States.

In filmmaking, Indian Americans also have great names. Important in the list are: Pratik Basu's *Welcome To The Family*, Punam Sawhney's *The Goddess Method*, Mehreen Jabbar's *Beauty Parlor*, David Dasharath Kalal's *Five Minutes To Cloud Boundary*, Anmol Chaddha and Sonya Mehta's *Yellow Apparel: When The Coolie Becomes Cool*, besides Mira Nair's *Mississippi Masala*, *Salaam Bombay* which has been appreciated all over the world. Mira Nair's movie *Monsoon Wedding* has won the Venice Film Festival *Golden Lion Award.*

Asian Indian ethnic media plays an important role by keeping in touch with fellow ethnic members in the diaspora. The Indian ethnic media in the United States has evolved gradually from radio, to print and then to ethnically owned radio and TV channels. Some of the important Indian ethnic media that have flourished in the United States today are recorded during the Pravasi Bharatiya Divas meet at New Delhi in January 2007

The important media outlets are as follows:

Newspapers, Journals and Magazines: *India Abroad, News-India Times, Globe, Awaz, Biz India, Desi Talk, Express India, Greet Gujrati, Gujarat Mitra, Gujarat Samachar, Gujarat Times, Himalayan News, The Hindi Times, Hindi Jagat, Hindu Vishwa, Indo-US Business Journal, India Currents, The Indian Express (North American Edition), India Focus, India Journal, Indian Life & Style Magazine, India light, India Living Magazine, India Monitor, India Positive, India Post, India Reporter & World News, India Today, India Tribune, India Weekly, India-West, Jhankar, Khabar Magazine, Lokmat, Lokvani, Malayalampathram, Malayalee Sabdam, Mantram, Marathi Vishwa, NRI Times, NRI Today, The Pittsburgh Patrika, Prasaar Bharati, Punjab Times, Rajani, Ranauk Mela, Rang Taranga, Sandesh International, Sher-e-Punjab, Silicon India, Spirit of India*, etc.

Radio: Bharat Vani, Jhankar (Hindi), RBC Radio, Vividh Bharati Radio Programme.

Television: Channel-80 Aap Aur Tum, Chitrahar Broadcasting, Darshan TV, Ektara Television, Kerala Television, Manoranjan Channel 30, Namaste America, News India TV, Sanjha Punjab TV Network, Sikh TV/Sohna Punjab, Sony TV (EABC), S R Video and so on.

The High Level Committee on the Indian Diaspora chaired by Dr. L.M. Singhvi has made some recommendations to strengthen links between Indian organizations and ethnic media as well as prominent Indians in the foreign media. The important recommendations include creating a data bank on the ethnic media and a facilitation mechanism for interaction with the Indian ethnic media and so on.

Ethnic Associations

The steady growth of Indian population in the United States over the years has contributed to the emergence of various cultural, religious and regional associations. The first major community based group was initiated in New York with the formation of Association of Indians in America (AIA) in 1968.[17] After ten years, in 1978, the Federation of Indian Associations (FIA) was formed as an umbrella organization in New York. In 1980, the Association of Indians in North America (AIINA) was formed in New York. Besides this, the National Federation of Indian-American Associations (NFIA), the American Indian Associations (AIA), and the Indian American Forum for Political Education (IAFPE) was established to pursue and promote Indian interests in a more organized and sustained manner. Other important organizations, which have emerged to enhance and safeguard the Indian interests, are: Global Organization of People of Indian Origin (GOPIO) and the National Association of Americans of Asian Indian Descent (NAAAID). There are larger political organizations like American Indian Foundation and various professional organizations like The Indo-US Entrepreneurs, Indo-American Chamber of Commerce, Network of Indian Professionals etc., which function as umbrella organizations.

The ethnic, linguistic, and cultural diversities among the Indians in the United States have manifested in the formation of separate associations over a period of time. Among these are: the Bengali Association, the Bihar Cultural Association, the Tamil Nadu Foundation, the Telugu Association, the Punjabi Cultural Society, the Maharashtra Mandal, the Kerala Associations, Gujarati Association, Kannada Koota, Oriya Society of America, Rajasthani Association, etc. There are organizations which has striven very hard in evoking a more comprehensive notion of 'Indianness' among Indians in the United States such as Indian Classical Music Circle, which sponsors recitals by major Indian musicians, and the Chicago chapters of various professional organizations of Americans of Indian origin.

The religious, regional, linguistic and caste factors unlike in India plays an important role in the everyday lives of the Indians in the United States. For example, besides the language and religion, the caste and sub-caste identity of Telugus provides them an additional forum for closer interaction. Telugus are generally classified into several caste groups, the important among them being the Brahmin, Reddy, Kamma, Kapu, Naidu, Mala, Madiga, Yeraka and Yanadi. These caste differences have made their presence in the socio-economic and political interactions among the Telugus in the US For example, the members of Kamma caste dominate the Telugu Association of North America (TANA) while the Reddy caste on the otherhand promote the American Telugu Association (ATA).

Conclusion

This study aims in establishing a baseline for observation of the sociological parameters of the Asian Indian community. Proponents of assimilations have always taken the stand that rapid Americanization is the most desirable goal. Even if one accepts its viability, one is never sure what it means or connotes. If it means a monoculture, then obviously the assimilationists have reason to be utterly disappointed. Even in the days when the assimilationists' view was dominant, diversity in American society was very much in existence. In the final analysis, it is safe to conclude that there is room for flexibility, tolerance, freedom, openness and opportunities in American society. From Asian Indian perspective, one can argue that the American society may not be fully ideal, but it is fair to suggest that it has been considered better than many other societies of the world. This is validated by the continuing flow of immigrants to the United States from various parts of the world, representing diverse languages, religions, regions and cultures.

The major flow of Asian Indian immigrants started in 1965 in the aftermath of change in the immigration laws that removed the quota system. The Indian population is marked by its high educational credentials, concentration in professions, known history, strong family ties, and at the same time represents splendid diversity in terms of language, religion, custom and religion. They represent a history which strongly recognizes the Indian motto of 'unity in diversity'. In spite of the existence of internal diversity, there is still that sense of Indianness that has solidified the community. This aspect is also clearly noticeable to outside observers.

The Indian population recognizes a pluralistic society as a desirable goal, and wishes to flourish without the pressure for Americanization. Government policy in the United States today is maintaining foreign languages and cultures through various bilingual and bicultural programs. Despite its diversity and preference for pluralism, the Indian population shows its clear commitment to participate actively in the structural side of it, that is in the spheres of education, economics, mass media, and slowly but surely, in political arena as well.

Asian Indian community wants to become part of the mainstream of American society by exhibiting itself as a 'model minority'. The Indian experience has also shown that neither complete assimilation or acculturation, nor separatism or alienation, have any place in the context of American society. On balance, the cultural pluralism model certainly has the potential to bridge the societal and cultural divide and in helping Americans of all backgrounds to take pride in, maintain and enrich their identities. As agents of 'cultural pluralism' model, the Asian Indians want to become full, proactive participants in the American society. There is near unanimity on the cultural pluralism model, at least in the context of the Asian Indian population. The real challenge is to work out a suitable middle ground which can provide for support to the basic institutional arrangements of American society and at the same time fulfill the wishes and aspirations of these who are Americans, yet Asian Indians.

REFERENCES

1. Cohen, C, *Global Diaspora: An Introduction*, UCL Press, London, 1997; also see, Safran, W. diasporas in modern societies; Myths of homeland and return" Diaspora, Vol.1, 1991; also, see, Harpreet Kaur, "Diaspora: Some General Expositions", *Punjab Journal of Politics*, Vol.XXX, No.1, 2006, pp. 109-120
2. See, Paramatma Saran, *The Asian Indian Experience in the United States*, Schenkman Publishing Company, Cambridge, MA; 1985, pp. 1-10; see, see, Anjali Sahay, *Indian Diaspora in the United States: Brain Drain or Brain Gain?*, Lexington Books, New York, see, also, Tambiah, Stanley J. 2000 "Transnational Movements, Diaspora, and Multiple Modernities." *Daedalus*, No.129: p. 163-194.
3. For details, see K.N.Vaid, *The Overseas Indian Community in Hong Kong*, Center for Asian Studies, University of Hong Kong, 1972, pp. 5-6.
4. H.S. Morris, "Ethnic Groups," in *International Encyclopedia of the Social Sciences*, ed. David L. Sills (New York: Macmillan & Free Press, 1968), p. 167.
5. For a theoretical analysis of the Caste systems, see Baidya Nath Varma, "The Caste System of India," in *Contemporary India*, Asia Publishing House, New York, 1964; pp. 59-81.
6. Milton J. Esman, *Ethnic Conflict in the Western World*, Cornell University Press, Ithaca, New York, 1977.
7. Safran, W. "Diasporas in Modern Societies: Myths of Homeland and Return" *Diaspora*, Vol.1, 1991; also, see, Harpreet Kaur, "Diaspora: Some General Expositions", *Punjab Journal of Politics*, Vol.XXX, No.1, 2006, pp. 109-120
8. Sheffer, G, *Diasporas Politics: At Home Abroad*, Cambridge University Press, London, 2003; also see, Ma, J.C and Cartier, C, *The Chinese Diaspora: Space, Place, Mobility and Identity*, Rowan & Littlefield Publishers, Lanham, 2002
9. Nathan Glazer's article, "Cultural Pluralism: The Social Aspect," in *Pluralism in a Democratic Society*, Melvin. Tumin and Walter Plotch, eds; Praeger, New York, 1977, p. 248
10. *Ibid*
11. B.N. Varma, *The Sociology and Politics of Development: Theoretical Study*, Routledge and Kegan Paul, London, 1988
12. See, Ajaya K.Sahoo, "Contemporary Appraisal of Indian Diaspora in the United States", *Man and Life*, Vol. 30: Nos. (3 & 4), July-December 2004, pp. 81-92, ISRAA, Kolkata
13. M.K. Mohapatra, "Overseas Indians in Urban America: A Study of their Attitudes and Experiences involving Discrimination in American Society," *Nagarlok*, Vol. 11, No.1, 1979, pp. 120-41
14. Parmatma Saran, "New Ethnics: The Case of East Indians n New York City" in *Sourcebook on the New Immigration: Implications for the United States and the International Community*, Roy Simoh, Bryce Laporte, ed. (New Brunswick, N.J.) Transaction Books, 1980

15. Lal, Vinay, 1997, "Ambiences of Hinduism in the Wild West of America: Perspectives from Two Citadels, The Grand Canyon and Las Vegas", *Suitcase,* Vol.1, No.1-2, pp. 84-97; also, see, Prentiss, Karen Pechilis, 2004, 'The Pattern of Hinduism and Hindu Temple Building in the US'. Committee on the Study of Religion, Harvard University, www.pluralism.org., see, *Ibid*, Ajaya K. Sahoo, No.9
16. Mohapatra, *Ibid*, also, see, Ministry of External Affairs, 2001, *Report of the High Level Committee on Indian Diaspora,* New Delhi: Indian Council of World Affairs.
17. Abraham, Thomas, 2003, *The Power Of Community Involvement: Successes in Indian Communities Across America*. Keynote address at the 40th Anniversary of India Association of Nashville, March 8, 2003., see, Ajaya K. Sahoo, *Ibid*, No.9

8

Non-Alignment to Emerging Defence Co-operation

Monish Tourangbam

India's rise as an economic power to reckon with and its ramifications at the global stage has brought new dividends in Indo-US relations. The past decade since the path-breaking visit of President Bill Clinton in March 2000 has turned a new leaf and now the relationship is being touted as the "defining relationship of the 21st century". President George W. Bush during his two terms brought great strides—the nuclear deal being the center-piece, which has served as a platform to develop habits of cooperation across diverse sectors of interactions, both governmental and non-governmental.

The Bush administration as well the Manmohan Singh government had to face a lot of criticism internally, from political parties as well as analysts for going ahead with the nuclear agreement. The Singh government in New Delhi even put its power at stake, distancing itself from the Left, its then coalition ally. President Bush who evidently took extra steps to open a new chapter for India, with new understanding at the International Atomic Energy Agency (IAEA) and Nuclear Suppliers' Group (NSG) waiver, was popular in India, even when his foreign policy misadventures plummeted his popularity internationally. During the initial days of the Obama administration, suspicions were raised in Indian strategic circles regarding the fate of the emerging strategic partnership. Uncertainty amounted regarding US approach to the Kashmir issue, India's envisioned role in the Afghan conflict, China's role in South Asia, etc. But, it did not take much time for the astute politician in President Obama to correct the misgivings, engineering highly successful bilateral meets like Secretary Hillary Clinton's visit of 2009, the state welcome given to Prime Minister Singh in Washington later the same year and the eventful Obama's November 2010 visit thus giving credence to his policy that India remained one of America's partners for the century ahead.

The relationship now spans across a broad spectrum of issues. There is a more matured and nuanced understanding of differences and divergences. Increasing meeting of political minds in the last decade has created major dividends in defence relations. While the United States will remain the pre-eminent world power, American commitments across the globe are stretched thin. Moreover, while the United States and China continues to have inevitable economic linkages and an open confrontation is almost impossible, a cold confrontation on various political and economic issues is also inevitable given the undeniable rise of China in every department. As the United States strives to maintain a status quo in the international order and India equally strives to raise its power status, the two democracies more than ever needs to cooperate with each other. America's new rebalancing strategy towards the Asia-Pacific; called America's 'Asia Pivot' envisions a vital role for India. Indo-US relations has indeed come a long way since the Cold War days when America's obsession with anti-Communism and India's adherence to Non-Alignment created gaps that could not be easily be bridged.

Cold War Estrangement

India-US relations have had a checkered history. As the United States confronted the Soviet Union in a race for global supremacy during the Cold War, American foreign policy decision-making was largely defined by its perceptions regarding the threat that communist Soviet Union presented. India's Non-aligned policy was highly distrusted by American policymakers, with US Secretary of State John Foster Dulles calling it "an immoral and shortsighted conception."[1]

Amidst the overarching structural influence of the Cold War, Indo-US relations suffered despite continuing people-to-people contacts and a convergence of democratic ideals. Indians always resented the political strings they believed were attached to American aid. Occasional opportunities of a rapprochement (like the arms assistance to India during the 1962 border with China) did not materialize. Johnson's approach to the Indian food crisis during the mid 60s created much discomfort for those who wanted to see convergence between the two countries. The Imposition of arms embargo on India and Pakistan during the 1965 Indo-Pakistan war further aggravated problems because Johnson's approach was seen in India as equating the aggressor and the victim. America's involvement in the Vietnam War and the difference of perception with India on this issue made matters worse, negatively affecting relations. During the Indo-Pakistan war of 1971, the Nixon Administration had sent the USS Enterprise to the Bay of Bengal, showing the American tilt towards Pakistan. India signed the Treaty of Peace, Friendship and

Cooperation with the Soviet Union in 1971. Pakistan served as a conduit for Nixon's rapprochement with China. As such, it is easy to understand why relations between the two democracies were called "estranged".[2] Despite various efforts made to improve the ties between the two countries in the realm of defence and security in the successive periods, differences of perception and opinion towards issues deemed vital to American national security such as the Afghan conflict of 1979-89 created hindrances towards closer Indo-US partnership. America's deepening relationship with India's arch rival Pakistan and the kind of overtures that the former made toward regional issues like the Kashmir dispute did not help matters.

According to Indian strategic analyst C. Rajamohan: "India's de facto alliance with the Soviet Union to manage the difficulties in its regional security environment, its commitment to state socialism and its leadership of the Non-Aligned Movement were three factors that reinforced the inherited legacy of anti-colonialism and anti-imperialism. These factors also masked the essential political similarity between India and the West."[3]

Post-Cold War Developments

The end of Cold War and the changing international order thereafter made the United States and India see the relationship through a different lens altogether. New Delhi also had realpolitik reasons to try and bridge gaps with Washington because the demise of the Soviet Union led to American predominance in international politics. Indian policymakers in the 90s put utmost emphasis on the new opportunities for building ties with the US, in an effort to leave behind years of mistrust and hostility. On the other side, US policymakers found conditions much more conducive to forge economic as well as political links with India after structural impediments created by Cold War priorities gave way to prospects for a new thaw in the relationship that had to be capitalized on.[4] The end of Cold War removed from American mindset the long harboured doomsday view of Asian countries falling like "dominoes" into the lap of Soviet communism. Although India still retained its adherence to the general tenets of Non-alignment, the end of the Cold War removed its anti-western edge. India's economic liberalization close on the heels of Cold War's end increased its integration into the international market, creating more opportunities to initiate and build on linkages between the two countries. The real promise of the Indian market and the vitality of the Indian private sector were slowly being unleashed and American leaders and firms were watching the developments closely and positive fallout in the political and economic field were soon to come. The importance that the United States under Bill Clinton's administration accorded to India's economy was evident quite early. American policymakers showered praises on the

Indian economic reforms and envisioned a continued expansion of trade and commercial ties between the two countries.[5]

Towards the end of the Clinton administration, the Kargil conflict led to a dramatic change of perception and opinion. In 1999, as the Indo-Pak conflict at the border intensified, Pakistani Prime Minister Nawaz Sharif dashed off to Washington asking for American assistance. But President Clinton refused to help unless Pakistani forces had withdrawn to their side of the Line of Control (LoC). According to reports, Clinton had informed Vajpayee after intensive parleys with Sharif in Washington in early July 1999 that he was "holding firm on demanding the withdrawal of Pakistani troops to the Line of Control."[6] This episode was the 'trigger moment' in terms of bringing a fresh new perspective in Indo-US relations, providing the best platform than ever before to find more convergences between the two countries. Another important initiative of the Clinton administration would be the sustained talks between External Affairs Minister Jaswant Singh and Deputy Secretary of State Strobe Talbott on nuclear issues. An intensive dialogue between the two countries at the highest levels, unprecedented in the history of the relationship enabled the two countries to better understand each other's security concerns contributing in a big way years later towards India and the US signing the historic civilian nuclear deal. As Talbott remarked, "We are getting better at disagreeing without being disagreeable with each other."[7]

Then came the unprecedented Clinton's March 2000 visit to India that lasted for five days. In contrast, he spent only a few hours in Pakistan, thus signaling the transforming intent of the United States. Setting the tone of the new enthusiasm seen in Indo-US relations, Foreign Minister Jaswant Singh, on the eve of Clinton's visit, summed up independent India's relations with the US as "five wasted decades."[8] President Clinton's visit was public diplomacy at its best. In contrast, America's uneasiness with Pakistan was palpable after the General Musharraf led military coup. President Clinton questioned the democratic deficit in Pakistan. Reflecting Indian concerns, he emphasized that the Kashmir dispute could only be solved by India and Pakistan bilaterally through dialogue.[9] India was seen as a vital partner in Clinton's 'community of democracies' initiative making democracy a major factor in developing relations. India, as an original member of the convening group in Warsaw in 2000 played a prominent role, also leading one of the working groups.[10]

Paradigm Shift in Indo-US Relations

The closing years of the Clinton Administration did signal a major thaw in Indo-US relations, but it was during the George W. Bush Administration that policymakers in Washington D.C. took the extra mile to take ties towards an unprecedented upward trend. A strategic partnership was visualized and implemented during this period. A major breakthrough was achieved in the form of the Indo-US nuclear deal. India's nuclear programme has created a lot of unease in Indo-US relations. India's nuclear tests in 1974 and in 1998 created major stumbling blocks in the relationship, raising the ire of American policymakers and non-proliferation lobbies. Various rounds of sanctions followed isolating India from international nuclear commerce. The US policymakers followed a strategy to cap, roll back and eliminate India's nuclear weapons programme, which of course did not materialize. Interestingly, India's loud and clear decision to become a nuclear power left no doubt about India's intentions and the US was then left with no other choice but to see the whole situation in a more pragmatic way. It took some years but eventually, Washington did come round to finally acknowledge India as a responsible nuclear power despite having refused to sign the Nuclear Non-proliferation treaty (NPT) and the Comprehensive Test Ban Treaty (CTBT) calling them discriminatory in nature.

India unlike some other nuclear powers including Pakistan and China had a clean record on non-proliferation and had a unilateral moratorium on further nuclear testing. The Bush administration saw the positives of the relationship and toned down the differences. Moreover, the presence of officials at the top level who wanted an Indo-US convergence helped bring about a paradigm shift. Otherwise discredited for his foreign policy misadventures like the ill-advised intervention in Iraq, George W. Bush helped open up an international platform for India in the form of the Indo-US nuclear deal and the Nuclear Suppliers' Group (NSG)-waiver.[11] India and the United States developed hitherto unseen habits of cooperation during negotiations leading to the civilian nuclear deal, at the International Atomic Energy Agency's Board of Governors and in the Nuclear Suppliers Group.[12] Another event that helped galvanize India's convergence with the United States in the early days of the Bush administration was the September 11 terrorist attacks. India wasted no time in giving support to America's war on terrorism. In the words of former American Diplomat, Dennis Kux: "New Delhi's prompt support for the war on terrorism marked a further step in the rapprochement with Washington that had begun in the final years of Bill Clinton's presidency.[13] India even provided naval escort to American military assets transiting the Malacca straits during Operation Enduring Freedom in Afghanistan in the summer of 2002.[14] During the Bush administration, the US-India relationship was differentiated from that of US-Pakistan relations. It was argued that the two relations had to have their own trajectories. That the Bush administration had every intention to follow a path of dehyphenation towards the subcontinent was quite evident in official American comments that wanted Indo-US relations to "stand on their own" without being "directed against any third party" and wanted "no hyphenated linkages emanating from Washington regarding South Asian nations."[15]

The diplomatic milestones achieved during the Bush administration entailed increased defence trade, military exercises and the importance accorded to India in the Asian and international scheme of things. President Obama's succession in the early days brought some concerns in India. Unsought policy advices were being offered for the Kashmir issue. Non-proliferation issues seemed to be taking centre-stage; creating unease among those who wanted to see implementation of the Indo-US nuclear deal. President Obama who inherited an economic crisis raised decibel levels against outsourcing. Moreover, the Obama administration went to the extent of hinting at a prospective Chinese role in the Indian subcontinent. But, efforts made to dispel the misunderstandings yielded quick results. Secretary of State Hillary Clinton's India visit in July 2009 was a significant step in this effort. The visit, coming after much negative speculations, managed to infuse a lot of positive energy. Although many commentators alluded to her skipping India during her maiden visit to Asia as Secretary of State but the July visit more than compensated. India's importance in the American scheme of things was elevated. As the US struggled to fix its economy, it could not address major global issues on its agenda without India.[16] This positive trend was quickly followed by Prime Minister Manmohan Singh's visit to Washington in late 2009, significantly the first state visit hosted for any foreign dignitary by the Obama administration.

Reflecting on its increased attention on India and its intention to substantially increase bilateral engagement, US National Security Strategy documents over the years beginning from the Bush administration to Obama's presidency have outlined similarities between the US and India across diverse sectors, with shared interests both in the political and economic field. India-US Strategic Dialogues and the increasing frequency of high-level visits are testimony to increasing importance given to India's pivotal role on both regional and global issues.[17] President Obama's visit in November 2010 during his first term in office helped accentuate the importance of the Indo-US partnership described as the "defining relationship" of the 21st century. His speech to a full-house Parliament was welcomed with thunderous applause. He signed about 20 deals worth around $10 billion dollars, intended to create more than 50,000 job opportunities in his country. He denounced the continuation of terrorist safe havens in Pakistan and promised to lift sanctions from Indian R&D organizations, such as ISRO, DRDO and BDL. Subsequently, it was reported that the US had removed nine Indian space and defense related companies including those from ISRO and DRDO from its export control 'Entity List'.[18] Most of all, President Obama extended America's support to India's inclusion in an expanded UN Security Council in the future. People-to-people contacts between the two countries that survived even the Cold War years and which have galloped in recent times has played an important role in enabling closer understanding between the two political systems. The Indian Diaspora's influence is on the rise in the US visibly creating major dividends across diverse sectors.

The US as a global power with interests to preserve in different corners of the world assumes certain dividends that it desires from a relationship but India consciously preserves its autonomy in foreign policymaking. Hence, like in any relationship that is entrenched across diverse sectors, there are differences that have to be resolved and loopholes that have to be mended. But at the same time, the larger vision of Indo-US relations has managed to override these issues. As often said, the sum of the relationship is greater than the parts. India is much more than a market for American products and technology but forms an inevitable part of the balance of power calculations in Asia. And defence cooperation between the two countries spanning across all the forces is an inevitable component of any American strategic plan to share more with India in terms of maintaining security and sustaining strategic stability in Asia-Pacific.

Defence Cooperation: Emerging Convergences and Enduring Challenges

Significantly, the two democracies are making major strides in defence cooperation which is the true hallmark of any strategic partnership. In the last decade, Indo-US defence ties have undergone a sea change. In fact, a strategic partnership cannot be envisioned without a robust defence component. In recent years, India has awarded $9 billion worth defence contracts to US companies.[19] The Indian military is undergoing modernization, planning to spend $100 billion on buying new weapons in the next ten years. Thus, analysts say that arms sales may be the best way for the United States to revive stagnating US-Indian relations.[20] The India-US Defense Policy Group (DPG)—moribund after India's 1998 nuclear tests and ensuing US sanctions—was revived in 2001 and meets annually. In June 2005, the United States and India had signed a ten-year defense pact outlining planned collaboration in multilateral operations, expanded two-way defense trade, increasing opportunities for technology transfers and co-production, expanded collaboration related to missile defense, and establishment of a bilateral Defense Procurement and Production Group.[21]

Cold War constraints and relatively easier access made New Delhi look towards Moscow for most of its defence armoury. Recently, New Delhi has diversified its weaponry destination to Israel. Many officials in the Indian government and the Indian armed forces still remain wary of going too close to the Americans for procuring weapons partly for historical reasons, partly for many hurdles that remain in the form of weapon sales laws, cost factor and also for the fear that leaning too much on the Americans will lead to relative weakening of India's strategic autonomy in the face of possible American demands for political concessions and compromises.

The issue of dual use exports is one of the major areas of contention, between the two countries, wherein stringent domestic laws and matters of strategic constraints and India's cautious sustenance of strategic autonomy will continue to constrain Indo-US defence trade in the future. The US-India High Technology Cooperation Group (HTCG) was conceived in November 2001. By November 2002, the US and Indian governments began work on a set of principles regarding bilateral cooperation in high technology trade and the first session was held in 2003. By this time, India had also obtained official commitment to increase cooperation in the areas of civil nuclear energy, commercial space applications and high-technology trade. Since the lifting of sanctions on India in 2001 and the creation of the HTCG, the number of dual-use exports to India requiring licenses has dropped significantly.[22] As such, there is definitely an upward trend in streamlining defence transactions between the two countries, a noticeable progress given that defence trade was minimal at best during the Cold War and only sporadic a decade ago.

Since 1998, a number of Indian entities were subjected to case-by-case licensing requirements and appeared on the US export control "Entity List" of foreign end users involved in weapons proliferation activities. But since 2004, as part of the Next Steps in Strategic Partnership (NSSP) implementation, the US has over the years increasingly shown resolve to modify its export licensing policies towards India and removed major Indian defence and space related organizations and subsidiary entities from the Entity List. As the US aspired to increase its defence ties with India through increased transactions and exchanges, the continuation of sanctions on India's premier defence research institutions was anomaly of sorts. Hence, the decision to lift sanctions was a much needed step. US State Department's approved licenses for defence articles for India as well defence services for India through Technical Assistance and Manufacturing Licensing Agreements have also seen an upward trend.[23] Increased defence sales to India assumed more importance for an America facing unemployment problems as bigger contracts to the Indian military would mean more job creation in American defence firms. On the other hand, US-India defence trade would also open doors towards knowledge and skill upgradation for Indian firms working in this field.[24]

Besides technology transfer, trade in military weapons and equipment also saw an upward trend as part of the efforts to strengthen strategic partnership. The first-ever major US arms sale to India came in 2002, when the Pentagon negotiated delivery of 12 counter-battery radar sets (or "Firefinder" radars) worth $190 million to India. Other defense purchases by India included $44 million worth of *USS Trenton*, a decommissioned American amphibious transport dock which became the second largest in the Indian navy when it was commissioned as the *INS Jalashwa* in 2007.[25] The acquisition of the *C130 J Super Hercules* was a major defence purchase from the US, one of six military transport aircraft ordered from the US in a deal worth almost $1billion. Aimed at enhancing the special operations capacity of the Indian armed forces they have already been successfully employed to provide critical humanitarian assistance following an earthquake in Sikkim in September 2011.[26] India's Defence Ministry has also cleared its long-pending $660 million proposal to buy 145 ultra-light howitzer guns 27 long years after the Bofors guns payoff scandal broke out in the late 1980s. India's Defence Acquisition Council (DAC) cleared the deal for the M777 BAE Systems guns that will be bought through the Foreign Military Sales (FMS) route of the US government.[27]

But, differences persist over a host of other issues. Licensing process in the US for export of munitions is more cumbersome and opaque than the dual-use licensing procedures, causing yet another major hurdle in Indo-US defence trade.[28] For instance, the requirements of End-Use Monitoring Agreement (EUMA), Communications Interoperability and Security Memorandum of Agreement (CISMoA), the Logistics Support Agreement (LSA) and the Basic Exchange and Cooperation Agreement for Geospatial Cooperation (BECA) have hampered the pace of Indo-US defence trade. EUMA seeks to establish a standard set of procedures governing the proper end-use of US-origin defence items, as well as the on-site inspection of such item; CISMoA aims at ensuring the secrecy and interoperability of US communications and intelligence systems; and the LSA seeks to provide US and Indian military aircraft and vessels access to each country's ports, airfields and other facilities for refuelling and refurbishment. Even though US officials continually insist on India to sign these agreements in order to further streamline trade flow in defence items of the most sophisticated and advanced nature, overriding political sentiments in India resist the US attempts for fear of losing strategic autonomy in the backdrop of historical unreliability of the US, as a defence partner. The United States scores above other weapon suppliers when it comes to the quality and technological superiority of weapon systems. But differences persist between the two countries when it comes to US stringent laws regarding transfer of technology that has military uses, its heavy cost and India's procurement system that analysts contend is plagued with lack of transparency, legitimacy and corruption problems.[29] The hard bargaining between the parties finally led to the signing of the EUMA in 2009 by the two countries, but not without some Indian conditions untypical of EUMA agreements between the US and other countries. Prime Minister Manmohan Singh defended the agreement in the parliament arguing that the Indian sovereignty was not compromised and that the agreement did not allow "unilateral" US inspections.[30] All three outstanding accords have faced political opposition in India; and some technical issues remain to be clarified. Talks over these contentious topics have been put on the back burner for the time being and are not being discussed openly during major bilateral strategic dialogues and meetings. But high level efforts are being made to clear differences and bring more clarity to the process currently impeding more streamlined Indo-US defence trade.[31]

India's quest for 126 new medium, multi-role combat aircraft (MMRCA) in a deal worth some $11 billion could have been the most lucrative Indo-US defence contract. But in 2011, New Delhi announced that it would not look to American firms for this sale. Many analysts and even pro-India voices in the United States felt let down by the Indian decision, with some regretting that the Indian government had short-circuited a brilliant opportunity to take the Indo-US strategic relationship to the next level. But, not all agree with such an assessment. It is important to note that a strategic partnership of the kind that India and the United States envisions should not be based on the pedestal of business alone, and the failure of a single deal, however large, should not be trumpeted as the ultimate symbol of India's inconsistency and unreliability in the issue. India's decision to settle for fighters from European consortiums should be seen as an independent autonomous decision arrived at under internal consultations. India, as a rising power at the global arena wants to maintain sustainable relationships with a host of countries around the world, and it would be unnerving for the United States too if other major partners started objecting against every other major project the US concludes with India.[32] In any case, various other significant deals amounting to billions have more or less compensated the presumed monetary and strategic loss resulting from failure of the US companies in striking the deal for the multi-role aircraft.

Another significant area of military-to-military cooperation between India and the US has been joint military exercises. Since early 2002, the United States and India have held a series of unprecedented and increasingly substantive combined exercises involving all military services. The US now conducts more joint exercises and personnel exchanges with India than with any other country. These embrace "Cope India" air exercises, joint Special Forces Training, "Vajra Prahar" exercises (focused on advanced rifle marksmanship, combat marksmanship, close-quarters combat, helicopter insertion, medical evacuation, combined mission planning, and scenario-based missions), annual "Malabar" joint naval exercises and "Yudh Abhyas" which is a recurrently scheduled bilateral exercise hosted by the Indian Army. The 2009 Yudh Avyas exercise involved 17 Stryker vehicles – the largest deployment of the US vehicles outside of Iraq and Afghanistan in recent years.[33] The Yudh Abhyas 2011-12 brought the US and the Indian armies for exercises at Mahajan and Bathinda in India that also saw for the first time engineer brigades participating from both the countries teaming up to train on a United Nations-modeled peace support operation.[34] Indo-US military exercises have infused a habit of cooperation and interoperability between the two militaries. This is important in view of the lack of such habit earlier and due to growing convergence of security interests, such as combating international terrorism to keeping the sea lanes of communication trouble free from piracy. Moreover, the United States might have an indirect interest in showcasing the sophistication and high-end efficacy of its weapons, thus hoping to create more leverage towards increasing its defence sales to a modernizing and expanding Indian military.[35] In 2010, the US Pacific Command (USPACOM) and the Indian Integrated Defence Staff (IDS) conducted the inaugural Joint Exercise India (JEI) tabletop exercise that involved officers from more than one services. "Shatrujeet", another exercise, focuses on amphibious doctrine and operations. Cope India is the premier exercise between the two air forces.[36] Besides the large-scale "Malabar" exercise, The US and Indian navies also conduct three other naval exercises, namely "Habu Nag" (naval aspects of amphibious operations), "Spitting Cobra" (explosive ordnance destruction focus), and "Salvex" (diving and salvage). The US Coast Guard has also begun engagement and training with the Indian Coast Guard.[37] Naval cooperation assumes increasing importance in view of projected shared interests of both the countries in securing the sea lanes and in allowing freedom of navigation under international law of the sea, and with the Indian Ocean gaining increasing strategic attention.

Indo-US Defence Ties and America's Asia Strategy

From "estranged democracies" to sharing an "evolving strategic partnership", India and the US have travelled a long distance. US Defence Secretary Leon Panetta during his India visit prior to the 3rd India-US Strategic Dialogue, stressed on the US decision to reorient its foreign policy and put emphasis on the Asia-Pacific region. The US saw an inevitable role for India in its "rebalancing" strategy towards Asia-Pacific and managing China's rise. America through this strategy intends to "expand" its "military partnerships" and its "presence in the arc extending from Western Pacific and East Asia into the Indian Ocean Region (IOR) and South Asia". "Defence cooperation with India is a linchpin in this strategy," Panetta said.[38] A US Department of Defense strategy paper 'Sustaining US Global Leadership: Priorities for 21st Century' released earlier in January 2012 also emphasized the necessity to "*rebalance toward the Asia Pacific region*" and noted that the US was "investing in a long-term strategic partnership with India to support its ability to serve as a regional economic anchor and provider of security in the broader Indian Ocean region." The same paper raised concerns over the "the growth of China's military power" and sought "greater clarity of its strategic intentions in order to avoid causing friction in the region.[39]

One of America's most prominent strategic commentators, Fareed Zakaria in his well known book *The Post-American World and the Rise of the Rest* calls China "the Challenger" and India "The Ally".[40] Top officials in the Bush administration including National Security Adviser Condoleezza Rice and the US Under Secretary of State for Political Affairs Nicholas Burns had consensus regarding India's increasing importance in American strategic calculations.[41] Managing China's rise does not imply preparing for another war, which is hardly imaginable in this globalized world where China plays the banker to the United States and India-China trade figures increase each passing year. But, the presence of economic linkages may not translate into strategic convergences. China's increasing military budget and Chinese Navy's deliberate march towards becoming a blue-water navy, have become a major cause of concern for the United States, India and many Southeast Asian nations, raising fears that the rise of a "hegemonic" China would disturb the balance of power in Asia and across.[42] China's increasing military expenditure (it is believed that the actual budget would be bigger than is officially projected), and its increasingly aggressive behaviour, especially in the South China Sea have increased concerns.[43]

China's relentless drive for power and influence around the world is sought to be disguised under the propaganda of the "Peaceful Rise of China". But, the problem is that others, more so countries in geographical proximity, do not perceive it in the same way. Washington policymakers see India's rise as a stabilizing force in the Asian continent. India's economic growth with an enduring liberal democratic base and the growing vitality of its private sector is something that finds resonance in the US. The probable rise of a "hegemonic" China in the Asian region presents a scenario in which the present pre-dominant power of the United States would resort to balancing the Chinese power with the assistance and partnership of other major powers in the region, especially India which has had a long, messy relationship with China. Ashton B Carter, a US national security professional argued that the US and Indian governments do not wish "....to talk publicly, let alone take actions now, to advance this shared interest, but they very well might in the future."[44]

As many other states in Southeast Asia see a threat in China's increasing power projection in the South China Sea, India's increasing closeness to the Southeast Asian nations via its reenergized 'Look East Policy' is a welcome development. As a response to China's aggressive assertion in the South China Sea, many Southeast Asian nations want a continuance of US primary role in this region. Now, given India's increasing convergences with these countries, a US-India combined attention should be directed to assisting these countries towards safeguarding against any future belligerence from China. With concerns of a rising China that increasingly sees Asia as its exclusive zone of sphere, the US as well as Japan would more than ever realize the importance of India as a power balancer in Asia. India, US and Japan share common interests in preserving strategic stability in Asia. The initiation of the ambitious India-Japan-US trilateral dialogue on regional and global issues of shared interest is a significant development.[45] It is indeed an opportune time for the formulation of such a framework, looking at the trajectory of the relationships between the countries involved. Clearly, the rise of an aggressive China will not serve the interests of any country in the Asian Continent, and this is something clear to most policy makers and analyst across boundaries. Consequently, this trilateral framework should serve as leverage for Indian policymakers and be a sober reminder to the Chinese that their strategic moves are being watched quite intensely.

Although there is a broad consensus both in New Delhi and Washington regarding the centrality and salience of Indo-US strategic partnership, there are concerns in Indian minds regarding the possibility of a US-China condominium, or G2 as it is nowadays referred to. Indians are concerned that Washington, because of its economic problems, the economic interlinkages with the Chinese state and massive Chinese growth, might eventually end up giving too much leeway to the Chinese in South Asia and in the Asian continent at large.[46]

Undeniably, things are more complex when one looks at the bigger picture. The US, India and many Southeast Asian countries have major differences with China regarding freedom of navigation, especially in the South China Sea over which Beijing claims uncontested authority. But, at the same time, economically, New Delhi, Washington and most of South-East Asia are so interlinked to Beijing that one can hardly foresee any major conflict. Thus, when it comes to hedging China, responses are subtle and attention geared more towards: "How to manage rising China without provoking any major untoward incident having global ramifications?" Hence, if Defence Secretary Panetta outlined America's new defence strategy in New Delhi, Foreign Minister SM Krishna was seen emphasizing the importance of India-China relations at the Shanghai Cooperation Organization (SCO) summit in China around the same time. Pertinently, Chinese leaders too understand the importance of sustaining India-China ties. Just as Washington and New Delhi look for ways to control Beijing' aggression, they also prepare various diplomatic cushions so as to prevent any crash landing.

Conclusions

As India's influence increases and its voice begins to matter more in issues global in nature, it has to take some hard decisions and take sides and form pragmatic partnerships if not alliances in order to protect its own interests. Despite domestic constituents that will come out with guns blazing at a closer working relationship with the US, accusing whichever government in power of selling out 'India's independent foreign policy", New Delhi should recognize the salience of US support for its rise globally and the US at the same time should recognize India's importance for maintaining strategic stability in the Asian continent, as China rises across a wide spectrum of areas. Keeping in mind that both the countries are thriving democracies with political structures that are not monolithic in nature, negotiations and differences are well expected. Countries have to make choices in international relations, which may often be not popular. But, when it comes to choosing between national interests and popularity, the former should win. Clearly, as during the Cold War wherein New Delhi and Washington did not share the best of relationships, there are lingering skeptics on both sides of the fence. For cynics in the US, India will always be a reluctant partner and for those on the Indian side, Washington will always be an unreliable power. Long held suspicions towards US imperialistic policies and India's non-aligned tendencies would continue to raise heads.

As an emerging or an "emerged power" as President Obama preferred to call, India is fiercely guarded about its decision-making autonomy, and its independent foreign policy. But, the strength of India as an ally lies in the fact that India will never blindly toe the US line, in the fact that an emerging power like India, will never become the kind of ally that Pakistan typifies. But, when India is convinced of a shared interest and rational convergence, it will leave no stones unturned to work hand in hand with the United States.

REFERENCES

1. Dulles as cited in Dennis Kux, *Estranged Democracies: India and the United States, 1941-1991* (New Delhi: Sage Publications, 1993), 128.
2. For an in-depth analysis of US Cold War policies and its impact on South Asia, see Robert J. McMahon. *Cold War in the Periphery: The United States, India and Pakistan* (New York: Columbia University Press, 1996) and H. W. Brands, *India and the United States: The Cold Peace* (Boston: Twayne Publishers, 1990.
3. C. Rajamohan, *Crossing the Rubicon: The Shaping of India's New Foreign Policy* (New Delhi: Penguin Books, 2003), 58.
4. *Ibid*, 58
5. Chintamani Mahapatra, *Indo-US Relations into the 21st Century*, (New Delhi: Knowledge World, 1998), 21.
6. "Vajpayee stood firm during Kargil conflict: Clinton aide," *The Times of India*, May 19, 2002, http://timesofindia.indiatimes.com/world/Vajpayee-stood-firm-during-Kargil-conflict-Clinton-aide/articleshow/10341644.cms (April 9, 2011). Also see Chintamani Mahapatra, "Analyzing American Approach to Kargil Conflict," *Institute of Peace and Conflict Studies (IPCS)*, 17 July 1999, http://www.ipcs.org/article/indo-pak/analyzing-american-approach-to-kargil-conflict-227.html (25 June 2012).
7. C. Rajamohan, *Crossing the Rubicon*, 94.
8. *Ibid*, 83.
9. "Clinton Addresses Pakistani People," *CNN.com Transcripts*, March 25, 2000, http://transcripts.cnn.com/TRANSCRIPTS/0003/25/bn.01.html (April 16, 2011).
10. C. Rajamohan, *Crossing the Rubicon*, 64. Also see Community of Democracies, http://www.community-democracies.org/
11. Interestingly, the 2005 Pew Global Attitudes survey found that about seven-in-ten Indians (71%) had a favourable view of the United States. Moreover, President Bush who was globally unpopular by then was widely admired in India. Just over half (54%) of Indians said that they had a lot or some confidence that Bush would generally do the right thing in world affairs. See Pew Research Centre, "India: Pro-America, Pro-Bush," *Pew Global Attitudes Project*, February 28, 2006, http://pewglobal.org/2006/02/28/

india-pro-america-pro-bush/ (June 4, 2011).

12. Evan A. Feigenbuam, "India's Rise, America's Interest: The Fate of the US-Indian Partnership," *Foreign Affairs*, 89, no.2 (March/April 2010): 79.
13. Dennis Kux (2002), "India's Fine Balance," *Foreign Affairs* 81, no.3, (May/June 2002): 94.
14. C Rajamohan, *Crossing the Rubicon*, 113.
15. Robert Blackwill, "Future of Shared US-India National Interests," *GlobalSecurity.org*, September 6, 2001 http://www.globalsecurity.org/wmd/library/news/india/2001/india-010906-usia1.htm (April 16, 2011.) For an astute analysis of the policy of dehyphenation, see Ashley Tellis, "Merits of Dehyphenation: Explaining US Success in Engaging India and Pakistan," *The Washington Quarterly* 31, No.4, (2008): 21-42.
16. Teresita C. Schaffer, "Hillary Clinton's Visit to India," *Center for Strategic and International Studies (CSIS)*, July 23, 2009, http://csis.org/publication/secretary-state-hillary-clinton%E2%80%99s-visit-india (May 19, 2011).
17. The White House, "National Security Strategy of the United States of America," September 2002, http://merln.ndu.edu/whitepapers/USnss2002.pdf (June 19, 2012): 27 and The White House, "National Security Strategy of the United States of America," May 2010, http://www.whitehouse.gov/sites/default/files/rss_viewer/national_security_strategy.pdf, (June 26, 2012): 43-44.
18. Lalit K. Jha, "US Removes ISRO, DRDO from Entities List," *Outlook*, January 25, 2011, http://news.outlookindia.com/item.aspx?709643 (April 11, 2011).
19. "Defence ties with India strong and growing: Pentagon," *The Economic Times*, March 30, 2012, http://articles.economictimes.indiatimes.com/2012-03-30/news/31261259_1_defence-ties-defence-policy-defence-trade (June 19, 2012); "Joint Statement 2012 US-India Strategic Dialogue," *Ministry of External Affairs*, June 13, 2012, http://meaindia.nic.in/mystart.php?id=530519618, (June 14, 2012).
20. Stephen Cohen and Sunil Dasgupta (March/April 2011), "Arms Sales for India: How Military Trade Could Energize US-India Relations," *Foreign Affairs* 90, no. 2, (March/April 2011): 22. For a critical analysis of India's military modernization, see by Stephen Cohen and Sunil Dasgupta (2010) "*Arming without Aiming: India's Military Modernization*," (New Delhi: Viking, 2010).
21. "India: Domestic Issues, Strategic Dynamics, and US Relations," *CRS Report for Congress*, September 1, 2011, 82, http://www.fas.org/sgp/crs/row/RL33529.pdf (December 21, 2011).
22. For details see Kenneth I. Juster and Ajay Kuntamukkala, "US-India Initiative Series: Unleashing US-India Defense Trade," Working Paper, *Center for New American Security*, (October 2010):5, http://www.cnas.org/files/documents/publications/CNAS_USIndiaDefenseTrade_Juster.pdf (December 12, 2011). Also see Kevin Wolf (Assistant Secretary of Commerce for Export Administration), "Remarks at the 7th US-India High Technology Cooperation Group Meeting," March 16, 2010, http://

www.bis.doc.gov/news/2010/2010_k_wolfs_htcg_remarks_final.pdf,(12 December 12, 2011) and C. Rajamohan, *Crossing the Rubicon*, 114.

23. For details see Kenneth I. Juster and Ajay Kuntamukkala, "US-India Initiative Series: Unleashing US-India Defense Trade", 6.
24. For details see "India: Domestic Issues, Strategic Dynamics, and US Relations", (September 1, 2011): 85-86 and Moska Najib, "Why India-US Defence Deals Have Become Big Business," *BBC News*, February 7, 2011, http://www.bbc.co.uk/news/world-south-asia-12381737 (June 13, 2012).
25. For details see "India: Domestic Issues, Strategic Dynamics, and US Relations", (September 1, 2011): 85-86.
26. Moska Najib, "Why India-US Defence Deals Have Become Big Business," and US Department of Defense, "Report to Congress on US-India Security Cooperation," November 2011, http://www.defense.gov/pubs/pdfs/20111101_NDAA_Report_on_US_India_Security_Cooperation.pdf (May 7, 2012).
27. "India Buys New Artillery Guns, 27 Years after Bofors," *NDTV.com*, May 11, 2012, http://www.ndtv.com/article/india/india-buys-new-artillery-guns-27-years-after-bofors-209582 (May 11, 2012).
28. Kenneth I. Juster and Ajay Kuntamukkala, "US-India Initiative Series: Unleashing US-India Defense Trade", 6.
29. Stephen Cohen and Sunil Dasgupta, "*Arms Sales to India*," 24-26. For more on the challenges of Indo-US defence ties, see Anit Mukherjee and Manohar Thyagraj (2012), "Competing Exceptionalisms: US-India Defence Relationship," *Journal of Defence Studies* 6, no. 2, (2012): 12-28.
30. For details see Jeff Abramson and Daniel Horner, "India, US Agree on Defense Trade Monitoring," *Arms Control Today*, September 4, 2009 http://www.armscontrol.org/act/2009_09/IndiaUS_trade (December 14, 2011).
31. For details see Sandeep Dikshit, "India averse to inking 3 military pacts with US," *The Hindu*, June 23, 2011,http://www.hindu.com/2011/06/23/stories/2011062366090800.htm (December 22, 2011). "CISMOA, LSA Not on Table of Indo-US Strategic Dialogue," *OutlookIndia*, July 15, 2011, http://news.outlookindia.com/items.aspx?artid=727872 (December 22, 2011); "US hopeful of selling more arms to India," *The Economic Times*, June 7, 2012 http://articles.economictimes.indiatimes.com/2012-06-07/news/32101083_1_defence-secretary-logistics-support-agreement-security-memorandum (June 7, 2012). Also see Secretary of Defense Leon E. Panetta, "Partners in the 21st Century", *Institute of Defence Studies and Analyses (IDSA), New Delhi, India*, June 6, 2012, http://www.idsa.in/system/files/LeonEPanetta.pdf (June 6, 2012).
32. Dan Twining, "Why isn't India buying American fighter jets?," *Foreign Policy*, April 29, 2011, http://shadow.foreignpolicy.com/posts/2011/04/29/why_isn_t_india_buying_american_fighter_jets (December 15, 2011). Also see Praveen Swami, "Why the critics of India's combat jet deal are wrong," *The Hindu*, May 2, 2011, http://www.thehindu.com/opinion/lead/article1983674.ece (December 15, 2011); Evan A. Feigenbuam, "New Delhi Buys a Plane, Not a Defense

Relationship", *Council on Foreign Relations*, May 2, 2011, http://blogs.cfr.org/asia/2011/05/02/new-delhi-buys-a-plane-not-a-defense-relationship/ (December 8, 2011).

33. "US-India Army Exercise Yudh Abhyas Underway, Largest US Stryker Deployment Outside Iraq, Afghanistan," *US Embassy, New Delhi*, Press Release 2009, http://newdelhi.usembassy.gov/pr101909.html (December 25, 2011).
34. "USARPAC Soldiers Train in India During Yudh Abhyas 11-12, *US Army*, March 22, 2012, http://www.army.mil/article/76343/USARPAC_Soldiers_train_in_India_during_Yudh_Abhyas_11_12/ (June 26, 2012); Bonnie Cowles, "Exercise Yudh Abhyas Bridges US, Indian Army Engineers, *US Army*, http://www.usarpac.army.mil/ya1112/fullstory.asp?file=20120412&id=0 (June 26, 2012).
35. "Military Pacts on Hold but India, US Continue with Exercises, Arms Deals," *The Times of India*, September 22, 2010, http://articles.timesofindia.indiatimes.com/2010-09-22/india/28238324_1_cismoa-military-pacts-joint-combat-exercises (December 25, 2011). Also see Rajat Pandit, "Flurry of Wargames on Anvil to Boost Military Diplomacy," *The Times of India*, October 20, 2010, http://articles.timesofindia.indiatimes.com/2010-10-20/india/28230625_1_combat-exercises-indian-warships-wargames (December 26, 2011).
36. "Pentagon to Enhance Indo-US Counter-terrorism Cooperation," *Financial Express*, November 2, 2011, http://www.financialexpress.com/news/pentagon-to-enhance-indous-counterterrorism-cooperation/8694130/0 (December 26, 2011).
37. (*Ibid*). For details see Byron C. Linder, "Carrier Strike Group 1 Completes Exercise Malabar 2012," *Commander US 7th Fleet*, April 17, 2012, http://www.c7f.navy.mil/news/2012/04-april/022.htm (June 26, 2012) and "US naval chief's visit to strengthen Indo-US defence ties," *Times of India*, April 24, 2012, http://articles.timesofindia.indiatimes.com/2012-04-24/india/31392491_1_indo-us-defence-ties-western-naval-command-joint-military-exercises (June 24, 2012).
38. "Leon Panetta Calls for Closer Defence Ties with India", *BBC News*, June 6, 2012, http://www.bbc.co.uk/news/world-asia-18336854 (June 27, 2012).
39. "Department of Defense, "Sustaining US Global Leadership: Priorities for 21st Century Defense," January 2012, http://www.defense.gov/news/Defense_Strategic_Guidance.pdf (June 24, 2012). Also see Vibhuti N. Hatй & Teresita C. Schaffer, "US-India Defense Relations: Strategic Perspectives," *South Asia Monitor, Center for Strategic and International Studies (CSIS)*, April 4, 2007, no. 105: 1-3.
40. Fareed Zakaria, *The Post-American World and the Rise of the Rest*, (New Delhi: Penguin Books, 2008).
41. Condoleezza Rice, "Promoting the National Interest," *Foreign Affairs* 79, no.1 (January-February 2000): 56 and R. Nicholas Burns, "America's Strategic Opportunity with India: The New US-India Partnership," *Foreign*

Affairs 86, no.6 (November/December 2007): 131.

42. Bruce Vaughn, "US Strategic and Defense Relationships in the Asia-Pacific Region," *CRS Report for Congress,* January 22, 2007, 2-3, http://www.fas.org/sgp/crs/row/RL33821.pdf (June 18, 2011).
43. Ben Blanchard, "China Defense Budget to Stir Regional Dispute," *Reuters*, March 4, 2011, http://www.reuters.com/article/2011/03/04/us-china-defence-idUSTRE7230ZN20110304, (June 27, 2011); James Hookway, "Tensions Flare Over Disputed Asian Sea," *The Wall Street Journal*, June 10, 2011, http://online.wsj.com/article/SB10001424052702304259304576375203724909870.html, (18, 2011) and John Pomfret, "Beijing Claims 'Indisputable Sovereignty' over South China Sea," *Washington Post*, July 31, 2010, http://www.washingtonpost.com/wp-dyn/content/article/2010/07/30/AR2010073005664.html (June 18, 2011).
44. Ashton B. Carter, "America's New Strategic Partner?," *Foreign Affairs* 85, no. 4, (July-August 2006): 42.
45. "First US-Japan-Indian Trilateral Meeting", *Hindustan Times*, December 20, 2011, http://www.hindustantimes.com/world-news/Americas/First-US-Japan-India-trilateral/Article1-784695.aspx (June 27, 2012).
46. Zbigniew Brzezinski, "The Group of Two that could change the World," *FinancialTimes*, January 13, 2009, http://www.ft.com/intl/cms/s/0/d99369b8-e178-11dd-afa0-0000779fd2ac.html (June 18, 2011.) Also see C. Rajamohan, "India's Quest for Continuity in the Face of Change," *The Washington Quarterly* 31, no. 4 (Autumn 2008): 150.

9

India-United States Cooperation for Rebuilding Afghanistan

Akhilesh Kumar Tiwari

After more than a decade of fall of Taliban, perpetual state fragility in Afghanistan is still the major concern for international community. A series of terrorist attacks in several cities, bombing after United States President Obama's visit and killing of peace negotiator are a sharp reminder that the country is still fragile and even capital Kabul, is vulnerable to raids by terrorist and criminal organizations. Reports suggest that the security forces and security analysts were surprised by the scale and ferocity of these attacks. Security scenario and strategic dynamics of entire region including Iran have become extremely complicated and appear to be highly unpredictable. Threats emanate from diversified actors with varied political and ethnic support and strategic interests. Now it will be oversimplification to argue that Taliban are only security concern for Afghanistan and international community. Concerns further aggravated as Western security forces have already set out their exit strategy and Afghan security forces are not in the position to take the charge of security of entire country. These attacks were also seen as a major setback for President Hamid Karzai, who is desperately trying to strike a peace deal with Taliban for ensuring stability and building confidence among Afghan people and international community before international forces leave the country. Now more than a decade of efforts of the international community led by the United States for maintaining security and establishing rule of law seem to be falling short. The implications of these attacks and state fragility are *writ large* on India's engagement and stakes in Afghanistan. India and the US are the main stakeholders in Afghanistan, and this paper attempts to analyze their role in reconstructions and development.

Challenges in Afghanistan

Due to large scale of fighting for more than two decades, Afghan state had ceased to function. The World Bank estimated in 2000 that Afghan state was in the lowest percentile in all six areas of governance that the bank tracks: voice and accountability, the rule of law, control of corruption, government effectiveness, regulatory quality, and political stability. At that time, the Taliban government collected less than one per cent of Gross Domestic Product (GDP) in revenue, compared to an average of 11 per cent across South Asia and 26 per cent worldwide. There was no professional army or police force, leaving warlords to wage mini wars against one another[1]. *The Economist* had named it as 'worst country' in the world in January 2001.[2] The country still ranks at 6th and 7th position in 2010 and 2011 respectively on FSI.[3] Historically, Afghanistan has always been weak in structure as well as in political sense. Warlordism, fragmented society, ethnic and religious cleavage, rentier economy and regional conflict have not been favourable to state-building and nation-building process. Located at the heart of Asia, Afghanistan occupies a unique geo-strategic position that makes it vulnerable to regional power struggle for strategic advantages.[4]

In the grip of extremism, it was isolated from the world community. Taliban regime violated the civilizing principles one after another. The catalogue of its atrocities included the treatment of women as second class citizens, the expulsion of international agencies, mass persecution of ethnic and religious minorities, gross violations of human rights, cultural vandalism and other artefacts of the country's non-Islamic heritage, promotion of an illicit economy through opium production and, finally providing a safe haven to international terror networks from which to strike international targets.[5] After the fall of Taliban in 2001, a democratic government is at the helm: Afghanistan continues to suffer from illegal drugs trade, Taliban insurgency, organized crime high incidence of poverty and underdevelopment, widespread corruption and so on. According to Brookings Afghanistan Index 2011, insurgent attacks are rising after March 2011[6]. In many parts of the country, a sense of insecurity among Afghan people is rife. Recent terrorist attacks in month of April in several cities of Afghanistan are a grim reminder that the country is still fragile and even capital, Kabul, appears to be vulnerable to raids by terrorist and criminal organizations[7]. Security scenario and strategic dynamics of region have become extremely complicated and appear to be highly unpredictable. During his visit to Kabul, the US President Barack Obama told that Taliban's momentum was broken and Al-Qaeda was devastated. But Taliban struck back less than two hours after he left Afghanistan. That was a stark reminder of the difficult task still ahead for Afghan troops[8]. Afghanistan is still a predominant supplier of illicit opiates in the world, accounting for more than 90 per cent of world production and trade.[9] The relation between drugs and state weakness is bi-directional.

Drug trafficking is prevalent where governments are too weak to enforce counternarcotics laws. On the other hand, drug trafficking also weakens the state further by providing criminal groups with greater financial resources to suborn law enforcement officials and the process corrodes the state control.[10]

Afghan economy has recovered to a considerable extent in recent years and Gross Domestic Product (GDP) has risen to 11.8 billion US Dollar in 2008/09 and estimated to be 17 billion US Dollar in 2010/11. It has achieved considerable success in infrastructure development and human development. But it still remains one of the poorest and least developed countries in the world with more than 42 per cent population below poverty line. According to UNDP Human Development Report 2011, Afghanistan stands at the 172 position out of 187 countries in the Human Development Index (HDI) and at 141 out of 146 countries in the Gender Inequality Index (GII)[11]. It has one of highest infant mortality and mother mortality rates and one of the lowest life expectancy and literacy rates. The National Risk and Vulnerability Assessment (2007-08) found that 7.4 million people, nearly a third of the population are unable to get enough food to live active and healthy lives. Another 8.5 million people, or 37 per cent, are on the borderline of food insecurity. Current government system of Afghanistan is riddled with corruption and malpractices. It stands third from the bottom level in Transparency International Index 2010[12] and is referred as "corrupt-istan".[13] Feeble economic base has been recognised as one of the major challenges of state building in Afghanistan. Afghanistan is a rentier economy that heavily relies on international assistance for its public expenditure. The gap between domestic revenue and operating cost is wide. Afghan economy is growing at a rapid pace and GDP has been tripled in less than a decade but its base is very small. Agriculture is the mainstay of economy and society. Around 80 per cent people have been involved in this sector for livelihoods and income but it has been able to generate only 31 per cent of GDP. It has been noted that prospect for agriculture growth is not very bright as only 12 per cent of land is arable and out of this barely four to five per cent of land is irrigated.[14] In addition, Afghanistan is mountainous desert and semi-arid region. It is vulnerable to projected climate change that can adversely affect the agriculture sector. Approximately 75 per cent of Afghanistan is vulnerable to desertification.[15] Some 85-90 per cent of the country's water is taken from surface sources and 10-15 per cent from below the ground and estimated that current groundwater resources feeding the Kabul water supply can only cope with increased demand until 2012. More than 2.5 million people in Afghanistan are affected by drought or water shortages.[16] Thus, prospect for a robust agriculture growth and more domestic revenue appears to be grim. Afghanistan has abundance of natural resources. If they are extracted, they can be base for a viable industry in the country. Due to insecurity, continuing fighting and lack of a conducive regional environment, it also appears to be not feasible in near future.

Rebuilding Post-Conflict Afghanistan: The Role of International Community

Today it has been well recognized that 'failed states' or 'states teetering on the brink of disaster' are the major sources of global threats and instability. The US National Security Strategy 2002, Investing in Prevention: An International Strategy to Manage Risks of Instability and Improve Crisis Response (UK Government Report 2005), European Security Strategy, 2003 and Organization for Economic Co-operation and Development (OECD) Donor Assistance Committee (Paris 2005 Report) have expressed concerns over the threats originating from fragile states and stipulated how international involvement is necessary to quell them[17]. According to the World Bank, about 600 million people live in countries affected by fragility and conflict. The annual global cost of conflict is estimated to be around $100 billion. World Development Report 2011 of the World Bank will be devoted to issue of conflict, security and development[18]. In his book, *the Bottom Billion: Why the Poorest Countries are Failing and What Can Be Done About It*, Paul Collier paints a more dismal picture of the fragile states. He notes that there are almost one billion people in very poor countries that are not delivering much, if any, growth in per capita incomes. He highlights the plight of the 'bottom billion' is that they are caught in one or often several of four traps namely conflict; mismanaged dependency on natural resources; weak governance in a small country; and economic isolation among other very poor economies, with access to big markets available only at high cost[19]. Therefore, in recent years scholars have been emphasizing the importance of role of international community in building capable states and legitimate structure of governance to prevent the collapse into conflict and facilitate sustainable recovery from violence[20].

Second, in the era of globalization, persistence of poverty, hunger, malnutrition, violation of human rights, discrimination, political instability, climate change, to name a few, are not only national problems, but also global challenges since they have their impact beyond national boundaries[21]. Third, global assistance to improve developing and fragile countries governance has increased at a steady pace. International donors have been devoting substantial resources to strengthening institutions of governance in the hopes of enhancing the rule of law, accountability, transparency, probity, decentralization and so on. Bilateral development assistance providers also have been involved in the governance issues, often with more explicitly political goals of promoting principles of good governance in beneficiary countries. After September 11, 2001, the stakes for successful state-building in poor countries were raised, and good governance was transformed into a full-fledged, global public good. The quality of institutional performance in the developing world morphed from a matter of mere individual country concern into a challenge that could determine the fate of humankind[22].

According to the World Bank, international community can help the process of reconstruction and development in the fragile states mainly in two ways. The first is by taking action at a regional or global level to reduce external stresses. International initiatives aimed at tackling natural and economic shocks, illegal trafficking, international corruption, cross-border and transnational forms of violence are crucial for creating a conducive environment for development of fragile states. The second is to provide supplementary support to help shift expectations and strengthen national response capability[23]. International community provides basic humanitarian relief such as food, medicine, nutritional supplements, shelter and repatriation, reintegration, and resettlement assistance in fragile country. For providing the services to people in the early stage of recovery, international community gives funds to national government with appropriate financial controls. This is the most important support to a fragile state without undermining the state capacity in itself. Coordinating the development funding is another crucial task that international community should fulfill in the state-building, reconstruction and development process[24].

India-US Cooperation for Rebuilding Afghanistan

Both India and US have vital national interest in Afghanistan. Therefore, after the fall of Taliban regime they have been engaged in reconstruction and development. Though the US has led the war against Taliban and has been constantly fighting insurgencies there, India has not engaged in it militarily. It is primarily concerned with reconstruction and development work. India has pledged around US$ 2.0 billion development assistance to Afghanistan and it is engaged in several areas of reconstruction and development. The US emphasizes that India should play a more active role in Afghanistan after years of keeping New Delhi's participation limited in deference to Pakistan. Recently, Defense Secretary Mr. Panetta said that India should get involved in training Afghan security forces after the US draws down most of its forces by the end of 2014. "We welcome [India's] playing a more active role in Afghanistan, a more-active political and economic role;" said US Defense Secretary Leon Panetta, "We welcome India's contributions to training the Afghan national army and Afghan national police." Last year, Indian and Afghan officials reached agreement for India to train members of the Afghan national army. The training is to take place inside India. The US encouragement of India may be designed to tweak Pakistan, or pressure Islamabad to take a more conciliatory position on Afghanistan. Pakistan has fiercely resisted attempts by India to forge closer relations with Afghanistan. An Afghanistan with close ties to India, many in Islamabad believe, would threaten Pakistan and deprive Pakistan of the "strategic depth" it wants in central Asia. "Over the last 10 years, for a variety of reasons, India has not played a particularly active role in Afghanistan even though it steadily increased its economic investments in Afghanistan," the senior official said. Another defense official said with Western powers preparing to wind down, Afghanistan was at a pivotal moment, and the US recognized that other countries in the region were going to play a more critical role. In a significant indication of alignment of interests, India and US decided to hold trilateral consultations with Afghanistan[25]. Both countries look for opportunities to work together to promote Afghanistan's development, including in areas such as agriculture, mining, energy, capacity building and infrastructure. Noting the importance of women's economic empowerment for Afghanistan's economic success, they plan to work to further increase their ongoing vocational training and empowerment initiatives[26].

Future Prospects: NATO Withdrawal

NATO endorsed the exit plan from Afghanistan at the Chicago Summit held on 20-21 May, 2012. It was decided to end the Afghan mission and complete the transfer of command of security to the Afghan National Security Forces by the end of 2014. Although international forces may have broken down the 'momentum of Taliban', security in Afghanistan is still fragile. Major parts of the country are vulnerable to terror attacks. A series of terror attacks in several cities in April, bombings just after the departure of US President Barack Obama from Kabul and the killing of peace negotiator in May, reflect the perpetual state of conflict in Afghanistan. It is widely believed that Afghan security forces are not in a position to take full charge of security of the entire country. As ensuring security without the international forces seems uncertain, NATO's withdrawal appears to be premature.[27]

Concluding Remarks

Though the condition in Afghanistan is still fragile, hope has not despaired yet. The country figures high on the strategic priorities of India, US and the major European countries. Security strategy of India, US or European security strategy explicitly recognizes that the threats emanating from failed or fragile states pose serious implications for their society and national security and spillover effects of socio-political instability and underdevelopment have been felt beyond national boundaries, and therefore, call for to take comprehensive measures both security and development to quell these threats. It is evidently possible that they would avoid heavy military engagement but supply of development assistance would not be stop in future. The US President needs to be more persuasive to convince American people that the US troops should be stationed for good reason to safeguard homeland. *The New York Times* writes, 'without a base in Afghanistan, the US would never have been able to carry out the raid that got Osama bin Laden'[28]. Now much of the onus lies with national government and leaders to strengthen governance and democracy, thus dividends of development can reach to common man. It is not expected from a foreign power to unify a socially fragmented country, rather is primary task of national leadership and government to bring back all sections of the society in nation-building and development process. Impacts of development assistance ought not to be evaluated in isolation. International development assistance yield positive results in fragile countries if prerequisites like institutional set up, socio-political stability and good governance, coordination, active participation of civil society organizations and transparency exist there. International community and Afghan government need to infuse advance information and communication technologies to strengthen governance and provide basic services to people in rural areas. Common wisdom on development says poverty, deprivation and underdevelopment exist due to not only lack of resources but also lack of good and effective institutions of governance. Dividends of democracy and development must be percolated to bottom level of the society, only then 'hearts and minds' of Afghan people can be won and peace would be durable and development would be inclusive.

While Washington's desire for more robust regional engagement in support of Afghanistan is understandable, the notion that a qualitatively more aggressive Indian posture in Afghanistan would serve to encourage more constructive Pakistani behaviour – and still less, as some US defence officials have actually suggested, genuine Indo-Pakistani cooperation inside Afghanistan borders on the hopelessly naive[29]

REFERENCES

1. Miller, Paul D., "Finish the Job: How the War in Afghanistan Can Be Won", *Foreign Affairs* (Volume 90, No.1. 2011), pp. 52-53.
2. Cited in Miller, Paul D, "Finish the Job: How the War in Afghanistan Can Be Won", p. 54.
3. Foreign Policy, The Failed States Index 2011, accessed on 3 November 2011, http://www.foreignpolicy.Co m/articles/2011/06/17/2 011failedstates indexinteractivemapandrankings
4. Goodson, Larry P., *Afghanistan's Endless War: State Failure, Regional Politics, and the Rise of the Taliban*, (Washington: University of Washington Press, 2001).
5. Mishra, Amalendu, *Afghanistan: The Labyrinth of Violence* (Cambridge: Politv Press, 2004), p. 107.
6. Brookings Institute, Brookings Afghanistan Index 2011, (Washington: Brookings Institute, 2011).
7. Taliban Strike Across Afghanistan, *the Hindu* (15 April, 2012).
8. Taliban Strikes Close on Obama's Heels, *The Hindu* (3 May, 2012).
9. United Nations Office on Drugs and Crime, *Afghanistan Opium Survey 2010*, September 2010, accessed on 3 November 2011, http://www.unodc.org/documents/crop-monitoring/Afghanistan/Afgopiumsurvey 2010_ exsumweb.pdf
10. Mahadevan, Prcm, "Narcotics as a Growing Security Concern", p. 93.
11. United Nation Development Programme, UNDP, *Human Development Report 2011, Sustainability and Equity: A Better Future for All* (New York, UNDP, 2011).
12. Transparency International, Corruption Perception Index 2011, http://www.transparency.org/public ations/publications/other/corruptionperc eptionsindex2011
13. Brookings Institute, Brookings Afghanistan Index 2011, (Washington: Brookings Institute, 2011); and Center for Policy and Human Development, *Afghanistan Human Development Report 2007, Bridging Modernity and Tradition: Rule of Law and the Search for Justice*, (Kabul: Kabul University and United Nations Development Programme, UNDP, 2007).
14. Roy, Arpita Basu, *Afghanistan: Towards A Viable State*, (Kolkata: Maulana Abul Kalam Azad Institute of Asian Studies, 2002), p. 21.
15. United Nations Environment Programme, *UNEP in Afghanistan: Laying the Foundation for Sustainable Development* (Geneva: United Nations Environment Programme, 2009), p. 5.
16. United Nations Environment Programme, UNEP, *UNEP in Afghanistan: Laying the Foundation for Sustainable Development.*
17. Organistaion for Economic Cooperation and Development, "Declaration on Aid Effectiveness and Accra Agenda for Action, 2008 (http://www.oecd.org/dataoecd/11/41 /34428351.pdf), European Commission, "A Secure Europe in A Better World: European Security Strategy", December 2003, Brussels, (http://www.con silium.europa.eu/uedocs/cmsUpload/78367.pdf), Cabinet Office, Prime Minister's Strategy Unit, UK

Government, Investing in Prevention: An International Strategy to Manage Risks of Instability and Improve Crisis Response (UK Government Report 2005), (http://www.cabinetoffice.gov.uk/media/cabinetoffice/strategy/assets/investing.pdf). The National Security Strategy of the United States of America, September 2002, (http://www.globalsecurity.org/military/library/policy/national/nss-020920.pdf)

18. World Bank, "Conflict, Security and Development: World Development Report 2011", 2010 (http://econ.worldbank.org/WBSITE/EXTERN AL/EXTDEC/ EXTRESEARCH/ EXTWDRS/EXTWDR2011/0,,contentMDK:22290397~pagePK:64167702~piPK:64167676~theSitePK:6406083,00.html)
19. Paul Collier, *The Bottom Billion: Why the Poorest Countries are Failing and What Can Be Done About It*, (New York: Oxford University Press, 2007).
20. Stewart Patrick, "Weak States and Global Threats: Assessing Evidence of 'Spillovers'", Working Paper Number 73, January 2006, Center for Global Development, URL: www.cgdev.org
21. Wil Hout, *EU Development Policy and Poverty Reduction: Enhancing Effectiveness*, (Aldershot: Ashgate Publishing Company, 2007).
22. Barbara Nunberg, "Generational Shifts in International Governance Assistance: The World Bank and State-Building after 9/11" *International Journal of Economic Development,* 9 (1 &2), 2007, pp. 33-44.
23. World Bank, "Conflict, Security and Development: World Development Report 2011", p. 12.
24. Asian Development Bank, Rehabilitation and Reconstruction: ADB's Role in Afghanistan and the Region, 2010, (http://www.adb.org/documents/reports /rehabilitation afghanistan/theme100.asp)
25. *Indian Express*, India, US plan trilateral talks with Afghanistan, Jan 15, 2012
26. *Ibid*
27. Dinoj Kumar Upadhyay, "Security Transition in Afghanistan: Implications for India", View Point, Indian Council of World Affairs, June 2012.
28. New York Times Editorial, "The Way Out of Afghanistan", 22 June 2011
29. Robert Grenier, The US, Afghanistan and the 'India card', http://www.aljazeera.com/indepth/opinion/2012/06/20126119229712686.html

10

Terrorism as a Factor in Indo-US Relations and Role of Pakistan: A Recent Study

Amulya K. Tripathy

Terrorism is not a new phenomenon. The world has experienced it, in different faces and different demonstration since ancient times—particularly the twentieth century, which is certainly the most blood-ridden century in the human history, has seen a persistent increase and evolution in the terrorist activities. However, it had never enjoyed the status of being the foremost challenge for the international community. This transformation of the status of terrorism is obviously the outcome of the attacks of 9/11 on the twin-towers of World Trade Center and Pentagon – the chief symbols of American economic and military supremacy. Wounded at the time of its zenith as the sole super power of the world, America understandably decided to strike back and launch a global campaign against terrorism.

It was a very unpleasant decision. What this American resolve to initiate a world wide war could have implied for the dynamics of international relations could be well-judged by what President Bush said in his address to the joint session of the US Congress on September 20, 2001: "Our response involves far more than instant retaliation and isolated strikes. Americans should not expect one battle, but a lengthy campaign. We will starve terrorists of funding, turn them one against another, and drive them from place to place, until there is no refuge or no rest. And we will pursue nations that provide aid or safe havens to terrorism. Every nation, in every region, now has a decision to make. Either you are with us, or you are with the terrorists."

It shall be more than clear from this policy statement of the American President that what America was going to start was not to be a limited military action; rather America would take the war to the doorstep of every nation in every region. Thus, every nation and every society had to bear its share of the impact of this global war. Stephen P. Cohen has said that no part of the world has more affected by the terrorist attacks of September 11, 2001 than South Asia.[1]

Today, if we look back at the five years history of the war on terrorism, it becomes clear that South Asia had to endure the strain of the consequences of the war. Perhaps it has been the centre of enormity in this unusual war. There were a number of factors which made South Asia a central point in the US war. First and prime, the alleged suspects of these attacks were traced back to the mountainous wilderness of Afghanistan. The propinquity with a Taliban-ruled Afghanistan brought the war on terror to the doorstep of South Asia. As we know Pakistan shares border with Afghanistan and was among the countries which had a formal diplomatic relations with Afghanistan. Secondly, and more importantly, perhaps, there was no other state in the world that knew the radical regime of Taliban better than Pakistan. The ample treasure of reliable intelligence, the ability to launch air strikes from adjoining Pakistani airbases, and the Cold War confidence in its pledge made Pakistan, and therefore South Asia, a sort of field headquarters for American military campaign. It may be said that General Pervez Musharraf calculated that if Pakistan did not cooperate with US, his nation at the very least would be marginalized and isolated by the US and the international community, at worst Pakistan itself could be targeted because of its support and relationship with Taliban. Thirdly, a deep study of the American foreign policy thinking in the last decade will reveal that Americans began to develop a feeling of threat from the Islamic revivalism, after the end of Cold War. South Asia happens to be home to quite a number of active Islamic revivalist movements. Accordingly, the presence of militant organizations in South Asia was an open invitation for the American war on terror. Fourthly, the danger of nuclear terrorism also was a factor for the revival of American interest in South Asia. In the last decade, a major and drastic challenge to international security has been the rise of the non-state actors and the stem possibility that the nuclear weapons may fall to their hands. The presence of strong radical elements in a nuclear South Asia made this threat highly plausible.

It was for these, besides other reasons, that South Asia was so pervasively involved in the American war on terror. As the U.S. prepared to launch its global war, it put a tough choice before the states of the region "Either you are with us or against us". It was not only a decisive message but also an indication of the future course of Pak-USA relations. India, stimulated by the hope of strategic gains offered its all-out support, in every possible way. Pakistan, given its historic ties with the elements in Afghanistan was caught in a predicament, for some time, whether to join the war or not. Nevertheless, when Pakistan was presented the famous list of seven demands, it did not take much but a call from Colin Powell, for Pakistan to take the bold decision of joining the American war, unconditionally. Pakistan became an indispensable allay after 9/11 when President Pervez Musharraf broke with the Taliban and Al-Qaeda to join in the US-led war against terrorism.[2]

On January 12, 2002 President Pervez Musharraf said, "we have decided to join international coalition against terrorism. We took this decision on principles and in our national interest. He further said Pakistan will not allow its territory to be used for any terrorist activity anywhere in the world.[3] It may be stated that whatever President Pervez Musharraf has done to help the US in its war against terrorism was to avert the grave consequences of saying 'no' to the US. Pakistan's support was vital for the US because it not only wanted to use the territory of a country which shares the border with Afghanistan but also to avert the support which was being given to the Taliban government by Pakistan. The proactive role of US in South Asia posed challenges for Pakistan. Pakistan wanted to safeguard its strategic assets, the Kashmir cause and economic recovery. However there is a sense of dissatisfaction and a belief that the US and its allies did not live up to the promises and pledges made to Pakistan for its support in the war against terrorism.[4]

It may be argued that as far as South Asia is concerned, the post 9/11 development worsened the security environment of the region. The South Asian countries decided to join the US led war against terrorism because of their own interests.[5] India was prompt in offering its support in the hope that such a configuration of the situation in South Asia. Pakistan decided to join because of predictable economic incentives, the need to save its strategic assets and salvaging its Kashmir policy from total destruction. President Pervez Musharraf's acceptance facilitated America's military needs of the moment and led to yet a commitment of aid to Pakistan, has earned the country the title "key ally".[6] But it is imperative to note that America has seen the wisdom of building up India as counterbalance to China.

We may agree with Moisi Dominique that thirteen years ago, Samuel Huntington argued that a "clash of civilizations" was about to dominate world politics, with culture along with national interests and political ideology, becoming a geo-political fault line ... today, the world faces what might be called a "clash of emotion" as well. The western world displays a culture of fear, the Arab and Muslim worlds are trapped in a culture of humiliation and much of Asia displays a culture of hope.[7] Now almost 5 years have passed and the profound effect of the war is gradually unfolding. As we have mentioned in the beginning, the impact of the war on the South Asian region has been particularly at three levels – regional level, at the level of bilateral relations among regional states and at the domestic level. At the regional level, the important impact has been the resurgence of South Asia as the region of highest priority for America. While during the closing decade of Cold War, since 1979, South Asia remained the highest point in American foreign policy thinking, it lost its prominence with the Cold War. While the first Clinton Administration wanted to establish a rapport with India, South Asia did not figure heavily in American interests. However, the start of the global war on terror has rediscovered South Asia for America. With the presence of two nuclear power friends, and an Al-Qaeda-strewn Afghanistan, South Asia assumed a strategic status in American eyes. The rebirth of South Asia prominence was not limited to America, rather for whole the world. There was a long chain of Heads of States, and highest officials visiting the region every alternative day were evidence of long term strategic interests of the US in the region. The main objective of the US during the stand off were (1) that the prevailing tension between India and Pakistan should not escalate into a nuclear exchange (2) that the deteriorating situation should not affect Pakistan's support to the US war against terrorism in Afghanistan. According to Vanni Cappelli, the Bush administration presented President Pervez Musharraf with an ultimatum to abandon support of Taliban and commit to the American-led war on terror or face the consequences of being considered an enemy of the US.[8] Moins Ahmer says, "there is no overwhelming strategic framework for South Asia and being against "terrorism" doesn't provide one," neglecting both the regions enduring historical relations and our most pressing current security challenges.[9] Resolution of the Kashmir issue was important for us to maintain good relations with Pakistan and India. It is imperative to note that the US later played a proactive role in the normalization of deteriorating Pakistan-India relations. It became the centre of global attention in the global media and the central battle-ground where the global war was either to be lost or won. Secondly, the war on terror has had a lasting impact on the regional stability. There are opposite views in this regard. One viewpoint is that the war on terror has improved the regional stability. The source of regional instability mainly has been the irregularly rising tension between the nuclear archrivals – India and Pakistan. The war on terror and the American military presence is a factor of stability for the region. This has been fully proved during the 2002 militancy standoff. Following the December attacks on its parliament, India had pushed the war hysteria up. There was an unprecedented mobilization of armed forces on a large scale. The armed forces stood eyeball to eyeball for several days, on both sides of the borders. Even nuclear threats were exchanged. An outbreak of war was believed to be certain. Then the American military presence entered as a stabilizing factor. America perceived that a war between India and Pakistan will certainly subvert, and disrupt its campaign against terror. Its war on terror could only be saved by avoiding the outbreak of a regional conflict. So America initiated a whole-hearted effort to defuse the situation. The tension came down. Those who believe that it was American diplomatic activism which prevented an outbreak of war and nuclear holocaust believe that the US war on terror is a factor for regional peace and stability.

On the opposite, a viewpoint upholds that the US war on terror has made the region highly unstable. There are many aspects of this instability. Firstly, the Taliban had been successful to restore a kind of stability in Afghanistan for the first time after a very long period of unrest. America, by dripping to pieces the Taliban regime, once again pushed Afghanistan into a new phase of insurgency and civil war. This unstable and troubled situation will not remain confined within the Afghan borders; rather will soon spread into the neighbouring states. We can see for ourselves that the unrest and turbulence in Afghanistan has leaked out into Pakistan.

The second aspect of war created instability in the region is related to the Indian effort to manipulate the situation in its favour with full vigour. India equated the self-determination movement in Kashmir with terrorist and accused Pakistan of support and cross-border terrorism. Lal Krishna Advani warned that Bush doctrine could be used against Pakistan.[10] The situation provided an opportunity for India to justify its previous allegation against Pakistan before the world community. India planned to capitalize on the emerging worldwide focus against terrorism, which gave New Delhi an opportunity to portray Pakistan as a state sponsoring Jihad and terrorism.[11] It may be said that, in this way, after 9/11 Pakistan-India relations took a new turn when New Delhi offered full support to the US war against terrorism and tried its best to establish a linkage between Pakistan support to the Muslim struggle in Jammu and Kashmir and struggling elements in Afghanistan, but India failed to stop Pakistan from joining the US-led coalition against terrorism. India's purpose was to discredit the Kashmiri's freedom movement and declare Pakistan as a terrorist state. Consequently Pakistan initiated measures to launch a crackdown on terrorist elements especially those having connection with Al-Qaeda and Taliban. It indicated a change in government's approach on supporting Kashmiris freedom struggle. It is imperative to note that such measures did not result in de-escalation in tension between Pakistan and India. It may be stated that even though Pakistan is currently the frontline state in the US war on terror, it is America who is essentially reaping benefits from the situation—the conditions in Indo-Pak hostility—to materialize its own selfish design vis-à-vis the south Asia region. The Indo-US nuclear deal is a proof of the fact that the US has given a military edge to India making Pakistan more apprehensive than ever as to what real motives of US friendship with Pakistan. Convinced of American support, India tried to manipulate the American doctrine of pre-emption to pressurize Pakistan. India had been accusing Pakistan of waging cross border terrorism in Kashmir. It gambled to justify a possible attack on Pakistan by borrowing the preemptive doctrine and bringing the Kashmir insurgency into the realm of US definition of terrorism. The Indian effort to built pressure on Pakistan on the unjustified pretext of doctrine of pre-emption threatened to destabilize the region.

The third aspect in which the war on terror generated regional instability is even more important and sensitive. The chief source of regional instability is the hostility between India and Pakistan. On the western border, Pakistan always likes to feel secure through the presence of a friendly regime in Afghanistan. The war on terror has brought the Northern Alliances to power in Kabul. The Afghan government is extremely antagonistic to Pakistan. This has made the western border of Pakistan highly troubled, thus adding to the regional instability.

Apart from its impact on the regional environment, the war on terror has largely influenced the bilateral relations of the countries in the region. The bilateral relations between India Pakistan, in the last decade of the 20th century remained as tense as ever, except for the temporary relief of Lahore Declaration. The nuclear tests in May 1998, and then the Kargil crisis in 1999 worsened the relations to the worst levels. However, after passing through the litmus test of the 2002 military standoff, the ice began to thaw. The peace process, starting after the friendship offer by Vajpayee on April 18, 2003 marks the dawn of a new era in the bilateral relations between India and Pakistan. The composite dialogue has completed its three rounds. Although it has not been able as yet to produce some meaningful progress on any of the major issues with India, nevertheless, the general normalization of relations and decrease in tension is no mean achievement in itself. It may be said that the success of composite dialogue could make both countries abandon wars and cherish peace. The long range of CBMs is accomplishing their objective of reducing the trust deficit. Resumption of road, rail and air links, exchange of visits by the parliamentarians, media men, and students, the opening up of trade ties, and the growing people to people diplomacy, will ultimately make the task of final resolution of all disputes including Kashmir, much easier to achieve. One can hardly deny that this peace process and the CBMs is not inclusively a product of realization on the part of India or Pakistan, rather the role of a third party is of key importance. America, keeping in view the demands of its war on terror, has been decisive in the initiation and continuation of the present peace process.

On the third level, the war on terrorism has had its effects on the domestic political dynamics of the South Asian states. The impact has been most evident and vital at the domestic level. It has been either a direct result of the American military activities, or indirect fallout of the policies adopted by the United States in the region. Perhaps no other country of the world, except America, has been as deeply affected by the war on terror as Pakistan.

Pakistan's geographical location, its nearness with Afghanistan, its close relations with the Taliban regime, its deep knowledge of the rugged terrain of Afghanistan, and its history of Cold War alliance made Pakistan obviously the most important strategic asset for the United States. As Pakistan was chosen to once again fight an American war, it had to make a number of difficult choices, which changed the course of its history. Pakistan had to take a U-turn on its Afghan policy by accepting the new regime, both parties relations could not become cordial just on pretence.[12] Pakistan was forced to leave its longstanding search for the strategic depth in Afghanistan. It made forceful efforts to convince the Taliban to act in accordance with the demands of international community, but as the Taliban were insolvent, Pakistan had to withdraw its hand from all kinds of support to the regime. With this major shift in its Afghan policy, Pakistan lost whatever influence it had in Afghanistan, Karzai's government was of the opinion in 2006 that it was a kind of hidden invasion propped up by outside interference .... Intended to tarnish the national identity and historical of Afghanistan.[13]

For decades it was the policy of Pakistan to support and sponsor the militant organizations in quest of its bleed-India policy. However, the US war on terror forced Pakistan to rethink its priorities, because America believed that these militant organizations formed a pool of terrorists as well as a ready-made basis for its organizational facilities for the Al-Qaeda network. So, Pakistan at once attacked the militant organizations. Some of the organizations like LAT, JEM, TNFJ, SSP, and TNSM were banned. Their bank accounts were frozen, and their offices were closed. That Pakistan's participation in the war on terror has come at a heavy domestic price is clear from the later tussle between the government and the militants. The militant organizations were not ready to disappear so easily. They put up a firm resistance, and the government had to face a severe backlash. Law and order situation go worse. The banned organizations re-surfaced under new names. The frequency of terrorist activities multiplied. There was a sharp increase in the suicide attacks on the government officials and assets. The President himself narrowly got away two suicide attempts at his life.

This backlash has been most alarming in the North West of Pakistan. The North Western mountainous terrain, the ethnic ties between the

Pashtoons on both sides of the border, and the tribal traditions combindly offered the region as an ideal safe haven for the Al-Qaeda and Taliban fighters running from Afghanistan. The prevailing religious extremism and the large chain of madarssas spread all over the area welcomed the fugitives Mujahideen with open arms. As the pressure mounted up on Pakistan to trace and capture the fleeing terrorists, the government was faced with the difficult choice of launching a military operation in the tribal region. The state forces initiated a full-fledged military campaign to drive out the Taliban scraps in mid-March 2004, when the armed forces came upon an Al-Qaeda shelter at Kaloosha near WANA, in South Waziristan. Since then, a high tension clash between the state forces and the foreign militants, along with their local supporters is going on. The government had to concentrate as many as 80,000 troops in its effort to bring the troubled region under control. It was almost an impossible terrain despite countless raids, siege and search operations as well as large scale arrests, the high value targets were still away from the iron hands. Thus the military operation failed to deliver required results at the expense of bloodshed by country men of their brothers. No Al-Qaeda figure of any note was caught, except their Pakistani supports.[14] Few observers have pointed out that Kabul is not a free agent and that they would not have done all this without the approval of Americans.[15] The terrorist put up a daunting resistance, claiming the lives of above 700 army men.

The indiscriminate shelling on the non-combatants by security forces, have also caused a large-scale displacement of tribesmen from the violence-hit areas. Hundreds of families are forced to live with relatives in the neighbouring towns. The government has alternatively tried various forceful and appeasing strategies. The turbulence originating in the restless west has penetrated into the far and wide of the country. Major Urban centers have been targeted by the irritated militants.

Pakistan feels itself unjustly targeted as the pressure from America continues to go up without reason for doing more. While Pakistan has started its military operation into the Northern areas at a very heavy domestic price, the Karzai Government in Kabul, and the aggressive elements in American think tanks continue to show lack of trust on Pakistan.

Besides the military clashes in the tribal agencies, the war on terror is making its impact on the more peaceful cities as well. There is a clear cut polarization in the society on the question of Pakistan's desirable role in the war. This polarization has further deteriorated the perennial challenge of national integration and social cohesiveness in Pakistan. One school of thought believes that it is a battle that Pakistan is fighting for its own sake. The militant organizations have become Frankenstein, and turned against their creator. Therefore, such forces need to be controlled by the government. The opposite viewpoint upholds that the government is unjustified for lashing at these very organizations which it established by itself. It is, for them, unethical on the part of government to unleash terror on the Jihadi organizations, by surrendering to the American pressure. This sharp divide has displayed itself emphatically in public protests and media opinion.

It needs to be emphasized that while Pakistan is genuinely committed to a war against all forms of terrorism, the United States is making the task difficult for the Government of Pakistan, with its unintended actions. The heartless adventures like the gruesome air strike on the village of Damodola on13th January, 2006 is but only one of the many examples of the American actions which make it more difficult for the Pakistan government to justify their stance before the masses. Similarly, the way Karzai government continues to cast aspersions on Pakistan's role in restraining the militants further complicates the situation. It may be said that five years after 9/11, Pakistan's Islamist parties are growing stronger; the continuous violence in Kashmir has as far as Mumbai.

All along this, we must not forget the heavy economic cost that Pakistan is paying for the war on terror. The adverse situation generated by the war has discouraged the foreign investors and impeded the domestic economic activity due to political uncertainty. No doubt Pakistan has been taking substantial financial inflows from outside, but this temporary aid and assistance cannot be a substitute for the genuine inflow of investment, and resulting industrialization of a backward economy.

One may argue that the political compromise on the constitutional engineering in Pakistan and the game being played with the democratic ideals is also a result of the war on terror. Had it not been for his all out commitment to the American war on terror, who knows what, would be the American level of tolerance and support for the military regime of Pervez Musharraf. This is a compromise that the West in general and America in particular, are willing to make, for the sake of their war on terror. In this way, the analysis at the various levels – regional, bilateral, and domestic – makes it sufficiently clear that the war on terror has been a factor of utmost importance in the political, strategic and military dynamics of the South Asian region. It has left a lasting impact on the regional strategic environment, on the nature of relationships among the various states in the region, and on their domestic politics. What we must not forget is the fact that the war on terror is still not coming to an end. Therefore, its consequences and implications for the region of South Asia will continue to be gradually known for an indefinite period of time.

Responses from India and the US

The widespread terrorist activities in the Middle East, Africa and South Asia force the US and India to recognise terrorism as an international threat to all democracies. In the last one year or so, South Asia has become increasingly vulnerable to Islamic fundamentalism, with Afghanistan-Pakistan becoming the epicentre of terrorist activities. The US Annual Report on Terrorism, Patterns of Global Terrorism: 1999, pointed out that in 1999 the locus of terrorism directed against the United States had shifted from the Middle East to South Asia.[16] In 1999, Pakistan was close to being named as a state sponsor of terrorism. It was not done primarily for the reason that Pakistan has been an old friend and ally of the United States. However, Pakistan's relationship with the Taliban and the militant groups active in Kashmir is a matter of concern for the US and India. In fact, Michael Sheehan, US State Department Co-ordinator for Terrorism, has stated that the United States keeps a serious watch on Pakistan and that it will continue to be under "serious and constant review".[17] Regarding the role of Pakistan in sponsoring terrorism cited in the annual report of the State Department, Pakistan Information Minister Javed Jabbar expectedly dismissed them as "erroneous and misleading conclusions."[18]

Sheehan said that Pakistan was not included in the terrorist list also for the reason that Pakistan carried a mixed response to the issue of terrorism. Remarking on the findings of the US Congress's Blue Ribbon Commission on terrorism, Sheehan said that Pakistan's record on co-operating on counter-terrorism remains a mixed one. He added that "despite significant and material co-operation in some areas – particularly arrest and extraditions – Pakistan has also tolerated terrorists living and moving freely within its territory."[19] The US could follow two types of policy with regard to this issue. Either keep Pakistan at a distance and impose sanctions on it for its non-democratic political set-up and continued support to terrorists, or follow a policy of engagement through which Pakistan is kept within the US' foreign policy reach, and at the same time tighten the grip on Pakistan, as and when the situation so warrants.

Analysing the rise of militancy by Pakistan, Sheehan makes a point that it is Pakistan's political and economic difficulties and the ensuing damage to its institutions that have provided a fertile ground for terrorism.[20] Collapse of the educational system has further forced the poor to seek education provided by the Pakistani religious schools (madarasas), which is the training ground for militancy. These schools, some of them at least, inculcate religious extremism and also anti-Americanism and anti-Indian feelings in their minds. The United States has continued its repeated requests to Islamabad to end its support for elements harbouring and training terrorists in Afghanistan and urged the Government of Pakistan to close certain madarasas that serve as conduits for terrorism. Reports have also indicated that there is official Pakistani support for Kashmiri militant groups, such as the Hizbul Mujahideen, and Harakat ul-Mujahidin (HUM) that have been engaged in terrorism. Several reports, including the one brought out by the US National Commission on Terrorism,[21] have said that Pakistan provides a safe haven, and transit and moral, political and diplomatic support to several groups engaged in terrorism. Pakistan has also very openly said that it will continue to support those who are fighting for Kashmir. Federal Minister for Kashmir and Northern Areas Affairs, Abbas Sarfaz Khan reiterated that Pakistan would continue moral, political and diplomatic support to the Kashmiris, struggling for the right to self-determination.[22] This explains the Pakistani support to militancy in Kashmir and elsewhere by Hizbul Mujahideen, Harkat-ul-Ansar or Osama bin Laden against India as well the United States.

The Taliban continue to provide safe haven for international terrorists, particularly Osama bin Laden and his network, in the portions of Afghanistan they control. Despite the serious and ongoing dialogue between the Taliban and the United States, Taliban leadership has refused to comply with a unanimously adopted UNSC resolution demanding that they turn Osama bin Laden over to a country where he can be brought to justice. Pakistan can act significantly on this front. The US has had a long history of friendship with Pakistan since the Cold War years and thus it should be much easier for the US to bring Pakistan into a co-operative framework on counter-terrorism.

It is here that India and the United States need to co-operate on the issue of terrorism. First, both India and the United States have a long tradition of democracy as the basic political norm and terrorism does not fit into the democratic framework at all. Also, the two countries have had a secular bent of mind, which opposes any form of extremism. Therefore, both share similar political values and an abhorrence to all kinds of terrorism.

Yet another reason for Indo-US co-operation on this front is because of the fact that both the countries have been the declared enemies of Islamic fundamentalism, as declared by Osama bin Laden and other militant groups like Jihad Group in Egypt, Islamic Group, Jihad Movement in Bangladesh etc.[23] These groups feel that the Americans have been entering the land of Islam, the holiest places, the Arabian Peninsula, plundering its riches and turning its bases in the Peninsula into a spearhead through which to fight the neighbouring Muslim peoples.

Hence, any strategy evolving to combat terrorism has to attack the issue at its base level i.e., their complex links with other groups across the world to meet their needs of fund-raising, procurement of weapons, maintenance of training camps etc. As Sheehan pointed out, there has to be a strategy of "draining the swamp" and some of the key principles involved are:

- We pressure state sponsors, isolating them from the international community.
- We criminalise terrorism through the process of designating Foreign Terrorist Organisations (FTOs).
- We de-politicise the message of terrorism through public statements separating actor from action.
- We build international consensus for zero tolerance by working with our G-8 and FU partners.
- We support the construction of an international legal framework to allow states and the UN, EU, OAS, and other organisations to legally be tough on terrorism.
- We work bilaterally to arrest, disrupt, and expel terrorists.
- Finally, we bolster the capacity of those countries that need it to fight terrorism, through our international training programme, which are run by state, law enforcement, and intelligence agencies.[24]

Through the strategy of "draining the swamp", the mobility of the terrorists are restricted and they could get easily exposed. This needs to be an important component in the Indo-US counter-terrorism strategy. This process would also bring pressure on the states and governments that provide material and moral support to terrorists. However, this necessitates a well co-ordinated international effort to pressure certain regimes like that of Taliban in Afghanistan that provide a safe haven for Osama bin Laden and other related groups that operate in and around Pakistan. As one scholar puts it, there has to be a determined policy to check all sources of terrorism within the domestic polity along with the building up of an international consensus on international terrorism by all nations (at least who have been victims of this menace).

Draining the swamp would also mean including a shift in the public rhetoric. Very often one hears terrorists being called freedom fighters. One has often heard the clarification and differentiation that General Musharraf has made between terrorists and freedom fighters and terms jihad as legitimate. In a recent interview with the New York Times magazine, General Musharraf said that, unlike the State Department, he did not consider Harkat-ul-Mujahideen as a terrorist organisation; it is a freedom fighters' group.[25] When the leader of the nation offers this kind of a statement, what more support could the terrorists ask for? International community offers groups legitimate means of expression, but violence and terrorism are not to be considered as legitimate ones. Just because the terrorists put forward a political or religious view does not mean violent acts are justified. They are to be viewed as simple and plain crimes committed by those groups and proper action needs to be taken against them.

Modern terrorism includes a variety of tactics like intelligence gathering, intensified security measures, and the use of force. Thus, gaining international support for multilateral treaties in combating terrorism is a very important goal for India and the United States. For most governments, the key question is how to fight against terrorism. There are, at present, eleven multilateral conventions related to states' responsibility in combating terrorism and India and the United States are party to most of these conventions. They are as listed below:

1. Convention on Offences and Certain Other Acts Committed on Board Aircraft (Tokyo Convention, agreed 9/63—safety of aviation);
2. Convention for the Suppression of Unlawful Seizure of Aircraft (Hague Convention, agreed 12/70—aircraft hijackings);
3. Convention for the Suppression of Unlawful Acts Against the Safety of Civil Aviation (Montreal Convention, agreed 9/71—applies to acts of aviation sabotage such as bombing aboard aircraft in flight);
4. Convention on the prevention and Punishment of Crimes Against Internationally Protected Persons (agreed 12/73—protects senior government officials and diplomats);
5. Convention on the Physical Protection of Nuclear Material (Nuclear Materials Convention, agreed 10/79, combats unlawful taking and use of nuclear material);
6. International Convention Against the Taking of Hostages (Hostages Convention, agreed 12/79);
7. Protocol for the Suppression of Unlawful Acts of Violence at Airports Serving International Civil Aviation (agreed 2/88—extends and supplements Montreal Convention);
8. Convention for the Suppression of Unlawful Acts Against the Safety of Maritime Navigation (agreed 3/88—applies to terrorist activities on ships);
9. Protocol for the Suppression of Unlawful Acts against the Safety of Fixed Platforms Located on the Continental Shelf

(agreed 3/88—applies to terrorist activities on fixed offshore platforms);

10. Convention on the Marking of Plastic Explosives for the Purpose of Identification (agreed 3/91—provides for chemical marking to facilitate detection of plastic explosives, e.g., to combat aircraft sabotage);
11. International Convention for the Suppression of Terrorist Bombing (agreed 12/97—expands the legal framework for international cooperation in the investigation, prosecution, and extradition of persons who engage in terrorist bombings.[26]

However, over the past few decades, the government and security forces have become more sophisticated in their approach to terrorist attacks. The modern terrorists, as one of India's earlier Prime Ministers I.K. Gujral said, "have access to not only funds but also the most sophisticated technology"[27] and as a result, the government needs to update their technology to stay ahead of the terrorists. The trouble is when the terrorists have committed to the use of suicide bombers (Hamas, Hizbollah, LTTE) and nerve gas as in the Tokyo subway in the 1990s, much needs to be done by the international community on the counter-terrorism front. The US and India, on combating terrorism, need to take a few factors into consideration:

- Carefully examine important incidents and prepare detailed action oriented reports for those areas.
- Build a sophisticated communication network as part of a wider modernisation drive which gives access to the latest technology.
- Better management of local contacts, their support bases and sources of funding.
- Develop new techniques of security and the maintenance of secrecy.
- Need to have specialists in affected areas.
- Develop capability to anticipate security needs.[28]

It is only in the 1990s with a wide spurt of terrorist attacks that the US has decided to come up with definite policies on terrorism. Listing of certain groups as terrorist organisations, as per the Anti-terrorism and Effective Death Penalty Act of 1996, has been a major step in this line. President Bill Clinton and Secretary of State, Ms. Madeline Albright have said that this step would ensure that the terrorist groups do not get any kind of support from the United States, and make the US totally a "no-support-for terrorism zone".

One important element in combating terrorism would be to ensure that the terrorists do not get any support from outside—be it in terms of arms, money, training or even moral support. Terrorist groups who operate at local level cannot create as much damage to the society as those who receive external aid. However, one reality with regard to terrorist groups is their complex and wide network all over the world. For example, LTTE has its strong presence, by way of offices and cells, in the UK, Canada, France, Germany, Holland, Switzerland, Italy, Sweden, South Africa, and recently in Thailand too. The latest report in Jane's Intelligence Review confirms the LTTE presence in Thailand. They engage themselves in activities related to fund-raising, propaganda, procurement and transfer of weapons etc. The network in South Africa is quite a strong and matured one with a full-fledged Tiger Brigade, LTTE Baby Brigade, Female Brigade forces etc, enabling training facilities and more importantly fund-raising activities through a large section of the Tamil Diaspora in South Africa. Until and unless these host states stop these slimy activities and take up a sincere and truthful role to put an end to such activities, these groups will carry on their activities very successfully as they have been doing for decades. It is really a hard task to break into those complexities and cut off their world-wide linkages.

In January 2000, the United States and India agreed to establish a Joint Working Group on Counter-terrorism. The agreement was announced following meetings between Deputy Secretary Strobe Talbott and Foreign Minister Jaswant Singh in London. The inaugural meeting of the US-India Counter-terrorism Working Group was held in Washington. Both delegations included an interagency group of counter-terrorism and law enforcement officials. The two sides expressed concern at the growing menace of international terrorism, extremism, and drug trafficking. The two sides unequivocally condemned all acts, methods, and practices of terrorism as criminal and unjustifiable, whatever the considerations of a political, philosophical, ideological, racial, ethnic, religious, or any other nature that may be invoked to justify them. The two sides also agreed to intensify their joint cooperation to ensure that the perpetrators of the hijacking of Indian Airlines Flight 814 are brought to justice, as part of their joint efforts to combat international terrorism.

Inter-agency teams from the two countries agreed on a range of measures to enhance cooperation between the two countries to combat international terrorism. The two sides would share experience, exchange information, and coordinate approaches and action. This working group is intended to enhance the effectiveness of our efforts to counter international terrorism world-wide. The next meeting of the US-India Counter-terrorism Working Group will be held in India on mutually agreed dates.

The Indian Government agreed to the US offer of Anti-terrorism Assistance programmes. Intelligence gathering and sharing of vital information between India and the United States should be important components in their efforts on counter-terrorism. Both India and the United States have a shared interest in strengthening a regime to counter international terrorism. This mutual interest in countering terrorism should be the ideal platform for a rich, enhanced cooperation between India and the United States.

REFERENCES

1. Stephen P. Cohen, *India Emerging Power*, The Brooking Institute Press, Washington D.C., 2002, p. 13.
2. Vanni Cappelli, "Containing Pakistan: Engaging The Raja–Mandala in South Central Asia", *Orbis A Journal of World Affairs*, Vol. 51, No. 1, Winter 2007, p. 55.
3. President Musharraf's Address to the Nation, January 12, 2002. www.forisb.org/CE-019.htmls.
4. Fazal-ur-Rehman, "Pakistan and the War on Terrorism", *Strategic Studies*, Islamabad, Vol. XXIII, No. 30, Autumn 2003, p. 58.
5. Stephen P. Cohen, *The Idea of Pakistan*, The Brooking Institute Press, Washington, 2004, p. 305.
6. Venni Cappelli, *op. cit.*, p. 66.
7. Dominique Moisi, "The Clash of Emotions", *Foreign Affairs*, Vol. 86. No. 1, January/February, 2007, p. 1.
8. Venni Cappelli, *op. cit.*, p. 66.
9. Moonis Ahmar, "9/11 and the Changing Parading of Conflict Resolution", "*IPRI*" *Journal*, Vol. 111, Winter 2003, p. 4.
10. *Dawn*, April 19, 2003.
11. Brahma Chellancy, "Fighting Terrorism in South Asia", *International Security*, Vol. 26, No.3, Winter 2001-2002.
12. Talat Masood and Agah Murtaza Poya, "The US-Iran Standoff: Options for Pakistan's in Policy Perspectives", Institute of Policy Studies, Islamabad, No. 2, Vol. III, July-December, 2006, pp. 11-13.
13. *New week*, New York, October 2, 2006.
14. Maria Madalena L. Carvalho-Fischer and Malthias Fishen, *Pakistan Under Siege: Pakistan After September 11, 2001*, Maktaba Press, Lahore, 2004, p. 39.
15. Dr. Noman Sattar, "War Against Terrorism: Implications for Pakistan" in National Development and Security, Foundation of Research on International Environment National Development and Security, Rawalpindi, No. 4, Vol. XII, (Summer, 2004), pp. 31-34.
16. US State Department, *Patterns of Global Terrorism: 1999* (Washington, D.C., 2000).

17. "Terrorism issue: Pakistan has mixed record, says US", *Dawn*, June 18, 2000.
18. "US allegations baseless, says Jabbar", *Nation*, June 7, 2000.
19. "Terrorism issue: Pakistan has mixed record, says US", *Dawn*, June 18, 2000.
20. "Pak—a fertile ground for jehad factories: US", *The Hindu*, July 14, 2000.
21. US National Commission was set up by the Congress in 1998 after the bombings of the two US embassies in East Africa. The commission has found that even if Pakistan cooperated in counter-terrorism efforts, it was never a consistent one. Pakistan and Greece are under the category of "not cooperating fully" and these states do face an US embargo on arms sales.
22. "Pakistan to continue supporting Kashmiris, says minister", *The News International*, April 13, 2000.
23. "Text of Fatwah Urging Jihad Against Americans", Published in Al-Quds al-'Arabi on February 23, 1998.
24. Speech of Ambassador Michael Sheehan, "Post-Millennium Terrorism Review" at the Brookings Institution, Washington, D.C., February 10, 2000.
25. "State of Pak-US ties", *Dawn*, June 27, 2000.
26. US Department of State, "International Terrorism Conventions", Released by the Office for Counterterrorism, August 17, 1998.
27. Sudhir Hindwan, "Combating Terrorism: Lessons From Around the World", *Peace Initiatives*, May-June 1997, p. 80.
28. Some of the suggestions have been taken from Sudhir Hindwan, "Combating Terrorism: Lessons From Around the World", *Peace Initiatives*, May-June 1997, p. 80.
27. Anthony Davis, "Bangkok discovers LTTE logistics cell", *Jane's Intelligence Review*, vol. 12, no. 11, July 2000, p. 3.
28. US Department of State, Office of the Spokesman, Press Statement by James p. Rubin, "Joint US-India Statement on Counter-terrorism Working Group," February 8, 2000.

11

Terrorism as Catalyst: Changing Dynamics of Indo-US Counter-Terror Cooperation

Rajendra Kumar Pandey

The recent deportation of a key Mumbai attacks handler and Lashkar-e-Taiyyaba (LeT) operative Abu Jundal from Saudi Arabia exemplifies the newer heights that the relations between India and the United States (US) are attaining with terrorism, *inter alia*, acting as an unmistakable catalyst. Being one of Pakistan's closest ally in West Asia, Saudi Arabia, along with the United Arab Emirates (UAE) act as safe heavens for hardcore terrorists carrying out devastating attacks on Indian targets often at the instance of Pakistan's Inter Services Intelligence (ISI). Despite its best efforts and having clinching evidences against them, India has repeatedly failed to get any of these terrorists deported for trial in the Indian courts for their acts of death and destruction till the turnaround came through the case of Abu Jundal. Interestingly, it is reported that this prized catch for India came not as a result of either pointed efforts of the Indian security agencies or eagerness of Saudi authorities to cooperate in India's counter-terror pursuits. Rather, it was a net result of the concerted support provided by the US to India in its counter-terror measures. 'It's clear that the voice intercepts that led to Abu Jundal came from US counter-terrorism authorities, and subsequently there would have been some persuasion of the Saudis by the US.'[1] That way, the case of Abu Jundal points to the dawn of a new era in the Indo-US counter-terror cooperation as probably for the first time the US seems to have gone out of way to ensure that India get hold of one of the masterminds of the 26/11to crack the dastardly terrorist attack and strengthen its case against Pakistan as the hub of terrorist organizations and individuals targeting the interests of both India and the US. As against this, till now, the Indo-US counter-terror cooperation was essentially an act of sharing global concern on growing menace of international terrorism, orchestrated by the network of Al-Qaeda, without any tangible outcome for both side. In the whole exercise, the US interest was to enlist the Indian support in its global war on terrorism, at the least, and to get some inputs, if any, from Indian counter-terror agencies to locate and bust the hideouts and modules of Al-Qaeda. Though the Indian stakes were very high in such counter-terror cooperation between the two countries, the US, for obvious reasons, was not very forthcoming in either putting pressure on Pakistan to desist from aiding and abetting anti-India terrorist activities from its soil, nor in sharing intelligence inputs or taking proactive measures against the terrorist organizations and individuals working against India. In such a scenario, the question of US pressurising its closest ally in West Asia to nab and handover to India the terrorist like Abu Jundal, who would definitely spill the beans on Pakistani hand in the 26/11 attacks, simply did not arise. But with the changing geopolitical long term interests of the US, on the one hand, and its search for a natural and dependable ally in both, countering terror and promoting international peace and security, on the other, appear to have catapulted India to a position where it becomes a coveted partner of the US, not only in the context of South Asia but in global politics as well.[2] Presumably, it is in order to reassure such a coveted partner that the US walked the extra mile in case of Abu Jundal and elevated its relationship with India to strategic levels. The paper attempts to analytically locate counter-terrorism as a catalyst to boost Indo-US relations in the post 9/11 period.

Genesis of Indo-US Counter-terror Cooperation

Indo-US counter-terror cooperation is a relatively new phenomenon in the long-standing tumultuous relations between the two countries. Incompatible positions of the two during more than four-decade long cold war kept them on reverse sides of the international political landscape. In many cases, the two nations turned out to be the bitterest critic of each other, and in 1971 Indo-Pak war, President Nixon's open support to Pakistan soured the relations between the two countries like never before. In such a scenario, the prospects of any strategic ties between the two remained a distant dream. Later on, when cross-border sponsored terrorism reared its head in Punjab, India was left with no option than to fend for itself. Subsequent disturbances in the Kashmir valley at the behest of Pakistan based terrorist organizations further complicated the matter for India. Despite having clear-cut cross-border overtones and involvement of state actors in various terrorist activities in India, the international community took it as an internal matter of India not meriting any support or cooperation from other countries of the world. But in the closing years of the twentieth century, the rise of Al-Qaeda brought about a sea-change in the prevailing global political scenario. The successive attacks carried out by this terrorist outfit at various interests and installations of the US and its friendly nations at far off locations such as Dar-e-Salam and Nairobi shook the Americans from slumber to note that the genie of international terrorism is out to devour all the liberal, democratic and secular polities in the world. The terrorism in India also got integrated with the global terror network of Al-Qaeda affording propitious circumstances for India and the US to join hands together to cope up with the challenge. Subsequently, the two countries decided to set the Indo-US Counter-terrorism Joint Working Group in early 2000. However, given the marginality of US interest in the project of counter-terrorism, this working group was considered no more than 'a confidence building measure'[3] in so far as the Indo-US counter-terror cooperation was concerned.

The momentous phase in the Indo-US counter-terror cooperation was heralded by the Al-Qaeda attack on the supposedly impregnable vital installations signifying the economic and military prowess of the US on 9/11 in 2001. Demonstrating the coming of age of Al-Qaeda as the pal-bearer of international terrorism, this unprecedented attack on the US homeland shook the American psyche and forced a rethink on the strategic and security priorities and perspectives of the country. Undoubtedly, in the wake of 9/11, the transformations brought about by the spectre of terrorism have been so perplexing to the policy makers in various countries, that in the age of globalization when most, if not all, leverages in the conduct of foreign policy are supposed to be revolving around economic considerations, huge efforts are required to be concentrated in the hitherto marginal states in order to help them not only save themselves from the scourge of terrorist violence within their own countries but also become a frontal state in the collective endeavour of the international community to take the menace of terrorism head on.[4] As a result, a subtle move was initiated to reassess the counter-terror strategy in the overall global strategic and security architecture of the US in which India was to figure prominently as leaders of the two countries considered combating international terrorism as one of the most important global challenges.[5]

The 9/11 attacks left the US groping in the dark for a while. Though its interests and installations were targeted by the terrorist groups even in the past, such attacks were carried out in the faraway places like Nairobi without any direct bearing on the homeland security of the country. Strangely, the country that was readying itself for a foolproof security on the ground, waters and even in space through the strategy of 'star wars' during the cold war was caught so unaware of 9/11 that the Al-Qaeda attacks came as thunderbolt forcing it to enter into another war called 'global war on terror'. The focal point of this global war on terror was bound to be Al-Qaeda given its primary responsibility in carrying out the

9/11 attacks. But what seemed inscrutable for the US was the strong backing and logistical support that Al-Qaeda used to find from the Taliban regime of Afghanistan and fundamentalist terrorist groups from Pakistan overtly, and certain quarters of Pakistani Army covertly. Hence, the global war on terror was to be planned in such a way that it paid maximum premium without much of economic and political costs. The resultant strategy called for two-fold involvement of the US in the region. One, it had to spearhead the global alliance of forces amassed to take on the Taliban regime in Afghanistan so as to dismantle the safe heavens for Al-Qaeda operatives located in the cosy environs of Afghanistan. Two, in view of the doubtful credentials of Pakistan in becoming a dependable ally of the US in its war against terror, the Americans were left with no other option than to rope in other important powers of the region to provide back up support in case of certain contingencies. Such a scenario presented a mutually beneficial opportunity for the two countries to go for a new kind of partnership including wide-ranging counter-terror cooperation.[6]

Geopolitical Dynamics of South Asia

Arguably, Indo-US counter-terror cooperation has never been autonomous of other significant strategic interests of US foreign policy in south and south east Asia. This was precisely the reason that in the early days of terrorism in India when the US support was sought in pressurising Pakistan to desist from providing moral and material support, including safe heavens and training facilities to terrorist groups operating in Punjab, the US response was not at all encouraging, if not in negative. At that time, Al-Qaeda had not raised its head and US was not afflicted by the menace of terrorism directly and substantially. On the other side, Pakistan was its principal ally in its covert war against communist regime of Afghanistan whom it could not have afforded to annoy by having any meaningful counter-terror cooperation with India. At the same time, China was in transitional phase with sluggish economic growth and blurred strategic vision. In other words, China also did not appear to pose a formidable challenge to the US designs in south and south east Asia to counter which any strategic partnership with India would have been required. Similarly, Iran, despite not being an ally of the US, did not present itself to be as belligerent as it is today bent upon undermining the assumed supremacy of the US in the region. Amidst such fluid and propitious circumstances in which it seemed to be well placed to dominate the international politics of the region without any perceptible challenge to its hegemony did not leave any incentive for the US to explore the possibility of forging any strategic relationship with India whose core could have been counter-terror cooperation. Consequently, the strident challenge of cross-border terrorism in Punjab having international linkages and support base was squarely portrayed as internal problem of India, and there was no scintilla of doubt in the minds of the US policy makers that counter-terrorism did not merit to be a ground for fruitful cooperation with India.

The beginning for a change in this dormant situation on Indo-US counter-terror cooperation was incidentally made by the rise of Al-Qaeda and its misadventure of 9/11. The terror attacks on the US targets deep in the heart of its homeland made it feel the agony of death and destruction wrecked by international terrorism just like India. Though its resolve and efforts for taking the monster of international terrorism head on was autonomous and steely, the US definitely started looking for valuable partners in its global war on terror with focus on those countries that themselves have been victims of international terrorism backed by Al-Qaeda. This undoubtedly proved to be a solid ground for initiation of counter-terror cooperation dialogues between the two countries. But what took these preliminary dialogues to the status of strategic partnership focused on counter-terror cooperation was the rapidly changing geopolitical dynamics of south Asia in recent times. These changes were unsetting of the established US foreign policy norms and partners in the region in which India emerged as the most valuable long term natural partner of the US. The most illustrative of these changes have been the turbulent US relationship with Pakistan and its subtle posturing vis-à-vis China in the global politics.

Pakistan's status as the prized ally of the US in south Asia since the times of cold war was almost totally undone with the theatre of the US global war on terror being located in the restive regions of Afghanistan-Pakistan border. Ironically, it was a shocking reminder for the US that it was the same Pakistan that have been providing moral and material support to the terrorist groups in India that has now become the biggest den of Al-Qaeda and Taliban cadres. Naturally, despite being dismayed and frustrated, US did not have any other option than to bank upon Pakistan for successfully carrying out its operations against terrorism.[7] However, as the US expedition against Al-Qaeda and Taliban operatives progressed vigorously, the two countries began to experience the ruptures underlying their joint operation against international terrorism. Two remarkable signposts of this rupture were elimination of Osama bin Laden in a daring operation by US marines and relentless drone attacks in the Federally Administered Tribal Areas (FATA) of Pakistan. Unsurprisingly, Laden's episode confirmed the long persisting impression that US did not have faith in the sincerity and capability of Pakistan in taking proactive measures to eliminate the fugitive elements of Al-Qaeda taking shelter in that country under the fortified protection of a section of army and fundamentalist forces.[8] Subsequently, instead of putting Pakistani forces in the forefront of flushing out the Al-Qaeda elements from the FATA, US took upon itself the arduous responsibility of identifying and eliminating the terrorist elements using deadly unmanned drones. Clearly, in such choose and hit operations, the US was not always right, and many times the drones either hit civilian areas or missed their enemies to hit unintended targets. The public outcry following such killing of civilians compelled Pakistani government to take strong exception to drone attacks that led to further deterioration of their counter-terror operations. Faced with the ensuing animosity with its erstwhile ally, thus, US found it appropriate to evolve a common cause with India on the pedestal of counter-terror cooperation. Further, emerging position of China in global politics, and Islamabad's strengthening of ties with Beijing as an alternative source of support to Washington, seem to have motivated for increased cooperation between New Delhi and Washington. While other components of relationship between India and the US had always been cordial and upwardly mobile, what was missing was forging of a strategic relationship keeping in view the mutual interests and priorities in international politics. Hence, given the magnitude and costs of tackling cross-border terrorism, India sought to put the counter-terror cooperation at the forefront of the deepening of Indo-US bilateral relations. In return, the US has also claimed its pound of flesh by forcing India to compromise with its traditional cordial ties with countries such as Iran. In brief, the unchartered and tumultuous turn of events in the geopolitics of south Asia has placed India and the US in such a position that the two have found a number of long and short term common interests to readjust their bilateral relationship. But given the urgency of tackling the menace of international terrorism on priority basis, the two countries have obviously put their counter-terror cooperation in top gear in recent times giving new dimension to the counter-terror operations in South Asia.[9]

Contours of Counter-terror Cooperation

The range and depth of Indo-US counter-terror cooperation have remained variable owing to the varying contours of bilateral relations between the two countries. An analysis of the trajectory of Indo-US counter-terror cooperation reveals the progression of this cooperation from just being a political rhetoric to the stage of enhanced military and strategic partnership and eventually graduating from just bilateral endeavour to extending strong support in dealing with terrorists and their organizations based in third country as well. Traditionally, being two vibrant democratic polities based on the liberal values of rule of law and constitutionalism, and having unflinching faith in the lasting international peace and tranquillity, it was obvious for the two to evolve a political consensus against any sort of political extremism, violent protest movements, and all such fundamentalist and extremist activities aimed at creating social and religious cleavages in society, and violent overthrow of the government. Hence, amidst the ongoing terrorist activities in various parts of India, when the US installations were targeted by terrorist groups during late nineteenth century, the two countries found common ground to give a new impetus to their bilateral relations by denouncing terrorism and all forms of violence and extremism. As and when the scattered and sporadic groups and organizations involved in terrorism and extremism on the basis of religion, ideology and sub-national aspirations started creating common chords with each other, the need for a political consensus against such activities was felt like never before. The picture got drastically transformed with the arrival of Al-Qaeda on the scene as it sought to galvanize all the sundry extremist groups engaged in terrorist activities in such faraway places as Chechnya, Kashmir, Lebanon, Afghanistan, Xinjiang, numerous African countries and some places in Europe. In the name of jihad, it called for a coordinated action amongst these groups, thus, turning localized and episodic streams of terrorism into international terrorism. To counter this, Indo-US counter-terror cooperation focused on building political and ideological antidote to jihad that was reflected in the periodic joint statements issued by the officials and working groups engaged in strengthening counter-terror cooperation between the two countries.

Political orientation of Indo-US counter-terror cooperation was elevated to concrete military and strategic collaboration in the wake of 9/11 when US declared global war terror. Interestingly, the initiative in this regard emanated from India which offered all out assistance to the US in its hour of need by showing its willingness to permit the use of various military bases in India to undertake counter-terror operations in Afghanistan. By providing satellite imageries of the terrorist hot-beds in Afghanistan in prelude to the beginning of Operation Enduring Freedom under US stewardship, India conveyed its fullest cooperation to the counter-terror operations in Afghanistan though its domestic compulsions dissuaded it from getting directly involved in that operation. Yet, its covert cooperation to the US continued as and when required. For instance, Indian naval warships provided safety escort to the supply vessels carrying essential items for troops engaged in Afghanistan through the Strait of Malacca and the Andaman Sea. Such unequivocal military support from India to US counter-terror operations in Afghanistan presumably persuaded it to go for extension of counter-terror cooperation with India to concrete measures for military-to-military collaborations. Aimed at honing the skills of the two militaries in counter-terror operations by learning from experiences and strategies of each other, such collaborations included company-level joint counter-insurgency training of army units, periodic ground, naval and air exercises, training in high altitude operations and jungle warfare, and ever-increasing US assistance to India under International Military Education and Training Programme. Moreover, the two countries also went for institutionalizing law enforcement cooperation and creating a regular channel for mutual assistance in the areas of de-mining operations, counter-insurgency training and humanitarian relief for persons internally displaced by conflicts and internal strife.[10]

The most advanced stage of counter-terror cooperation between India and the US has come with the extension of such cooperation even in third countries the result of which was the arrest and deportation of the dreaded terrorist Abu Jundal from Saudi Arabia recently.[11] However, even before this, the two countries had already started sharing common concern on counter-terror strategies at global forum such as the United Nations when they supported the adoption of UN Global Counter-Terrorism Strategy by the UN General Assembly in September 2006. Calls were also made to enhance cooperation among Indian Ocean navies to act as vital instrument to fight terrorism.[12] Nonetheless, in the context of Indo-US counter-terror cooperation, the path-breaking role of the Indo-US Counter-Terrorism Joint Working Group is unquestionably commendable. Acting as the dedicated platform for strengthening counter-terror cooperation between the two countries, this Working Group has 'proved to be a useful mechanism for exchange of information, intelligence sharing, anti-terrorism training programmes and for strengthening institutional links between crime prevention agencies in the two countries.'[13] Consequent upon the vigorous efforts made by the Working Group, the gamut of counter-terror cooperation between the two countries has been widened to newer and unconventional areas such as 'greater intelligence sharing, an upgraded Anti-Terrorism Training Assistance Programme (ATAP) for Indian law enforcement officials, the launching of a cyber security forum to focus on cyber-terrorism and information security, improving border monitoring, counter-terrorism equipment sales, counter narcotics, money laundering, and the ratification and implementation of the Treaty on Mutual Legal Assistance.'[14] All these initiatives seem to have convinced the two countries to make an all out effort to track and fix the wanted terrorists not only within the homeland of the two but also in third countries as well. Clearly, with the beginning of busting terrorist hide-outs and arrest of hardcore terrorists hiding in foreign countries with the US assistance, the Indo-US counter-terror cooperation is poised for a big leap though taking such cooperation to its logical conclusion is not an easy task given the risks and stakes involved in such measures.

Going Beyond the Normal

The crux of argument in the aforesaid analysis conclusively proves the fact that even the enhanced counter-terror cooperation between India and the US could not cross the threshold of the normal. As a result, the long span of counter-terror cooperation between the two could not bring about any dramatic transformation in the profile of vulnerability and probability of terror strike on either of the two countries. Rather, ironically, the growing counter-terror cooperation has led to increased probability of the two being attacked by terrorist groups as the terrorist groups aiming at one particular country might feel provoked to attack a soft target in the other country as well. Whereas on the ground, despite the counter-terror cooperation, the two mighty nations are found to be fending for themselves as far as dealing with terrorist groups are concerned. For instance, the US operations in Afghanistan and occasional drone attacks in FATA of Pakistan are being conducted by the Allied forces led by US without any substantial support from India. Similarly, the Indian armed forces are waging the lonely battle against terrorist groups in Kashmir without any tangible assistance from the US anti-terror agencies. In such a situation of helping each other in counter-terror operations within the limits of normal, the whole exercise is likely to be futile. Despite being collaborators in anti-terror operations, the two countries would land up fighting their battle individually. What is therefore needed on part of the two most terror-affected countries in the world is to go beyond the normal and shed their cold war time inhibitions to evolve at mutually beneficial and result-oriented counter-terror strategy in such a way they fill up the most vulnerable gap in the individual counter-terror strategy and operations of the two.

On the part of the US, the three crucial gaps in its entire counter-terror strategy seem to be (1) secure and assured source of supplies for the troops engaged in counter-terror operations in Afghanistan, (2) ensuring safety and security of its interests and installations both within and outside the country, and (3) developing a long term counter-terror intelligence and reconnaissance system. In all these three critical areas of US counter-terror policy, Indian support could be instrumental in ensuring cent percent filling up of these gaps. As regards the short term aim of ensuring a secure and assured source of supplies for the troops engaged in counter-terror operations in Afghanistan, India needs to be more forthcoming in extending a helping hand to the US in order to reduce its overwhelming dependence on Pakistan for the same. Pakistan, undoubtedly, will remain the most economical and efficient source of supplied for the US troops in Afghanistan but given the blow hot-blow cold attitude of that country, the US sometimes feel sketchy regarding the assured route of supplies to Afghanistan. Such a strategically volatile situation for US counter-terror strategy needs to be stabilized that can only be done with a proactive and unqualified support from India. The mid-term goal of ensuring safety and security of US interests and installations within and outside the country could again be materialized with whole hearted support from India given its long standing and, by and large, successful experience in protecting its missions and officials abroad. While US experiences in this regard are themselves commendable, what is being argued here is that supplementing the efforts of each other will surely be a beneficial and effective antidote to terrorism out to devour the two. In so far as creating a long term counter-terror intelligence and reconnaissance system is concerned, the joining hands of the two countries could be pioneering in the global war terror as more and more countries could join the bandwagon to ensure a terror-free run for them. These measures cumulatively might go a long way in helping US win the war on terror in both short as well as long term.

In comparison to the US perspectives on counter-terror strategy, Indian scenario is quite similar barring the short term aim of putting down the cross-border terrorism emanating from Pakistan. It is in this seemingly inscrutable challenge that India needs the support of the US the most. Notwithstanding the alienation of a section of people in Kashmir valley from the Indian state, there is no denying the fact that the monster of terrorism in Kashmir is active and kicking only with the moral and material support coming from Pakistan. What is more worrisome in this context is that apart from the fundamentalist and extremist groups, a section of the Pakistan army, particularly the notorious ISI, is found to be using the terrorist groups to carry out dastardly attacks on the chosen targets in India such as Indian Parliament, Red Fort, various landmarks of Mumbai, Akshardham temple etc. The Pakistani support to the terrorist groups ranges from fresh recruitments in the terror outfits to training them in carrying out deadly attacks and pushing them into India with huge cache of arms, ammunitions and counterfeit Indian currency. It is in breaking this vicious nexus of Pakistani support to the terror groups in India that the US could play an instrumental role. This role could be performed effectively by the US through pressurizing Pakistan (a) to desist from involving state actors in the terror strikes in India (b) curbing with iron hand the activities of several fundamentalist and extremist groups acting as political fronts for the terrorist organizations, and (c) making Pakistan dismantle the terror infrastructure such as training camps on its soil. Given the American clout in the economic and military establishments of Pakistan, all these measures are well within its competence. What is needed is only a political will in the US policy makers to walk the extra mile in support of India to make the country a land of peace and harmony.

The suggested framework of counter-terror cooperation between India and the US would not materialize as long as the two countries continue to refrain from overhauling their perspectives and priorities towards each other. What is, therefore, required from them is to move beyond the normal course of their counter-terror cooperation and venture into a creative proximity in which the problem of one becomes a challenge for evolving a suitable solution for the other.

Concluding Observations

The pedigree of Indo-US counter-terror cooperation has been so that in the whole exercise India appears as the recipient of the pointers given by the US. Understandably, there have been valid reasons for this inequitable relationship between the two countries given that India has been victim of terrorism from much earlier times than that of the US. But what is intriguing about the US position on counter-terror cooperation with India is the fact that it was not at all concerned about the problem of terrorism in India until the monster struck at its backyards making it rise from slumber to wage the global war on terror. Indo-US counter-terror cooperation, therefore, appears to be an afterthought for the American policy makers as there is probably no evidence to show the US appreciation and worry about the terror problem in India at the time when terrorism was not a challenge to the security and sovereignty of the super power. The recipient attitude of India on counter-terror cooperation with US seems to continue even today as at no point of time the country was found to be assertive enough to extract any substantive support from US if it was unwilling to do so. A case in point in this context is that of Headley whose interrogation by the Indian counter-terror agencies would surely have provided vital clues on the conspiracy and modus operandi of the 26/11 Mumbai attacks. But for reasons best known to the US security agencies, it denied Indian security agencies access to him thereby berefting them having significant leads in the investigation of 26/11 attacks. Moreover, neither India nor its partners put up the kind of intellectual fight necessary to counter the pernicious arguments that turned the victims of 26/11 into a part-culprit.[15] Even the current case of US support in the arrest and deportation of Abu Jundal to India appeared to be executed as per the calculations of the US without much perseverance of the Indian agencies. In such a scenario, India could not expect to carry forward the counter-terror cooperation with the US to any longer period than the one fixed by the dominant partner. In other words, once the US is able to decimate Al-Qaeda and wipe out all probable terrorist threats to its interests and installations, it would not be interested in carrying forward the counter-terror cooperation with India despite her being ravaged by unabated terrorist attacks. India must, therefore, guard against such a scenario before going beyond the normal in counter-terror cooperation with the US.

REFERENCES

1. Indrani Bagchi, "Uncle Sam pulled Jundal strings", *The Times of India*, June 27, 2012.
2. Teresita and Howard Schaffer, "Expanding strategic partnership", *The Hindu,* June 26, 2012.
3. Shanthie Mariet D'Souza, "Indo-US Counter-Terrorism Cooperation: Rhetoric Versus Substance", *Strategic Analysis*, 32(6), 2008, p. 1068.
4. Rajendra Kumar Pandey, "International Terrorism" in Tapan Biswal (ed.), *International Relations,* Macmillan, New Delhi, 2009, p. 439.
5. Mohammed Badrul Alam, "Analysing Indo-US Relations during Bush Presidency", *Area Studies: A Journal of International Studies and Analyses,* 3(1), January-June, 2009, p. 65.
6. Seema Sirohi, "US-India: Alignment & Autonomy", *The Times of India,* June 18, 2012.
7. Barkha Dutt, "A tricky terrain", *The Hindustan Times,* July 7, 2012
8. Narayan Lakshman, "US mistrust over Pakistan's terror links persists, says experts", *The Hindu,* July 5, 2012
9. For a valuable discussion on counter-terrorism in South Asia, see, ORF, *Counter-Terrorism in South Asia,* (ORF-Heritage Dialogue), KW Publishers Pvt. Ltd., New Delhi, 2011.
10. "India, US forging new phase of ties, says Hillary", *The Hindu,* June 14, 2012.
11. Deeptiman Tiwary, "US traced ultra, forced his arrest", *The Times of India,* June 27, 2012
12. Sandeep Dikshit, "Cooperation among Indian Ocean navies vital to fight terrorism, says Manmohan", *The Hindu,* February 15, 2008.
13. Cited in Bhabani Mishra, 'Indo-US Relations: A Paradigm Shift', *Strategic Analysis,* 29(1), 2005, p. 90.
14. Shanthie Mariet D'Souza, *op. cit*, p. 1071.
15. Frederic Grare, "A year after Mumbai: The global battle of idea", *The Hindu,* November 23, 2009.

12

India-USA Engagement and Partnership for Democratic Development in 21st Century: Scope and Limitations

Kaustav Padmapati

With 1.2 billion people and the practice of universal adult franchise, India is the largest democracy in the world. Despite many shortcomings and challenges, India's democracy has survived and it is still growing strong. Former US Ambassador to India, Robert Black stated, "India is a plural society with democracy, rule of law and individual freedom, community relations and cultural diversity. What a place to be an intellectual! ....I wouldn't mind being born ten times to rediscover India."[1]

It is really surprising that despite maintaining a stable democratic culture and making available democracy at the grassroot level, India is still not a priority in the foreign policy of the United States. From American side, many terms are used to describe the relations between India and the United States like "estranged democracies," and "distanced powers". However, from Indian side the relationship is described in a more positive way like "distanced democracies," "engaged democracies," and finally "natural allies." Although India refers the United States as the most powerful democracy and itself as the largest democracy in the world, the relationship between both the countries are still far behind from achieving common democratic goals. The United States and India bilateral relation is so complex that it cannot be defined by any specific terms.

In reality, India stands among the working partner of the United States, a country that Washington can never ignore responding to recent change to the international order. It's aim is to bring India under its hegemonic calculations. It has been noticed that the recent improvements of India-USA relation is largely based on defense and economic cooperation.

There is no doubt that in 21st century, South Asia emerged as one of the core areas for US foreign policy interest. Being the dominant actor in the region, India was considered as promising power and "indispensible partner" of the United States. However, the reality is that a major chunk of the US policy towards South Asia is still concentrated towards Pakistan. During the Presidency of George W. Bush, it was stated that the emerging "strategic partnership" between the United States and India is based on a shared respect for democracy and concerns about the threat of global terrorism as well as mutual concern about the long-term implications of the rise of China and beyond. [2]

Despite improvements of India-US relations in recent times, many foreign policy experts and observers remain skeptical about India-US cooperation. Still many US experts and Indian foreign policy analysts dismiss the idea that India is confident enough to promote democracy and human rights abroad especially in the neighbouring states. There are many issues that are bothering sound India-United States relations like issue of climate change, management of Iran's nuclear challenge, and most importantly Kashmir issue. The differences on these are visible from time to time in some of the international gathering or events. Even for the US corporate sector and business community, Indian economy is still not open enough to accommodate the growing US business demands. Considering the exceptional character of both democracies based on extraordinary size, history, diversity and giving respect to open and diverse societies, there are many common grounds of cooperation.

Background

Over the last sixty-five years, the relations between India and the US have changed in many aspects and there were many ups and downs and high and lows as well. In reality, India-USA relations basically started taking shape in a fitful fashion after the end of Cold War. Before that, the two states frequently found themselves at odds due to opposing grand strategies. The main factors that can be identified for the emergence of new relationship between the two countries are world economy and nuclearism. India is identified as a power that can no longer be ignored, must be brought under the hegemon's calculations.[3] The growing economic integration and the historic Indo-US nuclear deal are the examples of India's strategic importance in these calculations. There are four core areas of Indo-US relations in the 21st century: appreciation of democracy, anti-terrorism, institutional frameworks, and the agency exhibited by India in the international system, even under structural constraints.[4]

There are many common grounds of cooperation between the United States as the "oldest democracy" in the world and India as the "most populous" democracy. However, the pattern of Indo-US democratic cooperation was not swift in the past especially during the Cold War time. Different democratic process and culture in both the countries made the relation very complex and complicated. Moral resentment and mutual misunderstanding, even at times a sense of betrayal, were the defining characteristics of bilateral relations over the past half century. Both countries also suffer from many shortcomings and democratic deficits. Many foreign policy and international relation experts characterized this troubled relation as "Estranged Democracies."

Despite many shortcomings and deficiencies, India's democracy has survived facing many odds, which has strengthened international opinion, including the United States, about the country's democratic progress. As India and the United States is linked by common values and a shared commitment to democratic pluralism, so there are more reasons to cooperate and engage with each other. In recent years, the United States realizes India's emergence as a rising power and its development into a mature market economy are significant to the region and the world.

During Cold War, there was less emphasis on Indian democracy by policy makers due to internal and external factors. Although India pursued a Cold War strategy under its first Prime Minister Jawaharlal Nehru based on the principal of non-alignment, its policy was far from neutral. Theoretically, under the policy of non-alignment, India intended to pursue an independent interest free from influence either by Soviet Union or the United States. In reality, Nehru himself was inclined to support the Soviet Union owing to its repeated statements against Colonial rule.[5] India openly collaborated with USSR on wide range of issues, including rapid industrialization during Nehruvian era. The era of friendship also continued during the period of Nehru's immediate successors. Therefore, by 1970's, Moscow emerged as New Delhi's principal arms and technology supplier. India's mistrust about China also helped to cement this relation. In addition, US democracy aligning with military-ruled Pakistan, US support for Pakistan by selling arms and supporting its claim on Kashmir issue stand on the way of making any substantive cooperation with the United States.

Due to Cold War ideological differences, India and the United States could not commit to shared political values. India stood outside the US alliances system and it was adverse to the West on most political issues. The term used to define that phase of "India-US" relations was "estranged democracies." India was against anti-imperialism, which was made another goal along with non-alignment during Nehru's era. During 1960's, India's foreign policy even turned to more anti-Western as there was an influence economic populism and leftist orientation at domestic politics. India took the lead of third world countries in different international platforms, and its non-aligned movement even radicalized that aimed for a reformation of a global order against the West.

Even after the end of Cold War, India did not portray itself as the leading democracy in the world. In the new environment created after 1991, India was worried about US dominance in Asian continent and creation of a uni polar world. The United States was also critical of India for violation of human rights in Kashmir and had soft corner for Pakistan. The Indo-US relation started to move towards positive direction in mid-1990's during the presidency of Clinton. In early 1990's, India opened up its economy and committed to liberalization. India's commitment to economic reform and the growing political clout of the Indian-American community created positive thinking in the United States as the Washington started to give India-United Stated relation a new approach. Therefore Clinton in his second term sought healthier and meaningful cooperation with India.

India-US relations again dropped to the lowest point as India conducted series of nuclear tests on May 11 and 13, 1998. The tests posed a direct challenge to the Clinton's administration's nuclear non-proliferation policy. The United States imposed economic and military sanctions on India under the Glenn Nuclear Proliferation Act of 1994. As the air craft industry of the United States had significant contracts with India, attempts were made to make amendment to an omnibus appropriation bill. It gave the President the authority to waive most sanctions against India, including those under Glenn Amendments.

Many attempts were made to bring the India-USA relations on track. Following two years, a remarkable series of high-level discussions between then External Affairs Minister Jaswant Singh and the US deputy secretary of state, Strobe Talbott, took place. Those talks were aimed to "transform" bilateral relations between both the countries. Kargil War broke out in 1999 and Clinton's response was quite unexpected. Clinton persuaded Pakistan to withdraw its troops from Indian portion of Kashmir. In the same year, US Congress removed some of the sanctions against India. In the new millennium, a historic event took place as Clinton paid a visit to India in March 2000. He became the fourth American President who paid a visit to India. Six months later, Indian Prime Minster Atal Behari Vajpayee visited Washington DC, which opened another chapter of the India-US relations. India-United States cooperation took place on several fields as joint working groups on counter-terrorism, peacekeeping, energy, and environment were formed. During that point of time, US legislators had finally realized that India's economic liberalization can yield domestic dividends. Millions of potential customers created more attention among the US business community. The growth of and achievements of Indian-American community has also succeeded in changing the perception of Indians in the United States. While celebrating a "closer and qualitatively new relationship," both Clinton and Vajpayee "reiterated their conviction that closer cooperation and stronger partnership between the two countries will be a vital factor for shaping a future of peace, prosperity, democracy, pluralism and freedom."[6]

Despite all these developments, major differences between the two countries regarding nuclear issues persisted as India refused to sign the Comprehensive Test Ban Treaty (CTBT). In addition, Clinton administration failed to receive New Delhi's support to promote democracy worldwide. India was skeptical to promote democracy as India's new cooperation with Washington would likely to change fundamentals of US policy toward India.[7] The Washington was also puzzled by the Indian decision to turn down the US request to lead the UN Democracy Caucus.

Developments during Bush Presidency

After coming to power, President George W. Bush took the India-United States bilateral relations to a new level. His personal enthusiasm translated into policy initiative toward India in many areas. In contrast to his predecessors, Bush was ready to recognize India as a potential major power. In the early 21st century, India's growing role in the larger strategic picture of the new world order was visible. In addition, the growth of the Indian economy and its increasing importance in the new global knowledge-based economy also brought it closer to the United States. In the calculations made by foreign policy experts of Bush Administration for maintenance of Asia-Pacific stability, India's strategic importance was realized and recognized.

During his presidential campaign, Bush referred India as "emerging as one of the great democracies of 21st century." He was lauded by the American-Indian community in the United States. Bush also had a less absolutist view regarding the nuclear aspirations of New Delhi. There was a speculation among Indian circle that Bush might use India to counterweigh China. Being elected as the President, George Bush embarked on an ambitious review of decades-old American policy to integrate India into his strategic doctrine.[8] In the team of new administrators appointed by Bush, there were many supporters of sound India-US relations. US Secretary of State Colin Powel advocated solid India-US ties, the new US ambassador to India, Robert Blackwill, Secretary of State for South Asia all voiced support for lifting sanctions against India and advocated a more collaborative partnership with New Delhi. In addition, Bush showed "generous and unprecedented gesture of goodwill," which indicated that Bush had a personal interest to make India-United States bilateral relations better. Bush had placed India on its most valued Asian friends and viewed India as a major strategic power, a key security interlocutor, and a nation whose opinion mattered on any security related issues.

The 9/11 terrorists attacks in New York and Washington DC and Bush's war against terrorism opened greater scope of cooperation between India and United States. New Delhi immediately offered cooperation for US counterterrorism operations in South Asia in the form of intelligence and military cooperation, access to air bases, over flight rights, port facilities for US warships which were lauded at Washington DC. All these developments made the United States concern about terrorist groups based in Pakistan targeting India. Although, Pakistan was an ally to the United States in its war against terrorism, Bush administration mounted political pressure on Pakistan to stop cross border terrorism. President Bush also waived the 1998 nuclear sanctions against India and reduced the Entity List that prohibited Americans from doing business with certain Indian companies.[9] The common interests seemingly highlighted in the post September 11 attacks, bought closer both countries – in many areas like military cooperation by conducting joint military exercises, counterterrorism, arms sale, missile defense. However, there was not much cooperation in the areas of democratic promotion.

The India-USA relation slowed down a little bit when the United States invaded Iraq and made arms buildup in Middle East. In order to speed up the process of cooperation again, the "Next Steps in Strategic Partnership" (NSSP) was launched by Washington and New Delhi in January 2004. It was a phased effort to ease restrictions on India's access to US technology in four areas: dual-use items, civilian nuclear applications, civilian space cooperation, and ballistic missile defense. The India-US relations reached its peak as the framework for Civil Nuclear Agreement between two countries was made on 18 July 2005. As a part of this agreement, India agreed to separate its civil and military nuclear facilities and to place all its civil nuclear facilities under International Atomic Energy Agency (IAEA) safeguards and, in exchange, the United States agreed to work toward full civil nuclear cooperation with India. This agreement infused a new confidence in the prospects for a new partnership between both countries as the door for the global nuclear energy market was opened for India. This agreement generated lots of attention among the international circle.

In addition, President Bush and Prime Minister Manmohan Singh announced a joint global democracy initiative by committing to support the new UN Democracy Fund aimed at strengthening democratic institutions and promoting human rights. There was a severe opposition from the Communist allies of United Progressive Alliance (UPA) government against all these progress made by Bush and Dr. Singh. Again multilateral policy makers in Indian side was skeptical about supporting the UN development fund as it would present a negative picture of India to its NAM allies in the United Nations. There were also US critics that doubted India's credentials as a promoter of democracy.

President Bush built on the idea of supporting democracy abroad along with India. There were some progresses made by both countries on certain matters in South Asia. During regime change in Nepal, New Delhi and Washington showed unprecedented diplomatic coordination. Working along with other major powers like European Union and imposing arms embargo against Nepal, India and the United States became successful in preventing the monarchy from dividing the powers to its advantage. [10] Although, there were many political differences between India and the United States while managing Nepal's democratic transition, the whole experience started a new era of meaningful political cooperation between democracies in supporting positive changes in South Asia. The cloud of suspicion regarding US role in India's neighbourhood was slightly removed as both governments begin to understand each other's problems and looked for further cooperation in many areas. India's role and shared interests in South Asian region was widely recognized. In case of Afghanistan, India emerged as top donors and Washington widely applauded Indian contribution. There were frequent diplomatic interactions, which helped to get rid of many misunderstandings based on historical grounds.

Despite, all these positive developments both countries had significant difference regarding democracy in Pakistan. India also disagreed with the US strict approach to promote democracy in Burma by imposing sanctions and isolating it. India's approach was much softer and had evolved over a period of time. It wanted to invest in more constructive engagement. The United States was disappointed at India's role in promoting democracy in Burma. For India, many factors had to be kept in mind while maintaining a balance between spreading democracy and protecting its own interests. There was a significant difference with the United States on the question of sovereignty and non-intervention. India opposes intervention by developed powers that could set the precedent for potential interventions against itself. This role is quite controversial as within its own neighbourhood, however, India's policy mirrored those of great powers choosing to intervene when its interests or principles demanded so.[11]

India as a Case for Democracy

Indian Prime Minster Dr. Manmohan Singh in a speech delivered at India Today Conclave on 25 February 2005 underlined the importance of liberal democracy by stating that India is moving forward to be a liberal democracy based on the idea of an inclusive and open society, which is largely multiethnic, multilingual, and multicultural in nature.[12] For Indian foreign policy experts like Raja Mohan such descriptions about Indian democracy symbolize a major departure from the modern Indian tradition. In the last century, India did not contribute much towards promotion of democracy abroad and showing concern regarding violation of human rights in neighbouring countries.

Historically, Indian foreign policy was characterized by a non-aligned, post-colonial, and non-interventionist approach. Although India has a strong commitment to preserve democracy, promotion of democracy as a political priority has largely been missing from India's Foreign Policy. The main reason for this attitude is the impact of Cold War and India's commitment to non-aligned movement. Defense of its own national security and integrity was top priority in history of India's foreign policy.

India's attitude has started to change in the late 1990's after the end of Cold War. Giving support to democracies abroad became a factor in Indian policy making. Therefore, India-US engagement had started taking place sharing the same goals and objectives. It was mainly during Presidency of Bush, Washington emphasized the importance of India as the world's largest democracy and looked for options for working with New Delhi on the promotion of democracy worldwide.

Despite many internal challenges and struggles with security issues, today India considers itself as an emerging global power. In the 21st century, India has emerged as an increasingly important player on the global stage. India dominates the geography of the now strategically vital South Asia region, and its vibrant economy, pluralist society, cultural influence, and growing military power have made the country a key focus of the US foreign policy attention. It has started playing role in global platform through participating in various groups like G-20, BRICS etc. President Obama's endorsement of Indian membership at UN Security Council is another example of India's growing importance at new international order.

In addition, India has showed its responsibility in its neighbourhood by working towards strengthening democratic institutions in Nepal, Sri Lanka, Bangladesh, Bhutan, and most prominently, Afghanistan. India is Afghanistan's fourth-largest bilateral donor by funding 1.3 billion. India has invested significantly building the administrative mechanism by training Afghan civil servants, building the Afghan parliament constructing infrastructure around the country, and supporting Afghan elections. India's unique democratic experience has created demand for its expertise abroad, and it has taken some steps toward democracy assistance. Time by time, India deploys teams of election management experts in Asia and Africa and offers internships and study tours to its lively parliament as well as extensive capacity building programs. Other important contribution that included India is one of the founding members of the Community of Democracies and a leading cofounder of the UN Democracy Fund, which is dedicated to promoting good governance and human rights around the world. It should be noted that India's success in combining democracy and development in a highly diverse society provides a powerful argument in favour of democracy.

The cause of concern is that all these achievements and merits did not bring much change of attitude of the United States. Still there is scepticism of the United States and other Western powers regarding India's role in global affairs specially the promotion of democracy. Many factors explains this attitude, as anti-imperialism is a prominent feature of Indian foreign policy. India prioritized its ties with emerging nations rather than developed nations. So far, India has opposed trade and climate agreements seen as overly favourable to developed economies and is often accused of obstructing international negotiations rather than providing constructive solutions. India is mainly willing to support democracy abroad when such assistance coincides with its foreign policy goals of improving India's international standing, regional stability, and South-South cooperation[13]. India is suspicious of democracy promotion as an explicit foreign policy goal and is hesitant to confront dictatorships. India's role in democracy promotion cannot be ignored as it has the credit of combining democracy and development in a highly diverse society.

India and the United States have significant differences in their approach towards Iran and Burma. US alliances with Saudi Arabia and support to Pakistan always stand on the way to sound India-US cooperation based on democratic values. The United States was also irritated by India's cold attitude towards human rights violations in Sri Lanka and Myanmar. Despite persistent efforts of the US to include India in its democracy promotion initiatives, India has been reluctant to take a stronger pro-democracy stand or associate itself with US foreign policy. India still worries that Introduction of democracy and human rights concerns into its bilateral relations could create unproductive tensions and reduce India's room to maneuver on other issues.[14] All these limitations and differences still put a question mark on India-United States cooperation based on common commitment to strengthen good governance and pluralism within states as sources of security and stability as not always based on growing security and economic ties. For India, the United States is still an unreliable partner that ignores India's range of pressing problems. There is a more scope for value-based cooperation rather than defense ties between two democracies.

Still, there is a better scope of India-United States relations based on shared values and common commitment to political pluralism. It is sad that shared democratic values did not keep the two democracies from quarrelling in the past, nor will they guarantee a convergence of interests in the future.[15] To get rid of all skepticism, India should assume a leading place within the group modern democracies and coordinate its efforts with other like-minded powers in sharing responsibilities. Still much hard work remains to be done before this relationship meets the expectations of its most enthusiastic proponents.

The main challenge is that substantive differences over the nature and goals of Indo-American partnership are likely to complicate future relations between the world's two largest democracies. The issues where Washington and New Delhi finds difficult to collaborate includes Pakistan, China, Iran, Iraq, the World Trade Organization, and the future of the global non-proliferation regime. India still prefers a multipolar world order, which is not very much a part of US foreign policy goal. The United States determines its policies according to calculations of interest. To attract attention, India has to demonstrate more commitment by building a vibrant economy, accelerating reform, solidifying democratic institutions and values, investing in its human and capital infrastructure, improving relations with its neighbours, meeting the needs and aspirations of its people, which will make favourable ground for further cooperation between the two democracies.

Developments during Obama Administration and future scope:

So far, there is no breakthrough in India-USA engagement under the Obama Administration

However, President Obama issued a statement asserting that, "Our rapidly growing and deepening friendship with India offers benefits to all the world's citizens" and that the people of India "should know they have no better friend and partner than the people of the United States."[16] Even Secretary of State Hillary Clinton reaffirmed this commitment and gave assurance to work more closely with India. Despite such top-level assurances from the new US administration, many Indian experts doubted that Washington was not focusing on the bilateral relationship with the same vigour as did the Bush Administration. This uncertainty Obama Administration's excessive focused on China ignoring India's influence and visibility in South Asia. In addition, deepening relations with India's main rival Pakistan could be harmful to Indian security and perhaps lead to a more interventionist approach to the Kashmir problem. India also feared that US emphasis on non-proliferation and arms control put pressure on India join such multilateral initiatives as the Comprehensive Test Ban Treaty and the Fissile Material Cutoff Treaty.

During his India visit in November 2010, President Obama's historic speech at a joint session of the Indian Parliament characterized the India-USA partnership as serving three broad purposes: (1) promoting prosperity on both countries, especially through greater trade and two-way investment, and food security and health-related initiatives; (2) enhancing shared security by working together to prevent terrorist attacks, and; (3) strengthening democratic governance and human rights. Regarding the third objective, Obama mentioned that India is not serious about common values as sometimes it shies away from taking clear public stands in the face of gross human rights violations and the suppression of democratic movements, making a reference to Myanmar. [17]

Starting under President Bush and continuing with President Barack Obama, the US and Indian governments have been seeking to their leaders quite clearly and routinely express support for the expansion of liberal values. Despite many limitations and differences, the scope is really vast for cooperation on shred democratic values. In the future, India-US cooperation will be more meaningful and firm if both democracies put emphasis on issues of common concern like democratic assistance, global governance, assistance in development, institution building in many disturbed areas based on democratic values.

REFERENCES

1. *People, Progress Partnership – The transformation of US-India Relations*, (2004) Public Affairs Section, Embassy of the United States of America, New Delhi.
2. *Ibid.*
3. Sumit Ganguly, Brian Shoup, and Andrew Scobell, (2006) "US-*India Strategic Cooperation into 21st Century*" (New York, Routlage, 2006) 1
4. Anurag Sinha , "The Proximate Causes for the New Indo-US Relationship" URL: http://www.google.co.in/url?sa=t&rct=j&q=&esrc=s&source =web&cd=1&ved= 0CEwQFjAA&url=http%3A%2F%2F www.global indiafoundation.org%2FIndia-US.doc&ei=gEUDUJjZL4f OrQeekKigBg&usg=AFQjCNHzg 12g2Hej7u4VdAOHMHfAEJKL0g, accessed on 10 June 2012
5. Dipanker Banerjee "An Overview of Indo-US Strategic Cooperation: a rollercoaster of a relationship," Sumit Ganguly, Brian Shoup, and Andrew Scobell, (2006) "US-*India Strategic Cooperation into 21st Century*" (New York, Routledge, 2006) 68
6. Robert M. Hathaway, "The US-India Courtship: From Clinton to Bush," *Journal of Strategic Studies*, 25:4, (2003) 6-31

7. *Ibid.*
8. See *People, Progress, Partnership -- The Transformation of US-India Relations*, (2004) Public Affairs Section, Embassy of the United States of America, New Delhi.
9. Devin T. Hagerty "Are We Present at the Creation? Alliance theory and the Indo-US strategic convergence," Sumit Ganguly, Brian Shoup, and Andrew Scobell, (2006) "*US-India Strategic Cooperation into 21st Century*" (New York, Routlage, 2006) 4.
10. C. Raja Mohan, "Balancing Interests and Values: India's Struggle with Democracy Promotion," *The Washington Quarterly* 30, no. 3 (Summer 2007): p. 99, http://twq.com/ 07summer/docs/07summer_mohan.pdf. Accessed on 5 July 2012.
11. *Ibid.*
12. *Ibid.*
13. Thomas Carothers and Richard Youngs, "Looking for Help: Will rising democracies will become international democracy supporters?" *The Carnegie Papers*, Democracy and Rule of Law, July (2011).
14. *Ibid.*
15. Daniel Twining and Richard Fontain "The Ties that Bind? US-India Value-based cooperation" *The Washington Quarterly*, Spring 2011.
16. K. Alan Kronstadt, "India: Domestic Issues, Strategic Dynamics, and US Relations," US Congressional Research Service, RL33529, September 2011.
17. *Ibid.*

13

India-US Strategic Partnership and the Challenges of Enhanced Cooperation

Biswajit Mohapatra

There has been a thawing of relations between the two countries, after the joint statement, "India-US Relations: A Vision for the 21st Century" issued in New Delhi. Such positive development has laid a strong foundation for the growth of strategic partnership between the two countries. The Bush Jr Administration's efforts to broadbase its ties with India is a recognition to the fact that New Delhi does and can have a very important role to play in guaranteeing strategic stability in the Indian Ocean Region and in promoting a viable balance of power in Asia.[1] This is quite markedly a significant shift from the earlier phase of relation that was characterized as alternating from being tolerant and at times downright hostility, over the last six decades. Dennis Kux described this phase that existed between the two countries as, "Estranged Democracies".[2] The close alliance between United States and Pakistan and hostile relation between India and Pakistan are held to be the factors that marked India US relations in the gone by years.[3]

The end of cold War in 1991 brought a new perspective in the relation between these two.[4] The visit of President Bill Clinton to India after a long gap of 22 years and the signing of Joint Statement called Indo-US Relations: A Vision for the Twenty First century, in New Delhi, contributed towards a change in the India-US relation[5]. The vision statement underlined the desire, inter alia, for intensifying dialogue between both the countries. In the aftermath of 9/11, the immediate assurance of help extended by India to United States for tackling the problem of terrorism, made US appreciate seriously the threat that terrorism posed to regional peace and stability.[6]

"Until the late 1990s, the United States often ignored India, treating it as a regional power in South Asia with little global weight. India's weak and protected economy gave it little influence in global markets, and its nonaligned foreign policy caused periodic tension with Washington. When the United States did concentrate on India, it too often fixated on India's military rivalry with Pakistan"[7].

As India has started to achieve rapid economic growth, it is considered to have the capacity to act on issues of primary strategic and economic concerns. US presumed the reformist measures undertaken by India will contribute to global growth, promote market-based economic policies and will help maintain a mutually favourable balance of power in Asia. For its part, New Delhi also felt that United States will help facilitate its rise as a major power.[8]

There is ever-expanding partnership between the US and Pakistan and America's long-term commitment to the bilateral relationship and for a broad and lasting strategic partnership with Pakistan[9]. For India, this remains an issue of concern in view of the worsening security situation in and around Afghanistan, in the resurgence of the Taliban, terrorism in Kashmir, and the growth of Jihadi extremism and capabilities.

The US-India strategic partnership is being held upon to boost our shared values to enable our two countries to work together on global issues and to support our common strategic and security interests to increase mutual security against the common threats posed by intolerance, terrorism, and the spread of weapons of mass destruction. The successful transformation of the US-India relationship then can have a positive influence on the evolving future international system, which was again emphasized by President Obama in New Delhi.[10]

It proves that mere sharing of beliefs in democracy and freedom for people with different beliefs and long held traditions is not enough to boost friendly relations, because the interests of the two countries are either different or perceived to be different, which doesn't augur well for friendly India-US relations in the near future. Yet there continues to be concern and even fear about its consequences for regional and world security and for well-being in general. In order to sustain and consequently improve this existing Indo-US relations into the next millennium, it is of utmost priority to critically examine the tenuous relations between two countries and evaluate the various policy measures taken by US and to examine the response by India to see if the fear that is being voiced, whether US will truly respect the independence of the developing countries like India or will it throttle them as it emerges as a single most pre eminent powerful nation in today's world. In the light of these this paper critically analyses the changing nature of Indo-US relations after the signing of Indo-US Strategic Partnership and also evaluates the Indo-US Strategic Partnership's potential for closer Indo-US ties, on the regional security, and the issue of terrorism.

India and the United States are the world's largest democracies, with both committed to political freedom ensured by representative government. The US-India relationship as such is always believed to be derived from this common belief in freedom, democracy, and the rule of law, and is for seeking to advance shared security interests. These interests, inter alia, include maintenance of security and stability, fighting any form of terrorism and violent religious extremism, prevention of the spread of weapons of mass destruction and associated materials, data, and technologies.[11]

The US and India have also common interest in the free flow of commerce and resources, including through the vital sea lanes of the Indian Ocean and protecting the freeflow of commerce via land, air and sea lanes. The maintenance of safe and secure sea lanes, particularly those that link the United States with its partners in the Indian and Pacific Oceans, is at the very core of US interests.[12] They also share an interest in fighting terrorism and in creating a strategically stable Asia. Recently India has also been gradually moving toward greater economic freedom and wider access to its market for outside goods.

Between the two, there have been some differences, which included US' concerns over India's Nuclear Weapons Programme and the direction of India's economic reforms. In the past, these concerns dominated US thinking about India, but now the US perceives India as a growing world power with which it shares common strategic interests. As such a strong partnership between the two countries always remained a possibility to address differences and shape a dynamic and collaborative future, should a need arise in the future.

India-US Strategic Partnership

With the non realization of the so called "New World Order" and "Peace Dividends" as planned by the United States policy makers after the end of the Cold War,[13] and further the emergence of the United States as the unipolar global super power after the disintegration of the Soviet Union, the US policymakers encountered newer and greater strategic uncertainties in the new era.

A new set of complex strategic developments of concern to United States are believed to be behind it to seek the forging of a strategic partnership with India. Some of these are as follows:

China's emergence as a major military threat in the Asia Pacific with the perceiving threat that it might think of challenging the US predominance in the region[14] and the Russia's growing assertiveness in the European affairs and so also in the Asia-Pacific and with possibilities in the Middle east posed a great challenge to United States global strategic equations. Further emerging strategic partnership between Russia and China, made the strategic equation on the Western rim of the Pacific much more complicated. The rise in the Islamic fundamentalist challenges in the Gulf, Afghanistan, Pakistan and some of the Central Asian Republics, appeared to aim at challenging the pre-eminence of the United States and the West. The threat of potential Talibanisation of Pakistan and the recurrent instability in the South West Asia region along with Afghanistan appeared to be more of a formidable challenge for the United States, which was then forced to court newer strategic partnerships beyond its erstwhile Cold War alliances and relationships to face the emerging global challenges. The US realized that natural partners to overcome such challenges for it can only be vibrant democracies.[15]

India's Strategic Partnership with the US — Compulsive Factors

Following various political and strategic developments in the international and regional security environment, like the emergence of China being a potential threat to India's security and its intransigence in terms of its various acts being carried on by it against India, its preponderance of nuclear weapons and military might, cause serious concerns for the Indian policy makers.

Further, Pakistan turning into a nuclear weapon state in South Asia with sustained Chinese assistance and its growing missile armoury complicated the regional security more. The unabated China-Pakistan strategic nexus in South Asia and its likelihood of being reinforced with Clinton administration's policy pronouncements on South Asia and the widening estrangement between US and China posed security dilemma for India in its neighbourhood.

Further, the Islamic fundamentalists being sponsored and launched by Pakistan with aid from other Islamic countries, who were proving to be much of a security threat to India, both externally and internally and Russia, strategically a longtime friend, indicating its desire of forging a quasi strategic alliance with China for keeping US's design under control in the Asia-Pacific [16] and with the thought that Russia might not use its power in favour of India for the fear of annoying the Chinese, strongly persuaded India has to shed its so called non-aligned mindsets and to break out of its earlier politico-strategic straitjacket strategic thinking and to consider United States as probably the most important, dynamic and a strategic ally for protection of its national security interests.

India-US Strategic Partnership: Is it Convergence of Interests ?

With this realization, gradually it was realized that India-US strategic partnership can be of great help given the many areas of convergence of political and strategic interests, with the United States having enduring vital strategic interests in the Middle East, Gulf region and South East (SE) Asia, connecting the world's largest reserves of the energy and the SE Asia providing the strategic choke points linking the Indian and Pacific Oceans, which are also of critical importance to India's national security interests. The sea-lanes stretching from the Hormuz Straits and going towards its West and Eastern sides, are of special economic importance to both the countries. Islamic fundamentalism as a common threat and both USA and India having been declared as enemies by several Islamic fundamentalist organizations, require concerted action by both USA and India. Besides maintaining the existing status-quo in the prevailing strategic equilibrium in the Asia-Pacific security architecture, wherein USA and India both have equal stake.

In the present days, the fact of geo-economics supplanting the geo strategic and geo political considerations in the prevailing international relations, the joint potential for USA and India appeared to be very vast and something that these two countries could ill afford to let it pass, in the midst of security challenges to their national interests which are at stake. With India starting to redesign its own strategic interests, United States-India strategic partnership became unavoidable.

Long considered to be rather a regional hegemon, in the US strategic calculations, from Washington's perspective, India somehow went up as a big factor in the 21st century strategic calculus as US felt India to be a power increasingly vital to US core foreign policy interests. Some say India, with more than one billion citizens, has always been characterized as a nascent great power but to be considered as "indispensible partner" of the United States,[17] struck many analysts as somewhat surprising. It is true many analysts view the sudden warmth in India-United States ties, as a potential counterweight to China's ever growing clout.[18]

The occasion of President Clinton's five day visit to India in March 2000, marked some kind of shifts in US policies towards the South Asian region in terms of an India-US strategic partnership. For more than fifty years the United States and India stood apart as 'estranged democracies' when there were more than enough political and strategic compulsions on both sides in the late 1940's and early 1950's to have entered into a strategic partnership. This partnership has had the effect of recognizing India as a very key ally to US strategic interests, for which the United States sought to strengthen its relationship with India.

When President Bush lifted sanctions imposed under the terms of the 1994 Nuclear Proliferation Prevention Act following India's nuclear tests in May 1998, in late September 2000, this helped in bridging many of the gaps in understanding between the countries, following the non-proliferation dialogue initiated after the 1998 nuclear tests. The 9/11 attack against the US in 2001, has been an event of great reckoning as it has marked a sea change in the perception of Unites States toward India. This had the effect of President George W. Bush to actively think of collaborating with India for keeping control over the extremely crucial Indian Ocean sea-lanes from the Suez to Singapore, which can secure US interests.

In a meeting, President Bush and Prime Minister Vajpayee in November 2001, had expressed a strong and abiding interest in transforming the US-India bilateral relationship[19]. After several high-level meetings and contacts between the two countries during 2002 and 2003, in January 2004, the US and India mutually agreed for launching of, the Next Steps in Strategic Partnership (NSSP), which was hailed as both a milestone in the transformation of the bilateral relationship and a blueprint for its further progress.[20]

Since 2004, Washington and New Delhi began discussions on pursuing a "strategic partnership" based on shared values and albeit somewhat convergent geopolitical interests[21]. In this direction numerous economic, security, and global initiatives, including plans for establishing civilian nuclear cooperation, got underway. This last initiative, first launched in 2005, had the effect of reversing the three decades long US Non Proliferation policy. In 2005, the United States and India both entered into a ten-year defense framework agreement for expanding bilateral security cooperation.[22] Subsequently the two countries are now engaged in numerous and combined military exercises and major US arms sales to India. As such the value of bilateral trade tripled in the period from 2004 to 2008 and has been growing ever since. In April 2005, the United States signed an Open Skies Agreement to boost trade, tourism, and business by increasing the number of flights and helping Air India to purchase 68 US Boeing aircraft, at a cost of $8 billion.

In July 2005, in Washington DC, President Bush and Prime Minister Manmohan Singh announced the success of the NSSP, as well as several other agreements to further enhance cooperation in the areas of civil nuclear, civil space, and high-technology commerce besides US-India Economic Dialogue; Technology Cooperation; Democracy Initiative; an Agriculture Knowledge Initiative; a Trade Policy Forum; Energy Dialogue etc. During the President's reciprocal visit to India in March 2006, the progress of these initiatives were reviewed besides launching of other new initiatives.

In December 2006, with the US Congress approval of the historic Henry J. Hyde United States-India Peaceful Atomic Cooperation Act, the road became clear for direct civilian nuclear commerce with India for the first time in 30 years during which US policy had opposed nuclear cooperation with India because of the country's nuclear weapons programme and for unwillingness to sign the Nuclear Non-Proliferation Treaty. This legislation paved the way for India to buy US nuclear reactors and fuel for civilian use.[23]

In July 2007, the United States and India reached a historic milestone in their strategic partnership by completing negotiations on the bilateral agreement for peaceful nuclear cooperation, also known as the "123 agreement." This agreement, signed by Secretary of State Rice and External Affairs Minister Mukherjee on October 10, 2008, governs civil nuclear trade between the two countries and opens the door for American and Indian firms to participate in each other's civil nuclear energy sector. The US and India seek to elevate the strategic partnership further to include cooperation in counter-terrorism, defense cooperation, education, and joint democracy promotion.

After President Barack Obama's swearing in as the New President Of United States, both Secretary of State Hillary Clinton and the Minister Of External Affairs, India, reiterated their determination to "further strengthen the excellent bilateral relationship" between the United States and India. Soon after, President Obama also said in a statement, "Our rapidly growing and deepening friendship with India offers benefits to all the world's citizens" and that the people of India "should know they have no better friend and partner than the people of the United States." During the confirmation hearing at the Senate, Hillary Clinton also told Senators that she would work to fulfill President Obama's commitment to "establish a true strategic partnership with India, increase our military cooperation, trade, and support democracies around the world."[24]

Despite all these top-level assurances from the new Administration, during 2009 and into 2010, many in India expressed apprehension that Washington was not focussed on the upgrading the bilateral relationship with India in the same vigour as the Bush Administration had pursued for a both broader and stronger ties with India.[25]

Further there is fear that as the Obama Administration is more focused on US relations with China, which would reduce India's influence and visibility. For sometime Indian strategic thinkers started to hold that US is also intent on deepening relations with Pakistan, India's main rival, which might prove dangerous to Indian security and perhaps could invite a more interventionist approach on the Kashmir problem.

With New Delhi's continuous appeal for explicit US support for a permanent seat for India on the U.N. Security Council, not been lauded by United States, even though the Obama Administration's reiteration that there is a "need to reassess institutions of global governance" and that India's rise "will certainly be a factor in any future consideration of reform" of that Council, the warmth in the bilateral ties is probably missing.

Even after the Secretary of State Clinton's successful visit to India in July 2009 and inking several agreements and mentioning of the five key "pillars" of the US-India engagement: (1) strategic cooperation; (2) energy and climate change; (3) economics, trade, and agriculture; (4) education and development; and (5) science technology and innovation and Prime Minister Singh's visit to the White House as the first Head of the Government in the inaugural year of Obama presidency in November 2009 to hold bilateral talk with President Obama, the supporters of closer ties with United States felt disappointed in its outcome, as no "breakthroughs" in the bilateral relationship could be seen. It was argued that the strategic goals were increasingly well aligned; and that there were ample opportunities for taking advantage of commonalities and that the Obama Administration was not averse to India's potential role as a US partner.[26]

The subsequent noting by President Obama in the May 2010 National Security Strategy, that, "The United States and India are building a strategic partnership that is underpinned by our shared interests, our shared values as the world's two largest democracies, and close connections among our people" and then, "Working together through our Strategic Dialogue and high-level visits, we seek a broad based relationship in which India contributes to global counterterrorism efforts, non-proliferation, and helps promote poverty-reduction, education, health, and sustainable agriculture. We value India's growing leadership on a wide array of global issues, through groups such as the G-20, and will seek to work with India to promote stability in South Asia and elsewhere in the world," rekindled the hopes of closer strategic relationship between both the countries.[27]

The June 2010 Strategic Dialogue Reengagement

In June 2010, the United States and India formally again reengaged the US-India Strategic Dialogue initiated under President Bush, with the External Affairs Minister S.M. Krishna paying a visit to Washington, DC, accompanied by a large delegation of high-ranking Indian officials, Secretary of State Clinton, as the leader of the US delegation praised India as "an indispensible partner and a trusted friend."[28] President Obama also declared his firm belief that "the relationship between the United States and India will be a defining partnership in the 21st century."[29]

During this Strategic Dialogue, in a joint statement, both the countries pledged to "deepen people-to-people, business-to-business, and government-to-government linkages ... for the mutual benefit of both countries and for the promotion of global peace, stability, and prosperity." It also further outlined extensive bilateral initiatives in each of ten key areas: (1) advancing global security and countering terrorism; (2) disarmament and non-proliferation; (3) trade and economic relations; (4) high technology; (5) energy security, clean energy, and climate change; (6) agriculture; (7) education; (8) health; (9) science and technology; and (10) development and ended with Secretary Clinton confirming President Obama's intention to visit India in November 2010.

Unfortunately during his visit to India in November 2010, the US President had to face several bilateral issues that included, differences in perception over the proper regional roles which could be played by China and Pakistan; the status of conflict in Afghanistan; intensification of international efforts to address Iran's controversial nuclear program; restrictions on high-technology exports to India, outsourcing, and contentious issues on the conclusion of arrangements for both civil nuclear and defense cooperation, among others.

During the visit, President Obama saw India as prominent Future Power on world stage and declared it as one of the important ally to US. In a major policy shift Obama declared US support for India's permanent membership of United Nations Security Council, besides announcing removal of export control restrictions on several Indian companies. He also concluded trade deals worth $10 billion which were expected to create/support 50,000 jobs in the US during this visit.

United States' Af-Pak Policy

After the visit, analysts expressed their happiness at the fact that the US chose to see India with the same trust as it sees its main ally Britain —Australia and Japan, and that President Obama's India visit was seen by foreign relation experts as the most successful US Presidential Visit; yet India-US relations got strained over Obama administration's tackling of the Taliban insurgency in Afghanistan and Pakistan in its Af-Pak policy. M.K. Narayanan, India's National Security Adviser, seriously criticized the Obama administration for having linked up the Kashmir dispute to the instability in Pakistan and Afghanistan and said that by doing so, President Obama was "barking up the wrong tree"[30]. In a strong write up, *The Foreign Policy* criticized Obama's approach towards South Asia, mentioning that "India can be a part of the solution rather than part of the problem" in South Asia and also suggested India to take a more proactive role in rebuilding Afghanistan irrespective of the attitude of the Obama administration.

Dismissing any apprehension of rift with India regarding the United States' Af-Pak policy, Robert Blake, Assistant secretary of the United States' Bureau of South and Central Asian Affairs, said strongly that India and the United States are "natural allies".[31] He however outlined that the United States cannot afford to meet the strategic priorities in Pakistan and Afghanistan at "the expense of India[32].

Conclusion

Any close ties between US and Pakistan, and if the US's long-term commitment to the bilateral relationship with Pakistan is continued, then it may prove to be dangerous for the regional security and India as well.

Furthermore, current Western and US policies of extending continued support to Pakistan by generously providing of funds like a multi-billion dollar, multi-faceted assistance programme in the name of enhanced border security, including training, equipment, road-building, and logistic support etc., is being viewed with high degree of concern as it may become an important factor in the destabilization of the region. Such US policy has further encouraged Pakistan to trade democratization for its cooperation on terrorism, is also fraught with danger for India's security and regional stability. On this account there is currently too much mistrust and lack of understanding between our people.

In *Rethinking Western Strategies Toward Pakistan: An Action Agenda for the United States and Europe*, visiting scholar Frederic Grare while analyzing the cost of continued military rule in Pakistan, has argued that while Pakistan may partially cooperate with the West against international terrorism, without democratization Pakistan will continue its policies, resulting in continued regional instability.[33]

Indo-US relations have rather become much closer or as a result of enhanced cooperation and consultation between the two countries, even as economic cooperation between the US and India is continuing at an accelerated pace and is likely to grow substantially in the coming years. Likewise military cooperation also has increased. However with the US continuing to advocate the stability of the Indian sub-continent, its pursuance of Af-Pak policy with a Pakistan tilt, including the lessening of tensions over the Kashmir issue, and a renunciation of nuclear weapons proliferation and testing which are very contentious issues having the potential for a flashpoint, even as the interests of the two countries are becoming complementary which bodes well for friendly India-US relations in the near future. Yet there continues to be concern and even fear about its consequences for regional and world security and for well-being in general.

In order to sustain and consequently improve this existing Indo-US relations into the next millennium, it is of utmost priority that the strategic partnership is intensified while protecting each country's independence and independent way of promoting economic growth for the benefit of the large public.

REFERENCES

1. Terisita Schaffer, '*Rising India and the US Policy Options in Asia*'. http://www.csis.org/pubs/2003, accessed on 14/07/2012
2. Dennis Kux, *Estranged Democracies: India and the United States 1941-1991*, New Delhi: Sage Publication, 1994, p. 541
3. Thakkar Usha and Kulkarni Mangesh. (eds.), *India in the World Affairs: Towards the 21st Century*, Mumbai: Himalaya Publishing House, 1999, p. 125.
4. Barbara Leitch Lepore, "Foreign Affairs and National Defense Division", *CRS Issues Brief 93093: India-US Relations*, updated April 21, 1995.
5. N.E Elam Mathew, "Clinton Visit to India Generate Economic Optimism," Publication Travel News, Monday, June 26, 2007.
6. Guihong Zhang, "US Security Policy Towards South Asia after September 11 and its implication for China: A Chinese perspective", Jan. 2003. Accessed in *www.stimson.org/china/pdf/secpolsouthasia.pdf*
7. Evan A. Feigenbaum, *India's Rise, America's Interest, Foreign Affairs*, March/April 2010.
8. *Ibid*, p. 1.
9. Speech by Nancy J. Powell, US Ambassador to Pakistan, "US Foreign Policy towards Pakistan", at Karachi Council on Foreign Relations, Karachi, Pakistan, on November 13, 2003.
10. Available at http://www.whitehouse.gov/the-press-office/2010/11/08/us-india-partnership-fact-sheets.
11. Available at http://www.state.gov/t/nt/rls/rm/32293.htm
12. John F. Bradford, "The Maritime Strategy of the United States: Implications for Indo-Pacific Sea Lanes," *Journal of Contemporary Southeast Asia* 33.2 (2011): 183–208.
13. Dr. Subhash Kapila, "India-USA Strategic Partnership—The advent of the inevitable", available at http://www.southasiaanalysis.org/papers2/paper120.html
14. Andrew S. Erickson, Lyle J. Goldstein, and Nan Li (eds.), *China, the United States, and 21st Century Sea Power: Defining a Maritime Security Partnership* (Annapolis, MD: Naval Institute Press, 2010).
15. *Op. cit.*, Kapila.
16. Artyom Lukin, "Russia: between the US and China", available at http://www.eastasiaforum.org/2012/07/24/russia-between-the-us-and-china-2/
17. "The United States and India: An Indispensable Partnership for the 21st Century", available at www.state.gov/p/us/rm/2012/187401.htm

18. Congressional Research Service, "India: Domestic Issues, Strategic Dynamics, and US Relations", September 1, 2011.
19. Available at http://www.bis.doc.gov/internationalprograms/statementprinciplesindia.htm
20. Available at http://www.bis.doc.gov/news/2004/us-indianextstep.htm
21. *Op. cit.*, xii
22. "CRS Report For Congress, US-India Bilateral Agreements in 2005", September 8, 2005, available at fpc.state.gov/documents/organization/53616.pdf
23. Available at www.gpo.gov/fdsys/pkg/.../BILLS-109hr5682enr.pdf
24. Available at fpc.state.gov/documents/organization/150780.pdf
25. *op. cit.*, xviii
26. Available at http://fpc.state.gov/documents/organization/150780.pdf
27. Available at www.whitehouse.gov/sites/default/.../national_ security_strategy.pdf
28. Congressional Research Service, India-US Relations, October 27,2010, available at fpc.state.gov/documents/organization/150780.pdf
29. Hillary Clinton, "America's Pacific Century, Foreign Policy", November 2011, http://www.foreignpolicy.com/articles/2011/10/11/americas_pacific_century?page=full, accessed on 11July 2012
30. M.K. Narayanan (MKN), "India's National Security Advisor", in interview with Karan Thapar (KT), CNBC TV18's India Tonight, available at http://www.ft.com/cms/s/0/270d831a-f29d-11dd-abe6-0000779fd2ac.html#axzz21i1IuL28
31. Natural Allies "A Blueprint for the Future of US.-India Relations", By Richard L. Armitage, Co-Chair. R. Nicholas Burns, Richard Fontaine, see at www.cnas.org/.../CNAS_Natural%20Allies_ArmitageBurnsFontaine.p
32. Robert O. Blake, "New Strategic Partnerships," available at http://www.state.gov/p/sca/rls/rmks/2009/125503.htm
33. Frederic Grare, "Rethinking Western Strategies Toward Pakistan: An Action Agenda for the United States and Europe", available at http://carnegieendowment.org/2007/07/10/rethinking-western-strategies-toward-pakistan-action-agenda-for-united-states-and-europe/3p0b

14

Indo-US Relations and the Role of Indian Diaspora

Mukesh Bagoria

The presence of the Indians in the Unites States of America is traced back to 1790 in Salem, Massachusetts which is the first recorded arrival of an unnamed 'Man from Madras' according to the Dr. S. Chandrasekhar[1] (as based on an entry in the diary of Rev. William Betley, a Salem, Massachusetts clergyman). The migration of Indians can be divided into four phases—first phase till 1920s (as farmers, labourers, students, merchants and religious leaders), second phase till mid 1960s, third phase from 1965 to 1980s (as family members of the Indian immigrants, highly qualified professionals and businessman) and the fourth phase in the 1990s (with the information technology boom in the US). The population of Asian Indians has been increasing tremendously from one census to another. Various studies have revealed that the Asian Indians are the highest income earners as an ethnic community in the United States. From the late 1980s, the Asian Indian community started involving themselves actively in the American domestic political process by registering and voting. They now support both the Democratic and Republican parties and even independent candidates at various levels. Both the parties vie for their support in elections — financially as well as for their votes. The Indian Diaspora in the United States has been playing an important role in the improvement of bilateral relations between the two countries. The Indians as a community of one country origin have formed Caucuses in both the Congress and the Senate to promote better relations with India and to counter any move by Pakistan backed lawmakers to pass resolutions against India. The Congressional Caucus on India and Indian Americans since its inception in 1993 and Friends of India in the Senate since 2004 have been playing very important roles in discussing the issues concerning

India and the United States. The political clout of the Asian Indians can be measured by the fact that the Indian festivals are now being celebrated in the White House and the previous two presidents (Bill Clinton in March, 2000 and George Bush Jr in March, 2006) and the current president Barack Obama in Nov, 2010 have visited India.

The Asian Indian [2] community in the United States has been playing a prominent role in raising the issues of concern to India in the United States from the very beginning of their settlement in the US. Now with their numerical strength (as the second highest amongst the Asians) and affluence (the highest average income of US $ 90,525 as against the US national average of $ 51,222)[3], the Asian Indians are playing a major role in shaping the improvement of bilateral relations between the two countries. With time, they have grown demographically and have organized themselves into various associations. Their agenda has also not only grown from the issues of citizenship to sharp interest in American domestic political process and Indo-US relations. The phenomena discussed above have spurred fresh research to assess their role and impact on bilateral relations. The Asians- Indians with their various organizations have come together on issues and interests related to India and Asian Indians in the United States.

John Gunter Dean, former American Ambassador to India had once described the Indian community in the United States as a 'bridge'. "Indians in America he said, could 'soften' the edges in our relationship and bring technology and investment from the United States to India. Scientists, businessmen, and academicians of Indian origin in the United States could play the role of brokers in furthering American investment and collaboration agreements in Industry, for instance, there are now numerous technology agreements between United States and India and investments by American corporations in which United States- based Indian engineers, scientists, and managers play an important role".[4] This has been proving to be true as there has been a tremendous increase in the American investment and collaborations between the two countries.

The Indian Diaspora in the United States of America has a long history of establishing associations, beginning in 1910 when its population in the United States was 4713 (Census 1910). In 1900 the population was only 956; in 1950 it reached to 11534 and in 1960 to 13507. The population of Asian Indian had been increasing steadily in 1970 to 75000 approx., 1980 the population reached 3,87,223, in 1990 it was 8,14,538, Census Bureau of 2000 recorded the Asian Indian population as 16,78,765 and 28,46914 in 2010.[5] According to the latest estimates it is about 3.2 millions almost 1% of the total US population.

The Indian Diaspora had organized itself in the early 20th century to fight against the discriminatory American citizenship and naturalization Acts against the Indians. The Asian Indian community during the 1920s, 1930s and 1940s lobbied in the Congress and fought court battles to attain the right to naturalization as stated by Sripati Chander shekhar and US Commission on Civil Right.[6]

The long battle towards liberalizing immigration laws found its final shape in the Immigration act of 1946 also known as the Luce-Cellar Act, which amended the Immigration Act of 1917, grating the privilege of admission to the United States as quota immigrants and eligibility for naturalization races indigenous to India and persons of Filipino descent. The quota for Indians was raised to 100 immigrants annually. After the 1946 Act, Immigration laws were amended from time to time with the efforts of the Asian Indian community which resulted in the increase of Asian Indian population in the United States, especially after the 1965 Immigration Act (which allowed reunion with the family of the migrants) and 1990 Immigration Act (which came into effect in 1992).

On the aggregate, Indians who immigrated in the wake of 1965 immigration act were highly educated and technically skilled professional who, in a relatively short period of time found themselves in the middle and upper socio-economic levels in the American society. Although, despite their potential technical contribution and their financial affluence, the political involvement of Asian Indians in the mainstream American society is not commensurate with the professional success.

Many argue that in general, financial affluence provides freedom from other burdens that enables and encourage political participation. According to this view, Asian-Indians, who have consolidated and established their financial position, would predictably be attracted towards the United States domestic politics[7]. Evidence reveals however, that Asian-Indians have participated in some degree from early years of the 20th century. Influencing the political process extends from the act of voting, to working for the candidate, to contribution to funding for a candidate or a party, to contest an election for a public office; and for lobbying to influence the making of a specific public policy. The Indian Diaspora in America has had a checkered history in the field of political activism. Till around mid-1980s, it was more marked by individual, single issue-based efforts. Of late, it has become more organized and begun to shape itself as a focused efforts leading to its political efficacy and recognition at the top echelons of the American political system.[8]

There were many reasons for the lack of participation in the political process by the Asian Indians in the early period, such as not well established careers, traditional Indian distaste for politics and voluntarism and according to one view, Indian Diaspora in the United States, engaged with political events but viewed direct participation as exclusively reserved for "White Anglo Saxon Protestants" (WASPs) or "old money". In terms of the outlook towards voluntarism, the average Asian Indian feels a strong sense of responsibility towards his family, but not necessarily towards his community.[9]

The immigrant attitude towards the United States is also of relevance. The theories of marginal existence support the argument that perhaps many immigrants had not accepted the United States as their permanent home. The desire to participate in this country's affairs, then, remains minimal. It is not usual to see immigrants becoming more involved and emotional about Indian political and social issues then they are about American issues. Many first generation Asian Indians feel (point out) that they did not come to this nation as refugees but rather, because their skills were more desired and solicited by the American society, rather than back home. For them, the impetus to give back to the adopted land was not as great. Their occupations and residential patterns also point to difficulties in acting in a cohesive manner. Further, as an ethnic group, the Asian Indian community, is not united as one. Regional background in India often determines the people with whom one will associate. There are several associations on the lines of religious, castes and regional affiliation. The fact that there are a few areas in which Asian Indians are geographically concentrated, works both to the community's advantage and disadvantage. In other words, their geographical dispersal may generate a low profile and protect them from prejudices and resentment, but it also deprives them of strength in numbers needed at election times.[10]

The earliest effort on the part of the Asian-Indian community to involve in the issues related to India was the launching of Ghadar movement in 1913 in San Francisco. This movement was initially led by students of Indian origin in the United States such as Hardayal Singh, Kartar Singh Sarabha, and others. They held meetings in rural areas where the farmers donated generously to sustain the movement.[11] People from different religious backgrounds — Hindus, Sikhs, Muslims—participated in it. This movement was an attempt by Indians exile in United States to overthrow the British Raj by sending revolutionaries and arms to India. The Indian Home Rule league was founded in New York by Lala Lajpat Rai in 1915. He was a pioneer in enlisting American morale support for India's freedom in 1915 during his exile from India. The merchants and 'agro businessmen' financially supported India's Independence movement in the United States.

The Indian League of America led by Sardar J.J. Singh actively took up matters of India's interests with the members of the House of Foreign

Affairs Committee and writing to the American President. When India's official delegate could not bring up the questions of India's right to the United Nations Relief and Rehabilitation Administration, his perseverance got Congressman Karl E. Mundt, a member of the Committee and other Congressmen to finally succeed in the passage of amendment in the Congress to allow India the benefits of famine relief. J.J.Singh also took up the issue of the passage of an amendment to the immigration laws permitting a hundred Indians a year to enter America to become permanent residents and citizens. Meetings were organized in New York and Washington D.C. to gain support for this issue. The legislation co-authored by Emanuel Celler and Clare Booth Luce, was introduced in 1944, and passed by the House of Representatives in 1946 and by the Senate thereafter. During the later part of 1944, Vijayalakshmi Pandit joined the Indian nationalists in the United States. Both Pandit and Singh were on hand to press for India's liberation.[12]

After the assassination of Mahatma Gandhi on January 30, 1948, the Indian League lobbied for a Mahatma Gandhi Memorial Bill in the US Congress through Congressman Cellar from New York, which was passed by the Congress in 1949. The bill, was first of its kind, authorized the Indian League of America to erect a memorial of Mahatma Gandhi (the first non-American leader to be respected in this manner) on the US government land in Washington D.C. The memorial could not be constructed because fifty per cent funds had to be managed by the Indian community living in the United States and other fifty per cent by the Government of India within a period of 5 years.[13] The Asian Indians at that time were not prosperous enough to collect the required amount. In 1998 the Senate and the Congress passed resolutions to authorize the government of India to establish a memorial to honour Mahatma Gandhi in the District of Columbia.[14] In September 2000, Prime Minister Atal Behari Vajpayee unveiled Mahatma Gandhi's statue in Washington D.C. in front of the Indian Embassy.[15]

In 1950s and 1960s, Dalip Singh Saund, the first Asian Indian elected Congressman from California, arued to have better bilateral relations with India.[16] In 1970s, India tryst nuclear process derailed the Indo-US relations and since then had been a contentious issue between both the nations till the late 1990s. In May 1974, the Indian Atomic Energy Commission exploded an underground nuclear device at Pokhran in Rajasthan. The United States initially criticized the tests but was of the view that Indo-US relations should carry on and should not isolate India. The attention of the US nonproliferation lobby turned to the nuclear power plant at Tarapore, built as show piece AID project and the major element in Indo-US nuclear cooperation. Tarapore received US enriched uranium supplied under a 30 year commercial contract. After the explosion, the supply of enriched uranium for Tarapore became a major problem between India and the United States.[17] The National Federation of Indian American Association (NFIAA) had organized its members to pressure Congressmen and administration to relax the US policy over selling fuel to India for its Tarapore reactor, trade in garments, and sanctions.[18]

Since the late 1980s there has seen a steady growth of lobbying powers of the Asian-Indians in the US. The Asian Indians vigorously started to lobby for India on different issues, partly due to their dual roots. Many also carried the burden of Indo-Pakistan relations and continued to voice opposition to the United States assistance to Pakistan as detrimental to the US interest in regional stability.

The decade of 1980s and 1990s revealed interesting evidence to the growing political awareness of the Indian Diaspora in the United States of America. By late 1980s, the Asian Indians had become politically active. They held fund-raising campaigns for their favourite candidates for both the Democrats and Republicans and formed Political Action Committees (PACs) to gain affluence. The Asian Indians realized that money is a powerful tool, and since their dispersal residence patterns prevented them from exercising their power in voting blocs, they used their capital instead. Politicians such as Congressman Stephen Solarz (Democrat, Brooklyn) recognized this reality and actively campaigned for support among the ethnic Asian Indians. The Government of India benefited from his efforts, as he was instrumental in countering efforts to have the US development assistance to India cut off in 1989.

The Asian-Indian community staged a demonstration against the highly sophisticated airborne early warning surveillance system (AWACKs) to be sold to Pakistan. In 1987, the National Federation of Indian American Association (NFIAA) was invited by the US Senate to send its representative to the Senate Foreign Relation Sub-committee hearing on "Proposed American massive military and package to Pakistan" which included highly sophisticated airborne early warning surveillance system (AWACKs) to testify why AWACKs should not be given to Pakistan. NFIAA's the then Executive Director, Dr. Jagat K. Motwani, representing the two National Indians Organizations—National Federations of Indian American Associations (NFIAA) and Association of Indians in America (AIA) - testified on March 23, 1987 in Washington D.C. before the Senate Sub- Committee for Near eastern and South Asian Affairs chaired by Senator Sarbanes (Democrat, Maryland).[19] Dr. Motwani voiced strong opposition to the proposed supply of AWACKs to Pakistan under the pretext that they would be used to monitor the Soviet backed military movements near the Afghanistan border to blunt any border attack.

He asserted that there was sufficient evidence to show that the hilly border between Afghanistan and Pakistan would severely limit the effectiveness of such sophisticated system. They would be used, he said, by Pakistan against India. It would escalate arms race and upset military balance in South Asia. The US finally did not supply the AWACKs to Pakistan at the urging of the Asian Indians and the Government of India.[20]

The 1990s heralded a new phase of activities in the Indo-US relations. Though the breakdown of talks on NPT in 1993-94 and the turbulence in Kashmir coincided with the liberalization of Indian economy, the technological and defense cooperation continued between the two countries. The major political issue between India and United States remained to put Pakistan on the list of countries supporting terrorism—especially in Kashmir. Significantly a flurry of activities by the Asian Indians began to focus on the legislators in order to garner the support.

The Asian Indians with the help of the US lawmakers formed the India Caucus in 1993 in the House of Representatives. The Congressional Caucus on India and Indian Americans was founded with the official objectives of "pushing the Indian American community's agenda on the Capitol Hill and promote better Indo-US ties." It was founded by Congressmen Frank Pallone, a Democrat from New Jersey, and Bill McCollum, a Republican from Florida, with the help of Asian Indians, such as , Kapil Sharma, Himanshu Shekhar and others. The membership of India Caucus is 150[21] in the 112th Congress. Ed Royce (California, Republican) and Joe Crowley (New York, Democrat) are the two present co-chairmen. The Congressional Caucus on India and Indian Americans primarily focuses on:

a) US-India relations – to include trade, security cooperation, global terrorism and economic and humanitarian assistance.
b) Issues of interest to the Asian Indian community including the facilitation of trade and commerce with India, small business, visas, education, health care and promotion of Indian culture in the United States.
c) Developments in India and on the Indian Subcontinent include economic development, health care, inter communal relations, the status of religious and other minorities and corruption.

A new bipartisan group called "Friends of India" was formed in the US Senate on the lines of decade old Congressional Caucus on India and Indian Americans in the House of Representatives on 29 April 2004 with 32 members.[22] This is the first country specific body in the US Senate. The Caucus was co-chaired in 2004 by Texas Senator John Cornyn and

New York Senator Hillary Rodham Clinton, who is now the Secretary of States. In 2007 the membership increased to 37 with the same co-chairmen.[23] Today its membership is 40 with Senator Mark Warner (Virginia, Democrat) and Senator John Cornyn (Texas, Republican) as co-chairs.

Making a formal announcement about the Caucus at the simple but well attended event on Capitol Hill , Senator Cornyn said, " the US and India share commitment to freedom, representative government principles and the war against terror. So the Senate India Caucus provides forum for the US senators and Indian legislators to expand on agreements and candidly discuss issues of concern".

He said though a firm plan of action has yet to be evolved, one of the objectives of the Caucus is to have better relations with India and discuss a number of issues, including outsourcing, on which he said, "we have some disagreements but we also have the need for better understanding, and that India and United States have nothing to fear from one another. We have great potential". He also spelt out the primary goals that the Senate India Caucus proposed to achieve: support for war on terror, deeper defense relations between two countries, opportunities for trade and investments to benefit both sides, stronger economic ties, besides advancing peace, stability and democracy in both countries.

Both the Caucuses separately welcomed the newly appointed Ambassador to the US Nirupama Rao and were attended by William Burns, the Deputy Secretary of States and other high ranking officials and dignitaries. They spoke about the role played by her in the Indo-US Nuclear deal as foreign Secretary of India.[24]

The Asian Indian community is now financially funding the members of India Caucus and in return, they asked the Congressmen to support issues concerning India and Asian Indians. Not all times have the Indian Americans and their law maker friends succeeded. In 1995-96, this lobby founded hard to pursue matters that strained the Indo-US relations. For example, the State Department pronounced "Kashmir a disputed territory and the status of which need to be resolved", and added that "the 1972 Shimla Accord between Pakistan and India to resolve the issue bilaterally had been ineffective". There was a broad hint of plebiscite as the US policy to decide the future of Kashmir. Then, the Clinton Administration proposed the sale of 38 F-16 fighter aircrafts to Pakistan that are capable of nuclear delivery systems. This, despite the Pressler Amendment prohibiting the sale of any arms to Pakistan unless the President certifies that Islamabad neither has nuclear weapons, nor is it trying to develop them. Finally, this was achieved by the passage of the anti-India Brown Amendment leading to the dispatch of 370 million dollars worth of arms to Pakistan. "The vote on the amendment was close and if the Asian Indian community had been more organized and able to convince five more senators on this political injustice, the Brown Amendment could have been defeated."[25]

The highly fragmented structure of policy-making process of the American political system is being comprehended by some Asian Indian groups like Indian American Forum for Political Education (IAFPE) and Indian American Center for Political Awareness (IACPA). The other associations like Association of Indian American (AIA), Federation of Indian Association (FIA), Indian American Foundation (IAF), US-India Political Action Committee (USINPAC) etc. have been playing a vital role in improving the bilateral relations between the two countries and also taking up the issues affecting the Asian Indian community in the Unites States.

They have been trying to bring all the organizations and the Indian community together. They have been organizing Annual India Day Parade, celebrating Indian festivals and on these occasions they invite American political leaders. They have adopted politics of pressure and learnt how to deftly manipulate power structure (Congress and its Committees) in Washington DC by pursuing the productive contacts with those Congressmen having empathy for India's stand on various issues. In the process, they have shrewdly used their contacts for mobilizing relations and sub committees on South Asia.

IACPA organizes seminars/conferences to make American political leaders aware about India and the special concern of the Asian Indian community. It seeks to facilitate the goal of 'educating' the American populace and political leaders on foreign and domestic issues of importance to the community and India. The IACPA influences the process of policy making related to Asian Indians as well issues impinging in the Indo-US relations.

Most remarkable was the role of IAFPE, which led Swadesh Chatterjee to win over the die-hard anti-India critic Senator Jesse Helms (Republican, North Carolina) in 1997. Till 1996 he had supported the annually ritualized anti-India Burton Amendment in the Senate, seeking drastic cut in the US aid to India. Sometimes Helms was noted for caustic remarks highly critical of India. More than a decade ago, Helms had managed to enable the London based Khalistani separatist leader Jagjit Singh Chauhan by circumventing even a denial of visa to him by the US authority. He managed to do so by officially calling a separatist leader to appear before Senate Committee on the ground that his presentation before the Committee was necessary.[26] Senator Helms wanted financial and political support from the Asian Indians during his 1997 election. He approached Swadesh Chatterjee of IAFPE who asked him to listen to the issues and problems concerning the Asian Indian community, to change his views on India related issues and also to meet S .S .Ray the then Indian Ambassador to US, which he did after IAFPE raised funds. Senator Helms did not even convene the meeting of the Foreign Relations Committee for hearing, notwithstanding President Bill Clinton's plea for Senate ratifications of the Comprehensive Test Ban Treaty (CTBT). He was reported to have stated whether India signed the treaty or not, "is not relevant to us at this time". Earlier, after Pokharan test in May 1998, Helms had said, "India's action demonstrates that CTBT, from non-proliferation standpoint, is scarcely more than a shame". Thus Swadesh Chatterjee had been able to persuade such a tough leader, and see the rationale behind Asian Indians' move, positioned in the foreign policy-making structure.

IAFPE had organized a seminar "*Indo-U.S. Relations: Emerging Opportunities*" on June 17, 2000. In the seminar, the speakers included Michelle C. Maynard, senior advisor for South Asian Affairs, US State Department, Richard Harding, US Department of Commerce, Senator Leslie Byrne (Democrat, Virginia), and the Indian Embassy officials.[27] They pledged to engage the US lawmakers in a regular dialogue to enhance the relationship between the US and India towards mutual benefits and everlasting friendship and to share the information with the fellow Asian Indians.

The Asian Indian community lobbied with the India Caucus members after the May 11 & 13, 1998, nuclear tests by India. It even presented a memorandum to the President Bill Clinton and explained him the reasons as to why India carried out the nuclear tests.[28] The then President of the India Caucus, Gary Ackerman, wrote to the then US President Bill Clinton, asking him to lift the World Bank sanctions against India. He had argued that the sanctions imposed on India have had the unhelpful and unproductive effect on curtailing the US-India business ties and also pleaded for a re-adjustment of America's non-proliferation objectives in the light of India's security concerns.[29]

There were many Congressmen and Senators who had argued in support of the Indian nuclear tests and that the sanctions should not be taken far, as to hurt the Indo-US relations. For example, Senator Lauch Faircloth wrote a letter to the President Clinton, about the effects of sanctions imposed on India. Senator Daniel Patrick Moynihan, spoke in the Senate on May 13, 1998, in favour of India's nuclear tests, and elaborated on the positive aspects of the India-US relations and how India has been following the non-proliferation regime of not transferring the nuclear technology to rogue states and terrorist organizations.[30]

The Indo-US relation had been derailed after the May 1998 Nuclear test by India, and Prime Minister A. B. Vajpayee, presented a detailed report in the parliament about the Indo-US relation on December 15, 1998. [31] In the Kargil war (1999) episode President Bill Clinton, told Mr. Nawaz Sharief to unconditionally withdraw its forces from there. Although the Americans acted from fear that Pakistan's action might trigger broader conflict possibly involving nuclear weapons, India interpreted the presidential arm-twisting of Prime Minister (Pakistan) Nawaz Sharief as a sign that Washington D.C. no longer automatically backed Pakistan on Kashmir.[32]

The Asian Indian community played a vital role in lobbying with the members of the US Congress and India Caucus. The House of Representatives passed a resolution on July 1,1999, expressing the sense of the Congress in opposition to the Government of Pakistan's support for armed incursion into Jammu & Kashmir, India. The resolution was introduced by Benjamin A. Gilman, Gary Ackerman, Frank Pallone and others who resolved that it should be the policy of the United States to oppose the Government of Pakistan's support for the armed incursion into Jammu & Kashmir, India, to support the immediate withdrawal of intruding forces supported by Pakistan from the Indian side of the Line of Control, to urge the reestablishment and future respect for the Line of Control, and to encourage all sides to end the fighting and exercise restraint, and that it should be the policy of the United States to encourage both India and Pakistan to adhere to the principles of Lahore Declaration.[33]

In March 2000, President Clinton visited South Asia for five days, of which, three days were spent in India, and did not give much importance to Pakistan as he stayed for few hours. The US administration and policy-makers were keen that the visit should end Cold War suspicions. A distrust that arose out of India's close relationship with the USSR and dedication to non-alignment through which it exercised moral superiority to gain world status. But in the last few years, the current of higher morals has given way to a new pragmatic currency 'money'. Economically, the Americans are determined to get their share of the Indian market in a steadily liberalized economy.

Influential Asian Indians had persuaded the President Bill Clinton to visit India. Capitol Hill is awash with young ethnic Indian Congressional staffers. They are lawyers and lobbyists and are revolutionizing politics in the Congress. The new thinking of the Indian lobby is more pragmatic, frankly interested in business and contributes financially to political campaigns. They are second and third generations who link themselves with other strong lobbyists like the Jewish.

In September 2000, External Affairs Minister Jaswant Singh had said that there is now a 'completely altered equation' between the US and India as a result of the growing confidence in India and recognition of the country as a great democracy. The candor and confidence in the relationship is unique and the ability of the relationship in both the countries to contain their differences and forge closer ties has emerged as a new reality, he said at a dinner hosted by Indo-US entrepreneurs in the Silicon Valley. The essence of relationship between India and America, said Singh, is based on creativity, continuity, stability and confidence between them. "It is in this context that the role of successful Asian Indians as heroes needs recognition", he had said. He also commended the role of Asian Indians, referring to them as 'great ambassadors' and also said that their success has made every Indian proud and has boosted their aspiration in India and abroad.

In 2002, the US India Political Action Committee (USINPAC) was founded by Sanjay Puri in Virginia, now with its head office in Washington D.C. USINPAC's mission is to impact policy on issues of concern to the Asian Indian community in the United States and strengthen US-India bilateral relations.[34] USINPAC, America Israel Political Committee (AIPAC) and American Jewish Committee (AJC) are working in collaboration with each other to promote issues concerning India and Israel. In 2003, pro-Israel and pro-India lobbyists successfully worked together to gain the Bush administration's approval for Israel to sell four Phalcon early warning radar planes to India for about $ 1 billion, a deal that had alarmed the Pakistani government.[35] The organization also works on bilateral trade and scientific issues.

The USINPAC organized the first-ever India Caucus Day at the Capitol Hill on February 13, 2003 and urged all the members of the Congressional Caucus on India and Indian Americans, the largest Caucus in the House, to proactively engage with the Asian Indian community in resolving its concerns. USINPAC delegates urged the US lawmakers to link US aid to Pakistan with its pledge to permanently ending infiltration of the armed terrorists to India.[36] At the urging of the USINPAC, the International Relations Committee of the House of Representatives unanimously passed an amendment to H.R. 1950, on May 7, 2003.[37] The amendment titled, 'Section 710 Report on Action Taken by Pakistan', states, "For each fiscal years 2004 and 2005, the President shall prepare and transmit to the appropriate Congressional Committees a report that contains a description of the extent to which the Government of Pakistan has closed all known terrorists training camps operating in Pakistan and Pakistani-held Kashmir; has established serious and identifiable measures to prohibit the infiltration of Islamic extremists across the "Line of

Control" (LOC) into India; and has ceased the transfer of weapons of mass destruction, including any associated technologies, to any third county or terrorist organization".

This landmark vote marked the first time that Congress has acknowledged the role of Pakistan in abetting terrorism and in the proliferation of nuclear weapons technology. By focusing entirely on the behaviour of Pakistan in promoting terrorism as an instrument of state policy, and in the proliferation of nuclear technology, the US Congress had taken the first tangible step in decoupling the US relationship with Pakistan with that from India. The Asian Indian community rallied strongly behind USINPAC's efforts to petition lawmakers to bring peace to the sub-continent. USINPAC members from all over the United States, their representatives in the Congress, had urged them to support passage of this amendment.[38]

With the backing of Indian American Friendship Council (IAFC), pro India law maker Juanita Millender McDonald, introduced a Resolution in the House of Representative, 'lauding the role of Asian Indians and benefits of working with India to promote peace, prosperity and freedom. The Resolution noted that people of Indian origin who have for decades immigrated to the United States, have made extraordinary contributions to the United States, helping it to make the United States a more efficient and prosperous country'. It praised the generation of doctors and nurses, scientist who have helped in defense, space, medical and computational research. It also highlighted their participation in the space shuttle program, at great personal sacrifice, a reference to Dr. Kalpana Chawala, who died in the Columbia space shuttle disaster in 2003 along with six of her colleagues. It was passed on May 12, 2004.[39]

These positive orientations detailed above does not mean that there is an across the board agreement on issues affecting the Indo-US relations. The basic differences remain on nonproliferation issues between India and the US. But there is a qualitative difference in Bush administration on the issue towards India. The Bush Jr. administration has moved back from the admonitory and punitive postures against India on Nuclear issues. While remaining committed to the traditional nonproliferation's agenda, the US has now acknowledged the reality of India's nuclear weaponization.

The three years of joint negotiations between India and the US pertaining to the civil nuclear energy cooperation had finally materialized in the form of the 123 agreement. This agreement emphasizes the desire of both the countries to cooperate extensively in the use of nuclear energy for peaceful purposes as a means of achieving energy security on a stable, reliable and predictable basis. The significance of the Agreement lies in the fact that when brought into effect, it will open the way for full civil nuclear energy cooperation between India and the United States. The Asian Indian community played a vital role, through various organizations they represent, in pursuing the US lawmakers to support the civil nuclear deal.

The out sourcing of various jobs to India by US has become a very important issue in the bilateral relations between the two countries. India has become the major destination for outsourcing jobs from the United States, followed by China and Philippines. India – with its low wages and highly educated English speaking labor pool – increasingly is seen as the major rival for US high-tech jobs.

The US lawmakers in various states had proposed several bills in 2003 and 2004 to limit the number of guest-worker visas. To fight back, the Indian Government had lobbied in the various states. The Asian Indians also pressurized the lawmakers not to let these bills pass. The Asian Indians also outsource their jobs to India, as the wages are cheaper in India. In 2003, the Indian government with its alliances and few local Asian Indian lawmakers had succeeded in temporarily blocking the passage of out sourcing bills in the States of Maryland and New Jersey.[40] The Asian Indians, the Indian Government and the American businessmen are lobbying hard to get certain bills passed which would allow the highly skilled labour to work in the United States. President Barack Obama has appointed many Asian-Indians in his administration at key positions and they are mostly young second generation Asian Indians, who will play a positive role in shaping the bilateral relations between the two countries as well as stability in the south Asian region.

All this leads one to the conclusion that Indo-US relations have at last reached a stage where one can expect a stable and realistic structuring of Indo-US relations on practical and mutual understanding of benefiting both the nations. The Indian Diaspora in the United States has and will play a very important role in bridging the gap. The second and third generation Asian Indians are more practical. The framework of the Indo-US ties are ever expanding, demanding and requires a development of a new perspective – taking into account the common concerns of the super power on the one hand and the world's largest growing economy and democracy i.e. India, on the other hand. The two countries will be strategic partners in various fields as both require each other for the prosperity and peace in the world.

REFERENCES

1. Chandershekhar, S., ed, *From India to America : A Brief History of Immigration, Problems of Discrimination Admission and Assimilation*, California, La Jolla, Population Review Books, 1982, p. 55.

2. The term '*Asian-Indians*' has been used by US Census Bureau since 1980 to refer to the Indian community settled in the United States.
3. Census Bureau of United States of America 2010.
4. Myron Weiner, "*The Indians presence in America: what difference will it make*", in Sulochana Raghavan Glazer, Nathan Glazer, eds., *Conflicating Images: India and the United States*, the Riverdale Company, Maryland, 1990, p. 241.
5. Census Bureau of United States of America 1910, 1950, 1980, 1990, 2000 and 2010.
6. Chandershekhar, S., ed, *From India to America : A Brief History of Immigration, Problems of Discrimination Admission and Assimilation*, California, La Jolla, Population Review Books, 1982, p. 55.
7. Nimro Ban, Ung Thomas, *Political Pattern In America: Conflict, Representation And Resolution,* San Francisco, 1979, p111
8. Pravin Sheth, *Indians in America: One Stream, Two Waves, Three Generations,* Rawat Publications, Jaipur, Delhi, 2001, p. 332.
9. Some of the literature deals with the immigrant Indian attitudes in the United States. The following are noteworthy in as much as they identify the prevailing patterns of behaviour of the Indian diaspora in the U.S. 1) Pyong Gap Min, ed, *Asian Americans: Contemporary Trends and Issues,* Sage Publications, California, New Delhi, 1995, 2) Carolyn, P. Yoder, *Asian Indian Americans*, Hienmann Library, Chicago, 2003, 3) John W. Lee, *Asian American electoral Participation,* Novinka Books, New York,2002, 4) Kanjilal, Tanmay, *Indian American: Participation in the American domestic political process*, Calcutta, 2000.
10. Priya Agarwal, *Passage from India, Post 1965 Indian Immigrants and their Children – Conflicts Concerns and Solutions*, Yuvati Publications, Palos Verdes, 1991, p. 85
11. Suzane, McMohan, Ethoes of Freedom: South Asian Pioneers in California 1899-1965, in University of California Publication. online www.lib.berkeley.edu, p. 14.
12. Pravin Sheth, *Indians in America: One Stream, Two Waves, Three Generations*, Rawat Publications, Jaipur, Delhi, 2001, p. 334.
13. Jagat K. Motwani, *America and India in a Give and Take Relationship*, New York, 2003, p. 21.
14. US Congress, House of Representatives, Committee on Foreign Relations, "*To authorize the government of India to establish a memorial to honor Mahatma Gandhi in the District of Columbia*", Hundred Fifth Congress, First Session, October 28, 1998 (U.S. Government Printing Office, Washington D.C. 1998).
15. Jagat K. Motwani, *America and India in a Give and Take Relationship*, New York, 2003, p. 20.
16. Dilip Singh Saund, *Congressmen from India*, New York, 1960, p. 57.
17. Dennis Kux, *Estranged Democracy: India and United States 1941-1991*, Sage Publication, New Delhi, London, 1993, p. 317.
18. *Interview* with Dr. Parthasarthy Pillai on November 14, 2003 Washington D.C. Dr Pillai is Chairman, NFIAA and past President.

19. US Congress, Senate, Committee on Foreign Relations, Sub-committee on Near Eastern and South Asian Affairs, hearing on "*Proposed American massive aid package to Pakistan*" Hundredth Congress, First Session, March 23,1987 (U.S. Government Printing Office, Washington D.C., 1987)
20. *Interview* with Dr. Jagat K. Motwani on November 23, 2003 at Long Island, New York.
21. Membership of the Congressional Caucus on India and Indian Americans, Washington D.C., www.iacfpa.org also see www.usinpac.com
22. Vasantha Arora, "Senate India Caucus is inaugurated on the Hill with 32 members", www.iacfpa.org
23. See www.usinpac.com
24. www.embassyofindia.org accessed on June 15, 2012.
25. Pravin Seth, 2001, footnote, 6, pp. 347-48.
26. Parvin Sheth, 2001, footnote 6, p. 275. Also see www.iacpa.org
27. Third Biennial Luncheon Seminar organized by IAFPE on *"Indo-US Relations : Emerging Opportunities"* on June 17th, 2000. Washington D.C.
28. *Interview* with Dr. Sambhu N. Banik, Washington DC on November 14th, 2003. He had been appointed as Executive Director, President's Committee on Mental Retardation by President George W. Bush, Sr. He is now a functionary of the Global Organization of People of Indian Origin(GOPIO), Washington DC.
29. Nalini, K. Jha, "*Americans of Indian Origin: Bridging the Gap between the two Democracies*", in Sarva Dharam Singh, Mahavir Singh, eds, *Indians Abroad*, Hope India Publications, Grenwich Millenium Press, London, 2002, p. 60.
30. US Congress, Senate, Committee on Foreign Relation, Subcommittee on Near Eastern and South Asian Affairs, *"Senator Moynihan's statement in the Senate on the Nuclear test by India"*, Hundred Sixth Congress, First Session, May 13, 1998 (US Government Printing Press, Washington DC).
31. Prime Minister A.B. Vajpayee's statement in the Parliament on the Indo-US relation, 15 December, 1998
32. Dennis Kux, "A Remarkable turn around : US-India Relations", *Foreign Service Journal*, October 2002, p. 18-23.
33. US Congress, Senate, Committee on Foreign Relation, Subcommittee on Near Eastern and South Asian Affairs, Resolution 227, *"Expressing the sense of the Congress in opposition to the Government of Pakistan's support for the armed incursion into Jammu & Kashmir, India"*, Hundred Sixth Congress, First Session, June 29, 1999 (US Government Printing Press, Washington D.C.).
34. *Interview* with Mr. Sanjay Puri on October 28, 2003, at Langley Park, Maryland.
35. Alan Cooperman, "India, Israel Interests Team Up", *The Washington Post*, Washington D.C. July19, 2003.
36. USINPAC organizes first-ever India Caucus Day, February 18, 2003. www.usinpac.com

37. US Congress, House of Representatives, Committee on International Relations, Sub-committee on Asia and the Pacific, H.R. 1950, titled "*Section 710, Report on Action Taken by Pakistan*", Hundred Eighth Congress, First Session, May 7, 2003 (US Government Printing Press, Washington DC).
38. "US Congress Demands to Know about Pakistan's role in Abetting Terrorism and Nuclear Proliferation at USINPAC's Urging", *USINPAC*, Washington DC. May 7, 2003. www.usinpac.com
39. US Congress, House of Representatives, Committee on International Relations, H.R. 352, " commending the contribution of Indian Americans and benefits of working with India to promote peace, prosperity and freedom", Hundred Eight Congress, First Session, May 12, 2004 (US Government Printing Office, Washington DC 2004)
40. Jim Lorick, "The Politics of Outsourcing", August 18, 2003. www.larta.org

15

United States-Pakistan Ties: A Troubled Relationship?

M.J. Vinod

US-Pakistan relations has been fraught with lack of trust and shared goals. Pakistan has constantly remained in the eye of the storm due to what a former Pakistan Ambassador to the US calls the "tyranny of geography". Pakistan is situated in a very volatile part of the world which leads Pakistan to be a critical player in both regional and global security (Lodhi Maleeha: 2009). The US approach to Pakistan has also been heavily influenced by 'personal relationships' at the top. The relationship has also been highly 'militarised' and 'centralised', with very little trickling down to the average Pakistani.

Since 9/11 and 26/11, US-Pakistan ties have entered a troubled phase, primarily driven by the US response to the 'war on terror'. Since then Islamabad has assumed a strategically vital role in Washington's foreign policy calculations to combat terrorism. The US government since the 9/11 incident has declared that its larger strategic policy objectives toward Pakistan are grounded on the following goals:

1. Global War on Terrorism
2. Non proliferation of Weapons of Mass Destruction
3. Managing Pakistan-Afghanistan ties
4. Maintaining peaceful relations between India and Pakistan; and
5. Strengthening the democratic fabric in Pakistan

Given Pakistan's track record so far, it poses one of the 'greatest foreign policy challenges' to the Obama administration. It may be recalled that during his candidacy Obama had highlighted the following issues:

1. That there was the need to 'shift the strategic focus from Iraq to Afghanistan'.
2. That the Iraqi adventure was a 'strategic blunder'.

3. That Afghanistan-Pakistan-India are interconnected parts of the 'same strategic puzzle'.

The US has increasingly been using the phrase 'smart power' which is a combination of hard and soft power. Moreover, Washington visualises the need to use "the full range of tools at its disposal viz., diplomatic/ economic/military/legal/political/cultural. However there are serious limitations to the extent to which it can exercise leverage over Pakistan. The dilemma in the US approach is that:

- Traditionally Washington adopted a 'politically soft approach to Pakistan's military and ISI;
- a 'militarily hard approach towards Afghanistan; and
- a 'politically' confrontationist approach towards Iran – a country that could provide a viable supply route to the war zone.

However, much has changed since the elimination of Osama bin Laden, and Pakistan's complicity in the matter. The Bush administration it may be recalled had tried to de-hyphenate India-Pakistan ties. The rising economic profile of India also helped the Bush administration to look at India as a separate, sovereign power and not a conjoined twin of Pakistan.

The War on Terror in Pakistan and Challenges before the Obama Asministration

The Obama administration's policies and strategies towards Pakistan have been caught in a web of dilemmas, contradictions and challenges. The following are some of the major challenges before the Obama administration vis-à-vis Pakistan:

- To convince Islamabad that the real danger to Pakistan emanates within i.e., from the internal extremists and terrorists, and definitely not from India.
- That certain segment of the Pakistani army and the Inter-Services Intelligence (ISI) perceive the militant groups as a *'hedge'* to be used against India in Afghanistan and Kashmir.
- That training Pakistan's military needs to fight insurgents are quite different from the training required to fight a ground war against India. Presently a large number of American military advisers are working in Pakistan to train Pakistani army and paramilitary forces to fight insurgents.
- The need to reduce the 'trust gap' between Washington and Islamabad. When Richard Holbrooke, was asked on the "News

> Hour with Jim Lehrer" whether Pakistan's security forces were committed to rooting out terrorists, he replied bluntly – "I've rarely seen in my years in Washington an issue which is so hotly disputed internally by experts and intelligence officials."

Admiral Mike Mullen, then Chairman of the Joint Chiefs of Staff recognises that Pakistani military officers also have some grounds for 'mistrusting' Americans. According to him, the cutoff of US military aid in 1990 *led to* a whole generation of Pakistani military officers who have had no contact with Americans, and who suspect American motives. Prior to the Osama fiasco, Mike Mullen along with top military officials, such as Gen. David Petraeus, head of Central Command had regular meetings with Pakistan's army chief, Gen. Kayani, and the head of ISI, Lt. Gen. Shuja Pasha.

It may be recalled that General David Petraeus of the Central Command had said on April 1, 2009 that Islamist insurgents pose a growing threat not only to Afghanistan but to Pakistan's "very existence". Bruce Riedel in his book *The Search for Al Qaeda* observes that former president Gen Musharraf had allowed Al Qaeda to 'regroup' in 'Pakistan's tribal lands'. Moreover, Musharraf and his ISI stooges was 'more an enabler' 'than a foe' of terrorist state formation in Waziristan. Now, Pakistan seems to be paying a heavy price for all its follies.

On the one hand, the Pakistani's have been nervous about the US predator drone strikes against al-Qaeda and Taliban targets which not only cause collateral damage but also affect public opinion; on the other, Islamabad complains that the US isn't providing the equipment they need. Hence Islamabad has been demanding cobra helicopters, night-vision equipment, jamming equipment to block the radio broadcasts of the Taliban commander in Swat. They would also like 'small surveillance drones'. On the whole the 'surgical military strikes' of the US Air Force will continue to be an issue of contention in US-Pakistan relations.

Af-Pak: Issues and Challenges before the Obama Administration

It may be recalled that Richard Holbrooke had invited the Defense and Foreign ministers of Afghanistan and Pakistan to Washington to give him inputs into Obama's strategic review of the "Af-Pak" related issues. A large number of additional troops had headed for Afghanistan in 2009. Many of these troops have been deployed in provinces close to Kabul which do not necessarily have a significant international presence and are largely under insurgent control. The challenge for Washington is to hold onto the territory it has gained in Afghanistan and initiate reconstruction projects so that the local population can see the benefits of their presence.

A concern expressed by western officials has pertained to the propensity on the part of some elements of the Pakistani military of supporting militants based on Pakistani soil who cross into Afghanistan and launch attacks. Washington's biggest challenge is getting Pakistan's most powerful institution – the army – to revise its decade's old policy of supporting militant groups. Islamabad has been using these groups as proxies against New Delhi, as well as to project its influence in Afghanistan. This has long been a source of tension between the two countries, but in recent years some militants allied with Al Qaeda have also launched a war against Pakistan. The result is that Islamabad follows a dual policy of on the one hand, cracking down on such militants arrayed against the Pakistani state – which includes Al Qaeda; and on the other covertly tolerating/backing militants who restrict their fighting to Afghanistan. Perhaps Islamabad is now paying a heavy price for this dual policy.

The forty one NATO countries involved in Afghanistan – who make up roughly 55,000 of the 70,000 troops in the country – have differing rules of operation. Some refuse to deploy to combat-intensive zones and others have already set withdrawal dates. The battle cannot be won by military force alone. Alternative strategies also need to be adopted. The response has to be multi-pronged which requires an approach that encompasses the political, economic and social as well.

To succeed, this initiative must be fought and won on either side of the Pakistani-Afghan border. The US needs to stay focused on Afghanistan and put more pressure on the Pakistanis." Bill O'Reilly contends that "there's no winning the Taliban war unless Pakistan cracks down on the guys that are in Pakistan." Success in Afghanistan depends on success in Pakistan and vice versa. Many of the tribes and developmental challenges are the same on both sides of the border. Af-Pak will remain as long as the US does not move away from its failed policies.

Since 2008, insurgents have been periodically making attempts to interdict supply lines, especially near the Khyber Pass, connecting Peshawar and Jalalabad, and the route from Karachi to Kandahar. This route runs through Quetta and Chaman border crossing. These attacks have left behind a trail of destruction.

Perhaps the Pakistanis are quite hesitant to target the Haqqanis and other Afghan militant groups, based on Pakistani soil, as they could be of use to Islamabad when the American and NATO forces withdraw from Afghanistan. The Haqqani network and the Quetta Shura Taliban are often perceived as being tools of the Pakistani state. The latter refers to the central leadership of the Afghan Taliban under Mullah Omar based in the city of Quetta. Pakistan perceives the Haqqani network and the Quetta Shura Taliban as part of their larger framework to neutralise the influence of India in Afghanistan. It may be recalled that President Obama had made an announcement in June 2011 of the proposed US military withdrawal from Afghanistan in 2014.

US Aid to Pakistan

A large part of the US aid to Pakistan has gone to the Pakistan army in the hope that Islamabad will cooperate in the US efforts in combating terrorism. The US has pledged huge military/financial aid to Pakistan, though this is conditional on Pakistan's cooperation on the war against terror. Between fiscal years 2002 and 2008, the US has spent more than $11.2 billion. Of this amount, almost $5.9 billion was from the 'Coalition Support Fund' (CSF) programme. This is strictly meant to reimburse countries for the costs incurred in the support on the global war on terror. The funds were never intended to build 'capacity' within the armed forces of Pakistan. Washington generally pursues what Christine Fair calls 'supply-driven' aid to Pakistan. In the process large sums of money is pumped into Pakistan's coffers with 'few meaningful accountability requirements.

In a September 2009 cable, former US Ambassador to Pakistan Anne Patterson opined that no amount of US aid to Pakistan will get its security forces to sever links with the Taliban (Jayashree Bajoria: 2010). Pakistan seem to be using the war on terrorism to extract aid from the US. Pakistan has resisted such scrutiny, asserting that once such monies go into Pakistan's exchequer, they become sovereign funds (C. Christine Fair: 2009: 150-51). Coalition Support Funds account for the majority of the US assistance to Pakistan. Among all the countries receiving such funds, perhaps Pakistan is the largest recipient. Officially the fund is reimbursement for food, clothing, fuel, ammunition, billeting and medical expenses. Islamabad has been repeatedly submitting receipts to the US Central Command. Pakistan is also one of four countries along with Israel, Egypt and Jordan, to receive budget support from the US. The purpose of this direct cash transfer to Pakistan is to help it pay off its debt, so that it can spend more on the social sector. Needless to say that there is little accountability in the manner in which the money is being spent. (Craig Cohen and Derek Chollet: 2007).

Most of Washington's aid to Islamabad, has gone to the Pakistani Army, in the hope that the then military-led government of former President Pervez Musharraf would fully cooperate with the US efforts to prevent the Taliban and other radical groups from returning to Afghanistan.

The Taliban and its allies made a strong comeback in Afghanistan largely due to the safe havens they have enjoyed in the tribal regions on the Pakistani side of the border. Their brand of radicalism has spread outward from the Federally Administered Tribal Areas (FATA), where al Qaeda's leadership is believed to be based, into the North-West Frontier Province (NWFP) and beyond even into Punjab and other parts of Pakistan's heartland (Jim Lobe: 2009)

The Obama Administration, has increased 'non-military aid' to Pakistan. Islamabad needs to be held accountable for security in the border region with Afghanistan. It may be recalled that Joe Biden had in his capacity as Chairman of the Senate Foreign Relations Committee introduced a legislation proposing to triple non-military aid to Pakistan in the next five years; the legislation had authorised US$7.5 billion over five years mainly for building schools, roads and clinics. The US has moved ahead with the following two legislations:

1. The 'Biden-Lugar' legislation (the "Enhanced Partnership with Pakistan Act of 2008"); and
2. The "Reconstruction Opportunity Zones (ROZ)" legislation—which would allow for duty-free access to US markets for certain type of goods produced.

As a presidential candidate, Barack Obama had advocated putting more pressure on Pakistan since he feared that Islamabad is preparing for a war against India by using US military aid given to them for fighting terrorists. Asked how Islamabad could be pressurised, Obama said:

1. "we are providing them military aid without having enough strings attached;
2. They are using the military aid – for preparing for war against India." (US Presidential Election 2008, 'Pakistan using US aid for war against India', 5 September 2008, IANS).

Washington's ties with Islamabad have grown tense. Pakistan has been unhappy about the pace of deliveries of US military equipment and over congressional attempts to impose restrictions on its supply and use. "We are fighting this war today," a senior Pakistani military official said while describing US assistance as slow and stingy. "What good is it two years from now?" That official and others said there have been long delays in the delivery of helicopters, night-vision equipment and other supplies requested for the army's ongoing offensive against Pakistan-based insurgents. In recent interviews, civil and military officials in Pakistan drew a sharp contrast between the billions of dollars in assistance that George W. Bush's administration gave, with few strings attached, to the then President Pervez Musharraf – a general who came to power in a military coup – and what they see as efforts to condition assistance to the democratically elected government of President Asif Ali Zardari. (The Nation: August 30, 2009). However the fact is that by the end of 2011, the US Congress had appropriated about $15.3 billion in overt assistance over 10 years, including more than $8.3 billion in development and humanitarian aid, and nearly $7 billion in for security related programmes. In 2009 the Congress had passed a Pakistan-specific bill authorizing increased non-military aid to Pakistan – to 41.5 billion per year for five years. Certain conditions were also placed on future security related aid to Pakistan (Alan Kronstadt: 2012).

The Obama Administration and India-Pakistan Relations

The Obama Administration has been keen to revive the peace process between Islamabad and New Delhi after it was derailed following the terrorist attacks in Mumbai, popularly referred to as 26/11. Taking the relationship forward could be a key factor in helping stabilise Afghanistan. At the same time the Obama administration knows that the US-Pakistani relationship is too important to let the trust gap widen. Obama had argued out his case as follows:

> I will join with our allies in insisting, not simply requesting, that Pakistan crack down on the Taliban, pursue Osama bin Laden and end its relationship with the terrorist groups. At the same time I will encourage dialogue between India and Pakistan to work towards resolving their dispute over Kashmir and between Afghanistan and Pakistan to resolve their differences and develop the Pashtun border region. If Pakistan can look towards the east (India) with confidence, it will be less likely to believe its interests are best achieved through cooperation with the Taliban." (see Raja Mohan: 2009: 174)

In the process, there has been the risk that president Obama may kick-off a regional solution for the India-Pakistan impasse. The path to peace between India and Pakistan need not necessarily go through the Kashmir valley. New Delhi needs to be cautious of the US tendency of linking up Afghanistan's security with terrorism in Kashmir. Obama had pointed out the need to resolve the Kashmir problem to reduce nuclear dangers in South Asia. "I will continue support of ongoing Indian and Pakistani efforts to resolve the Kashmir problem in order to address the political roots of the arms race between India and Pakistan". Obama's comments in interviews to Time magazine in October and December 2008 and the reported consideration of former President Bill Clinton as a special envoy on Kashmir were at that point of time perceived as indications of a possible pro-interventionist stance. However, since then US-Pakistan relations have witnessed a variety of embarrassments for the Americans.

A few years back when Musharraf was at the helm of affairs, a Pakistan scholar Hussain Haqqani surmised the situation as follows: "Fifty eight years after partition, and in the absence of any incentive or compulsion on the part of India to revise the status quo, it might be prudent for Pakistanis to give priority to normalisation and stability in South Asia over settlement of the Kashmir dispute. To make that possible, the rhetoric fed to Pakistanis over Kashmir must end. Musharraf too should try to lower the rhetoric over Kashmir rather than raise his people's expectations in that regard." (Hussain Haqqani: 2005). ISI Chief Pasha told the German magazine *Der Spiegel* in January 2009 "We may be crazy in Pakistan, but we are not completely out of our minds. We know fully well that terror is our enemy, not India." These are signs at the top that Pakistani security officials understand the need for change. But Pakistani defence officials do not perceive the original Taliban, Lashkar-e-Taiba, the Haqqani network and other such groups as enemies of Pakistan. Rather they perceive them as a 'means' to extend their geopolitical reach into Afghanistan and the region as a whole (Malou Innocent: 2009).

The US must not fall into the trap of pushing for a resumption of official India-Pakistan talks as an end in itself but instead encourage changes in the dynamics of the relationship that will reduce tensions and uproot terrorism from the region. Without concerted action against the perpetrators of the Mumbai attacks it could well embolden groups like LeT to up the ante. The first step is for Pakistan to demonstrate that it will no longer tolerate the export of terrorism from its territory. As British prime Minister Gordon Brown has indicated almost three-quarters of all terrorist plots uncovered even in Britain in recent years, had links to Islamic terrorism in Afghanistan or Pakistan. The defence of the west begins in the Hindu Kush and Helmand. In other words as David Miliband, the British Foreign Secretary suggests "the badlands of Afghanistan and Pakistan are the 'incubator' of choice for international terrorism" (Roger Cohen: 2009). Former CIA director General Michael Hayden believes that the next attack on the US homeland is likely to originate from western Pakistan.

US-Pakistan Relations Post-Osama Bin Laden

A long standing worry for the Americans has been the propensity on the part of Pakistan to recruit American citizens in the cause of Islamic terrorism. Many of the most wanted terrorists reside in Pakistan. These include among others Taliban Chief Mullah Omar, Al Qaeda chief Ayman al-Zawahiri and Haqqani Network chief Sirajuddin Haqqani. Most of them receive protection from the Pakistani government (Newsweek, May 7, 2012). The terrorist group led by Jalaluddin Huqqani based in the FATA is perhaps the most dangerous of Afghan insurgent groups battling the US-led forces in eastern Afghanistan. In a testimony on September 22, 2011 before the Senate Armed Services committee, Mullen issued one of the most strongly worded US government statement on Pakistani malfeasance. To quote: "The Haqqani network, for one, acts as a veritable arm Pakistan's Inter-Services Intelligence agency. With ISI support, Haqqani operatives plan and conducted that September 13 truck bomb attack, as well as the assault on our embassy. We also have credible evidence they were behind the June 28th attack on the Intercontinental Hotel in Kabul and a host of other smaller but effective operations" (Mullen: 2011). The CIA also believes that the ISI continues to have links with some Afghanistan and India-focused militant groups such as the Haqqani network, Quetta shura Taliban and Lashkar-e-Taiba Daniel Markey: 2011). According to markey the "ISI has sought to wall off its interactions with the CIA". Moreover, the Wikileaks Cables have brought out US concerns over Pakistan's continued support for certain militant groups, Pakistan's nuclear programme, its civil-military relations and human rights abuses by Pakistan's security services.

Late November 2011 NATO troops in Afghanistan came under fire from Pakistani outposts. American retaliation resulted in the death of 24 Pakistani soldiers. This resulted in the closure of Pakistani ground lines of communication. Islamabad also renegotiated all existing bilateral agreements with Washington related to supply lines into Afghanistan. Pakistan sought as much as $5,000 per truck, which many American policy makers perceived as nothing less than extortion and "price gouging" (Levin and McCain: 2012)

Observations

Reducing the trust gap between the US and Pakistan depends on how Pakistan deals with the militants within Pakistan. Perhaps the militants have been briefed that the Taliban is making huge inroads into Afghanistan and that they perceive it as an opportunity to take over a nuclear-armed state. President Barack Obama's decision just days after his inauguration to authorise a new round of strikes by aerial drones within FATA – particularly in Waziristan—suggests that he is unconvinced by Islamabad's promises to curb militants such as JUD.

In the light of the recent developments, the fundamentals of US policy towards Pakistan 'have to be reworked'. There is 'no easy solution'. Some prioritising of issues would be necessary. Longer-term goals cannot be sacrificed for short-term gain. The US will have to strike a balance between short term measures – such as frequent air strikes against al Qaeda and Taliban targets on Pakistani soil; and the long-term goal of enhancing the 'credibility' and 'effectiveness' of Pakistan's 'civilian leadership and institutions'. The future direction of the region pivots on Pakistan's ability to overcome multiple socio-economic challenges as well as its willingness to fight terrorism in all its forms within its own borders. Washington will have to coax Pakistan into doing more against the home bred terrorist havens in the tribal areas and in Pakistan occupied Kashmir. Using the terrorists as a means of 'hedging' against India could only aggravate matters for Pakistan. Washington's success in Afghanistan will be contingent on fixing the problems and bottlenecks in Pakistan. Pakistan will continue to be the fulcrum of US policy in the region. This will be badly affected if the situation deteriorates in Pakistan. Ironically while cooperation between the US and Pakistan has increased, the 'mutual distrust' continues. Restoring '*trust*' between Washington and Islamabad will be the greatest challenge.

REFERENCES

1. K. Alan Kronstadt, "Pakistan-US Relations" Congressional Research Service, May 24, 2012, p. 54.
2. Levin and McCain, "Don't Pay Pakistan Exorbitant Trucking Fees", *Foreign Policy Cable* (online), May 22, 2012.
3. "America's Next Most Wanted," *Newsweek*, May 7, 2012.
4. "Senate Armed Services Committee hearing on Iraq and Afghanistan" CQ Transcripts, September 22, 2011.
5. "Route of Death: NATO supply tankers Bribe their way to the Border", *Express Tribune (Karachi)*, July 11, 2011.
6. Daniel Markey's (Senior Fellow for India, Pakistan and south Asia, Council on Foreign Relations) interview with Jayshree Bajoria dated March 4, 2011.
7. Jayashree Bajoria, "How Wikileaks Hurts US-Pakistan Ties", Council on Foreign Relations, December 6, 2010.
8. Roger Cohen, "AfPak: UK Resolves, America Ponders", *Deccan Chronicle*, October 28, 2009.
9. Malou Innocent, "Pakistan and the Future of US Policy", *Policy Analysis*, April 13, 2009.
10. Jim Lobe, "US-Pakistan: Obama-Tied think Tank Calls for a Dramatic shift", http://ipsnews.net/news.aspidnews=44739
11. The Nation, "Obama Administration Devising Metrics to Measure Progress Under Afghanistan-Pakistan strategy", August 30, 2009.

12. Lisa Curtis, "From Strategy to Implementation: Strengthening US-Pakistan Relations", The Heritage Foundation, July 8, 2009, http://www.heritage.org/research/asiaandthepacific/tst070809a.cfm
13. C. Christina Fair, "Time for Sober Realism: Renegotiating US Relations with Pakistan", *The Washington Quarterly*, 32:2 (April 2009), pp. 149-172.
14. C. Raja Mohan, "How Obama Can Get South Asia Right", *The Washington Quarterly*, 32:2 (April 2009), pp. 173-189.
15. Maleeha, Lodhi, "A renewed approach: finding stability in US-Pakistan relations", *Harvard International Review*, spring 2009 (Interview), http://www.entrepreneur.com/tradejournals/article/200271864.html
16. Craig Cohen and Derek Chollet, "When $10 billion is not Enough: US Strategy Towards Pakistan", *The Washington Quarterly*, 30:2, pp. 7-19.
17. Hussain Haqqani, 'The Eternal India-Pakistan-US triangle', *Gulf News*, April 6, 2005.

Contributors

Akhilesh Kumar Tiwari, Doctoral Research Scholar, Department of Political Science, Jamia Millia Islamia University, New Delhi.

Amulya K Tripathy, Head, Department of Political Science, D.A.V. Autonomous College, Titilagarh, Odisha.

B.V. Muralidhar, Professor, Department of Political Science, S.V. University, Tirupati, Andhra Pradesh.

Biswajit Mohapatra, Assistant Professor, Department of Political Science, North-Eastern Hill University, Shillong, Meghalaya.

Kaustav Padmapati, Fulbright Scholar and Junior Research Fellow, Observer Research Foundation, New Delhi.

M.J. Vinod, Professor of Political Science, Bangalore University, Bangalore, Karnataka.

M. Vishnu Prakash, Assistant Professor in the Department of Political Science, STSN Government Degree College, Kadiri, Anantapur, A.P.

Mohammed Badrul Alam, Professor, Department of Political Science, Jamia Millia Islamia University, New Delhi.

Monish Tourangbam, Doctoral Research Scholar, U.S. Studies, Centre for Canadian, US and Latin American Studies, School of International Studies, Jawaharlal Nehru University, New Delhi.

Mukesh Bagoria, Fellow, Multinational Institute of American Studies, Steinhart School of Culture, Education and Human Development, New York University, New York, USA.

Muzaffar Ahemad Ganaie, Doctoral Research Scholar at the Department of Political Science, Jamia Millia Islamia University, New Delhi.

Narottam Gaan, Professor and Head, PG Department of Political Science, Utkal University, Bhubaneswar, Odisha.

Rajendra Kumar Pandey, Assistant Professor, Center for Federal Studies, Jamia Hamdard, New Delhi.

Reyaz Ahmad Ganaie, Doctoral Research Scholar, Department of Political Science, Jamia Millia Islamia University, New Delhi.

Uma Purushothaman, Research Fellow, Observer Research Foundation (ORF), New Delhi.

Index